CARNAGE &
COURAGE

CARNAGE & COURAGE

A MEMOIR OF FDR, THE KENNEDYS, AND WORLD WAR II

PAGE WILSON

YUCCA

Yucca Publishing books may be purchased in bulk at special discounts for sales promotion, corporate gifts, fund-raising, or educational purposes. Special editions can also be created to specifications. For details, contact the Special Sales Department, Yucca Publishing, 307 West 36th Street, 11th Floor, New York, NY 10018 or yucca@skyhorsepublishing.com.

Yucca Publishing® is an imprint of Skyhorse Publishing, Inc.®, a Delaware corporation.

Visit our website at www.yuccapub.com.

10 9 8 7 6 5 4 3 2 1

Library of Congress Cataloging-in-Publication Data is available on file.

Cover design by Zoran Opalic for Yucca Publishing
Cover photographs courtesy of the National Archive

Print ISBN: 978-1-63158-061-1
Ebook ISBN: 978-1-63158-073-4

Printed in the United States of America

Contents

Preamble

Hyde Park

In August 1936 four of us, all in our late teens, friends of John Roosevelt, a sophomore at Harvard and son of the President, were invited to visit the Roosevelt family at Hyde Park on the Hudson River. The occasion was to celebrate the twenty-first birthday of the President's third son and namesake, Franklin Delano Roosevelt, Jr., known to his friends as Frank, on August 17. Our group consisted of two boys, one of whom would be our driver, a girl friend of mine, and me.

We knew the Roosevelt sons and some of their friends, many of whom had gone to what Scott Fitzgerald had referred to as the "St. Midas Schools." That term always made me laugh. Those are the schools, mostly named for saints, such as St. Paul's, St. George's, and St. Mark's, but the term included several others, such as Groton, all especially created for the sons of rich God-fearing Anglo Saxon Protestants. (My mother was always amused by the initials for the acronym "WASP" on the grounds of redundancy: If people are "ASP," they are, perforce, white.)

I and some other teenage girls I knew near where I lived then, in the country outside of Baltimore, had been invited by boys at these St. Midas schools to come to their in-school dances. On these occasions we were either chaperoned by the family of the boys who had invited us, or we were put up at the house of some hapless teacher and his wife. The Roosevelt boys, like their father, had gone to Groton and some of us on the St. Midas dance circuit had gotten to know them in that orbit.

I had broached the idea of visiting the Roosevelt family gingerly with my parents because if my father wasn't a rabid Republican, he at least frothed at the mouth at the mention of FDR. Mother was not political herself but she went along with my father in his anti-that-man-in-the-White-House sentiment. If anything, Roosevelt was even lower in Daddy's esteem than Al Smith had been in 1928, and to prove my inherited parental distaste for him, I had wrested a Smith button off of a schoolmate and cast it in the fishpond at my private school.

Earlier that summer there had been a smug picture of a friend and me in the *Baltimore Sun*, wearing buttons plugging Alfred Landon, governor of Kansas, the Republican nominee for the presidency. The photo of us was taken in front of the Republican headquarters in Baltimore, where we volunteered on occasional Saturdays, stuffing envelopes or doing some other such significant work. In the picture we are holding large sunflowers, the state flower of Kansas, further symbols of support for the Republican candidate.

It was already a hot steamy day, August 17, when we were to leave for our jaunt, but the weather didn't bother me: I was flushed with excitement for the adventure that lay ahead. We had a long way to go, so we planned to set off early. Mother had not finished dressing as I was ready to leave, so I told her goodbye inside the house. She hugged me tight and told me she was sure I would have a wonderful time. For a brief moment, I was afraid she was going to hint—tactfully, of course—how I should conduct myself in the august surroundings for which we were headed. For instance, not too many years back, she suggested every now and than that I not be "too peart," an odd word from her Virginia youth when they still used some old outworn English expressions, this one a rendition of "pert." Anyway, she didn't have any suggestions to make to me on my deportment this time, so I gave her an extra hug as I kissed her goodbye.

Daddy was already poised out by the driveway early to see us off. "Damn it," he said to me, as he put his arm around me. "If we let you go to Hyde Park you'll come back home a Democrat. I know it! You'll come back a damned Democrat." I pooh-poohed such an absurd notion and kissed him on the cheek as I headed for my friend's car.

We had a slow, pleasant drive and arrived at the Roosevelt home in late afternoon. As we turned into the driveway we saw a solitary soldier standing in front of a small shelter, which reminded me of the little guardhouse in my brother's collection of British lead soldiers. That was the only evidence of security that I saw all weekend.

We were greeted by John on our arrival. He guided us into a large, nondescript room full of antique furniture that appeared to have been collected over various generations and that seemed to be both mismatched and cohesive at the same time. There he introduced us to his grandmother, Mrs. James Roosevelt, and to his mother, Mrs. Eleanor Roosevelt, both of whom welcomed us cordially.

Then he showed us to our bedrooms. We girls shared a room, which was painted white and had crisp white curtains. There was a vase of paper-white tulips on the bureau and both beds were covered with white spreads. We threw our fancy dresses on the beds so they'd be unwrinkled by dinnertime. For fun, we each laid our stockings (nylon) on the bed as well, dangling to the floor. We put our evening shoes on the floor close to the toes of the stockings.

After we two had showered and made up our faces, we checked out each other's appearance. I surveyed my friend, centered the belt to her dress and told her she looked "nifty." I had borrowed a dress from one of my older sisters, although she did not know it. It was pleated black chiffon with a ruffle around the shoulders, threaded with elastic. When I'd tried it on at home I figured it made me look at least a couple of years older, which clinched my decision to take it.

This evening I looked at myself in the mirror next to the bureau and turned around to my friend. "Demure?" I asked her, with the shoulders covered. "Or dashing?" I asked, pulling the dress down to about the level of the smallpox vaccination, high on my arm. She nodded assent to the latter, and helped me fasten my simple gold link necklace.

We weekend visitors gathered in the living room with the President's mother and his wife, Jimmy Roosevelt, Franklin, John, and a few people from neighboring houses. The friend who had driven our group to Hyde Park had told us on the way that John had informed him that the President, since his polio attack of years ago, had no use of his legs, so when he stood or walked he had to be supported on both sides (generally by his stalwart sons) or had to use a wheelchair. This evening, he came into the large living room beaming, in a wheelchair being pushed by a young black man (I learned that his name was Prettyman) and waved sort of generally as a greeting.

I reckoned my dress was working all right when Jimmy, who I had not met before, offered to make me the house martini. He seemed affable and I thought that the sip I took of the drink was delicious, but it seemed strong, so after the one sip I tucked the glass away discreetly on a table. I had a little chat with Frank, who said he was so glad that our group had come to share his birthday with him. I knew he was sincerely grateful to have more young people around because his special girl, pretty Ethel du Pont—whom I'd gotten to know and liked a lot—was traveling in Europe this summer with her family, and I felt sure that he missed her fearfully.

At dinner, to my huge surprise, I found myself seated next to the President, on his left. He was there already, sitting in his wheelchair, when I came in. One of the local guests, Laura Delano, was on his right. She was a cousin of the President and I was awed by her casual elegance and her obvious self-assurance. She smiled at me and I smiled back, delighted. Then she got totally engaged in conversation with the person on her right as we sat down.

The President turned to me and mentioned that there had been a running acquaintance between our families, both Dutch. He asked me about a relative of mine, Cousin Wallis Huidekoper, who raised cattle on a ranch in Wyoming, and I told him the latest news I had. He seemed interested when I told him Cousin Wallis had lived there before barbed wire was introduced in the area. Apparently, in the days before barbed wire, the brand seared on your cattle identified them and thus they were allowed to wander afield.

Then he asked me what I did to keep myself busy in Baltimore. I told him I worked in a store there. He said I looked young to be working already. My dress apparently hadn't made me look older to him.

I smiled at his comment and said that's what my parents tell me all the time. And then I went on to explain what else I did to keep myself busy in Baltimore. I looked at him directly. "That is, I work in the store during the week," I said, speaking slowly and deliberately, and trying to smile at the same time. "But on Saturdays I volunteer at the Landon campaign headquarters in Baltimore, stuffing envelopes, passing out buttons and literature and such things."

The President threw back his head and roared with laughter. Then he told me two stories about my candidate. He said he had tried to talk to Landon about foreign relations, but Landon thought he was referring to immigrant cousins landing on Ellis Island. He said he tried again. This time he told Landon that he wanted to talk about the international situation, and Landon thought the subject was the drop in value of International Harvester stock on Wall Street. I smiled appreciatively at his obviously apocryphal tales.

Laura Delano said something to the President; he turned and now addressed his attention to her. I could overhear them talking about this and that in the easy fashion of people long fond of each other. At one point, I heard her mention some sort of dog she was breeding. The President seemed absorbed in discussion with her as they carried on with their dog talk.

Meanwhile I was thinking that although my mother and father had often told me that I was too young to even consider getting a job, which would mean quitting school just before my senior year, I was marveling once more that I was able to get them to change their minds. I had been able to convince them of my need to break out into a wider world than my all-girls private school. I also wanted to earn some money; the Depression had wreaked havoc on my father's plastics business. I knew my school was expensive. There were some nine million people unemployed in the United States, and I was fully aware of how hard it would be for me to find a job, but I felt hemmed in by what I considered the stifling homogeneity of my life. I longed for a more varied and challenging environment.

I was thinking about how lucky I was to have been able to find a job when I realized the President had turned to me and we started chatting again.

I don't know where we went from there, and I have tried often since to retrace the trail of conversation that led us into a discussion of Rudyard Kipling. I only remember that we pounced on the point that Kipling was a great storyteller.

We talked about several Kipling stories, the ones which were not so British-Imperial oriented, including "Kim." Then the President said he had one favorite Kipling tale which he had long felt would make a great movie and which he would like to direct someday. I asked him which one it was. He said it was an obscure story, one I surely had never heard of.

I asked him which one it was. It was a story called *The Brushwood Boy*, he told me. "It's one of my very favorite stories, too," I said. At once we set about casting the movie of *The Brushwood Boy*, arguing back and forth who would play the girl and who the boy. At some stage we tried to remember the names of those two characters but neither of us could. We were perplexed that although we each knew the story so well—we had talked about how one would direct the scene of the boy and the girl meeting in their childhood and the scenes of the recurring dream of the long ride—neither of us could remember the character's names. After dinner, the President promised, we'd look for the book.

We were still talking about our movie when the birthday cake was brought in. The candles were lit and Frank, after a couple of pretended unsuccessful tries for our amusement, blew all twenty-one out, and we clapped loudly and happily. The President made a warm birthday toast to his son, his namesake, and everyone smiled enthusiastically.

Then the President said he would like to drink another toast. He raised his glass, paused, looked at me, and smiled. I wondered what mischief he had up his sleeve. He proposed a toast, still smiling at me, to the poor Republicans who obviously can't afford to put clothes on their children's backs. I was so flustered at being the center of attention and everyone laughing good-naturedly, that first I put my hands over my face as if to hide, but promptly took them down, and now laughed heartily along with the others.

After the laughter died down and we had finished our slices of the birthday cake, the President and I set out to look for *The Brushwood Boy*. He was pushed in his wheelchair by Prettyman. Our pursuit took us first to a small room with various pieces of china sprinkled around on tables and on the mantle piece. There was a china chandelier, but what I especially remember was a china figurine, delicate but explicit, of a young girl wearing a full-skirted ball gown and leaning back in a chair. Obviously the dance was over and she was exhausted from excitement; also her feet were tired, for she had kicked off one shoe and it lay on the table an inch or so away from the figurine. I was entranced by the detached shoe and the President was so amused that he moved it away from the figurine another few inches.

We found books by Kipling but not the one we wanted—in that room or the second room we searched. We joined the group in the next room.

A few days later at home I found the book of Kipling short stories that included *The Brushwood Boy*. No wonder we couldn't remember the names of the main characters. Their real names are not memorable; most of the time they are simply called The Girl and The Boy.

***

I wrote letters to both Mrs. Eleanor Roosevelt and Mrs. James Roosevelt thanking them for the fine time. Later I heard from a friend of John's that the President was delighted that I'd sent him sunflowers as a bread-and-butter present. Actually, I had sent him nothing—but I was pleased with the joke—and I've always wished I'd sent him a copy of *The Brushwood Boy*.

And, of course, Daddy's dire prediction was absolutely right. I'd come home a damned Democrat—irrevocably, passionately, and permanently.

***

During that 1936 presidential campaign the conservatives threw the book at FDR. The epithets were not very original: the New Deal was Bolshevistic, or at least socialistic, and certainly un-American. Over 80 percent of the newspapers in the country were against Roosevelt.

In any event, he won the election with the greatest landslide in American history, losing only two states, New Hampshire and Vermont.

Part One

The Impending Storm

Dance at the White House

Sometime soon after Roosevelt's inauguration, the first lady had a dance at the White House. My sisters—Rosalind and Nancy—and I were invited to the party. We each knew some of the three honorees: Margo Delano, a cousin of the President, was a friend of both my sisters at Greenwood School; Marietta Peabody, daughter of the head of Groton School, the President's old alma mater which he had stayed close to over the years, whom I had gotten to know on the St. Midas's dance circuit; and Barbara Cushing, sister of Jimmy Roosevelt's wife—I had met Barbara several times and, of course, had met Jimmy at Frank Jr.'s birthday party. Anne Lindsay Clark, a dear friend, and classmate of mine at Greenwood School, was also there. I had introduced her to John Roosevelt. They fell in love and were married in 1938.

***

At one point in the evening Jimmy asked me to dance. He was a marvelous dancer and after twirling me around for a few minutes he suggested we sit down to talk. We chatted a little about the merry birthday party that past summer and, of course, talked a little about current political issues. I remember especially our agreeing that it was a huge step forward for democracy that Congress had agreed to the passage of the President's Social Security bill.

Jimmy asked me in a general way how my life was faring. "I am fevered with the sunset," I said. "I am fretful with the bay," and was about to go on when he filled in the next lines, "the wanderlust is on me and my soul is in Cathay." He smiled that big double Roosevelt smile, the result of both TR and FDR's smile genes.

"You're obviously restless," he said. "Are you serious about wanting to travel?"

1

I assured him I was and told him about the suggestion I'd made to my mother a while ago that I might try to take enough courses sometime to try to qualify for a job in the Foreign Service. I thought that could lead to lots of traveling and an adventurous life.

"Look," he said, "a good friend of mine, Joe Kennedy, is about to be appointed ambassador to England. Would you like me to find out if there is any spot on his staff where you might fit in?"

I told him I couldn't think of anything more exciting. He suggested I send him a few paragraphs about myself as soon as I could. The paragraphs I sent were few indeed. I didn't exaggerate my experience at working successfully in a popular store, or of my proficiency at typing and shorthand, but I took great pains to type my brief bio extra neatly. My letter was double-spaced.

One evening the next week Jimmy called me to say that Joe Kennedy wanted me to come to Washington to talk to him. "I have given him a copy of your bio and he may have a job for you," Jimmy said. "There is a spot open on his staff for which you might qualify," he explained. The appointment of Joseph P. Kennedy as ambassador to the Court of St. James's had just been announced. I had, of course, read about it with huge interest.

Jimmy told me to call Mr. Kennedy's office in Washington and set a date to go over to see him. His secretary would be expecting my call.

I was early for my appointment with Mr. Kennedy—I was always early for everything—but I was ushered into his office immediately. He greeted me warmly, indicated a chair and suggested I sit down. I noted how blue his eyes were. Maybe they seemed so blue because his face was so suntanned, I thought. He sat down in the chair behind his desk, leaned back, appeared relaxed and asked me to tell him a little about myself. He said Jimmy had given him the material I'd sent him.

I suggested that there really was not a lot more to tell, and confessed that I had practiced a little spiel on the train coming over. Basically I told him what I had already said in the note he had, that I could take shorthand and could type, and that I now was working in a store in Baltimore which sold riding clothes and anything else to do with horses, and that I had briefly attended an evening lecture series on international relations at Johns Hopkins University. Then I explained why I had only gone to the series briefly: because the professor was German and markedly anti-American, so much so that he insisted that the Americans has sunk the Lusitania in the World War and blamed it on the Germans. Furthermore, he hadn't wanted a woman in his course, and clearly resented my being there. Anyway, I explained that I felt compelled to quit that lecture course.

Mr. Kennedy smiled when I finished. It was a kind of gentle smile, as if to convince me that he was smiling at my frankness, not at my awkwardness. He said he had looked into the situation at the embassy in London and there was one vacancy in an office there which would be fine for me. He went on in the same voice to say that I could be working for the man he was taking over as his press attaché and who would help with speech writing.

"Sort of a clerk to him," he said. "Let's call it an assistant," he added. I tried not to seem overwhelmed with excitement. I kept nodding in agreement as he talked, and frowning because I thought that made me look businesslike. His secretary had some papers for me to fill out, he told me, winding down our meeting.

"I will send you a copy of a letter I'll be sending to the passport division of the State Department asking them to issue you a diplomatic passport," he added. I was so consumed with anticipation that I nearly left his room without thanking him. I recovered just in time to tell him how much I looked forward to the assignment.

"I hope you can be ready to go by the end of February," he said. My smile was all I needed to tell him that I'd be ready, with bells on.

On the way to his secretary's office, I passed the women's room. I decided to pop in there to look in the mirror. I still couldn't believe that this was happening to me. I was reassured to see that the face that looked out at me in the mirror was mine, perhaps a little flushed, but it was still mine.

On one of the forms his secretary gave me there was a space in which to write the annual salary I expected. I was prepared for that. When Jimmy had called me to tell me about the possibility of a job, after I had dropped down to earth we had discussed what my salary would be if I was lucky enough to be hired. He said it would be probably be in the neighborhood of $25 a week. I thought that sounded munificent.

Knowing there are twelve months in the year and figuring that there were four weeks a month, thus smartly calculating that there were 48 weeks a year. I multiplied that by 25 and came out with a salary of $1,200. A little later I realized that I had neglected to consider that there are actually 52 weeks a year. I understood now that the figure of $1,200 a year that I put down should have alerted anyone looking at this form that I was a total rube.

***

As soon as I got the copy of the letter Kennedy had said he'd send me, I went back to Washington and showed it to the woman at the passport division. She gave me a form to fill out. To my surprise, it said I had to have a witness to identify me in order for me to get my diplomatic passport.

I wondered who in the world I knew in Washington to perform that role. I told the woman there I would go out for lunch and come back in a little while. That would give me a little time to think, I figured.

I walked down the steps of the State Department trying to decide what I should do. Was it really true that the only people I knew in Washington were Jimmy or Frank or Johnny Roosevelt? In any case it would be too ridiculous for me to call one of them to help me on such a silly mission. And besides, I thought, I've no idea if any of them were in town.

As I was sweating out my problem, a nasal voice crept up behind me and said, "How'd they let you out of Baltimore?" The voice sounded as if it meant, "How'd they let you out of jail?"

I turned around and saw that it was a friend of Eddie's, the other salesperson at my emporium, the De Luxe Saddlery.

Eddie was in charge of things such as saddles, horse blankets, tools for mucking out stalls, and such items which were on display in a large space in the basement. Our boss at De Luxe, the man who had hired me, was Samuel Tissenbaum, a dear middle-aged man addicted to smoking cheap cigars, who had come from Poland some years ago. I soon learned that he was a fiercely patriotic American, and not only that, he had a markedly profound sense of rectitude. What Sam never knew, and would have died had he ever discovered, was that Eddie, in his empire in the basement, was not only selling equine paraphernalia but was also making book. Among Eddie's customers was Johnny, the cop from the corner up the street from our store, who came in to bet, I knew.

I now realized that the voice which just spoke to me at the bottom of the State Department steps belonged to Bootsie, another of Eddie's bookie customers. I liked all of Eddie's colorful pals, especially Bootsie. He was small and bandy-legged. I thought he must have been a jockey a long time ago. Now his more regular occupation was probably racetrack tout.

"Hi, ya, Bootsie," I said. "How come you aren't at the track? Although I must say I don't know where the ponies are running at this moment. Anyway, what luck to come across you!"

"My luck," he said, very friendly like.

"You asked what I'm doing here." I looked at him earnestly. "Well, Bootsie, you can do me a big favor, so I'll tell you what I'm doing here."

He came with me back to the passport desk and swore that I was who I said I was. To celebrate, we slipped into the closest bar we could find. He wouldn't even let me treat him and instead he insisted that he pay for my cola, as well as his beer. I thanked him warmly for the role he played in my getting a diplomatic passport.

Later Daddy asked to meet with Mr. Kennedy and we drove over together to Washington. The two men talked for a half an hour or so. Both mentioned their Harvard days proudly, and Kennedy promised that in the unlikely event that war broke out in Europe and he felt I would be in harm's way, he would send me home, just as he would send his own children home in the same circumstances.

Driving back home from Washington, Daddy said he suspected that Kennedy recognized that Europe was a "cauldron these days, what with a vicious Civil War in Spain, a maniac in Germany bent on havoc, and a mini-maniac in Italy with dreams of glory."

"Included Out"

"Button up your overcoat, when you're on a spree," I sang in my tuneless fashion as I danced onto the deck of the USS *Manhattan* on a bitterly cold day in late February 1938. And if "spree" wasn't the exact word, I figured it would serve as an adequate substitute for the adventure on which I was embarking: I was setting off with Joseph P. Kennedy to work for him in his spanking new post as the US ambassador to England.

"Take good care of yourself, you belong to me," I sang, smiling at my father, there to see me off on my journey. His old friend, "Uncle" Courty Moss, who had joined him for this occasion, picked up my nonsense: "Button up your overcoat when the wind is free," he sang. As he was singing, a blast of freezing air blew in off the Hudson. He looked hard at me and thought I was shivering. Now suiting his action to his words, he carefully buttoned up my overcoat all the way to my collar.

I wasn't shivering from the cold. I think I was just trembling with excitement about the job that lay ahead, and also I may have been quivering with apprehension about my qualifications for it. And so I was not as gracious as I should have been about "Uncle" Courty's kindly meant gestures. Further, by buttoning up my collar, he had hidden the beautiful Italian silk scarf that my mother—now stuck at home with the flu and thus unable to come to see me off—had given me some six weeks ago for my twentieth birthday present.

I tugged at my buttoned-up coat and wrestled out at least enough of my lovely scarf so that some of it could be seen above the collar.

Later the kindness of Harold Hinton and Harvey Klemmer, the other two members of the ambassador's entourage on this trip, subdued my nagging apprehension about my job. Our first night out to sea, when Kennedy had dinner at the captain's table, Harold, who was to be the ambassador's press officer, and Harvey, slated to be the ambassador's speech writer (with fine tuning by Harold), had already made me feel like a member of a seasoned team. We gossiped together about rumors of Kennedy's ambition to run for president if Roosevelt decided not to seek a third term, and about his passion to be the first Irish-American in the White House.

Harold pointed out that there were already four men who had been ambassadors to Britain who later became presidents. Then he named them (John Adams, James Monroe, Martin Van Buren, and James Buchanan) as if he had planned to all along, but I felt he had done it—gracefully—only for my edification.

Harold was on leave from the Washington bureau of the *New York Times* and he was to be my boss. I liked him immediately and looked forward hugely to working for him in whatever capacity he would find useful. "I'm going to be a happy drudge," I assured him.

I had ferreted out as much of their histories as I could beforehand. Harold, I had learned, was the son of an Episcopal minister. He had worked in England some years before for the *Times* and told amusing tales of London and other cities he had lived in or visited, all with a Southern raconteur's flair. He had a sophisticated little trick at dinner which fascinated me. He couldn't get the simple dressing he wanted for his salad, so he mixed his own, for himself at first, and then for me too. He held a big spoon in his left hand, added the ingredients for the dressing (oil, vinegar, mustard, salt, and pepper) with his right hand, and then stirred the mixture with a fork held in his right hand. It was delicious each time and I especially enjoyed the ceremony.

Harvey Klemmer had written much of the Maritime Commission Report for Kennedy when Kennedy was chairman of the Commission, the position he had just left on his appointment as ambassador to England. Kennedy had given Harvey much credit for his contribution to the Report. Harvey was grateful for this generosity, he told me, and added that generosity and frankness "are qualities not rife in Washington."

Where all the edges on Harold were smooth and rounded, those on Harvey were rough and sharp. To start with, he was the son of sharecropper parents in Michigan.

After working as a printer's devil at a local newspaper until he was sixteen, he had been a lumberjack, a factory worker and a merchant seaman. Somehow he acquired a formal education and was the principal of a high school near Detroit until he became a reporter for a Detroit newspaper. He had written several books, among them one called *Harbor Nights*, a copy of which he had with him. He gave it to me to read and since he figured Kennedy might not approve of my reading a book on the exploits of sailors on leave, Harvey covered the book with the jacket of a milder book, which he had gotten from the ship's library. He said he had tried to get a copy of *Little Women* for the use of its jacket, but there were none in the library.

We saw Joe Kennedy mainly at the evening meal when we all ate together. At lunch, however, there was no set hour, so we all ate at whatever time suited our fancies. On several occasions the ambassador and I hit the same lunch hour, and when we had finished we took a walk around the deck. They were brisk walks—he was not a stroller— and since it was windy we didn't try for protracted conversations, but on one of our walks we paused where it was quiet, near a funnel of the ship, and there we talked.

We chatted about this and that and he asked me how my family happened to know Courtland Moss, whom he had seen when he came over to say hello to Daddy and to welcome me aboard. Kennedy explained that when he was a freshman at Harvard, Courty was a senior and a devoted baseball player. Courty used to come to Joe Kennedy's pickup baseball team on Saturdays to coach the informal group "just for the fun of it," the ambassador said in an admiring voice. I commented that I had noticed with interest how fondly they had greeted when they ran across each other on the ship, and we laughed at the coincidence.

I explained that Courty (or Uncle Courty, as I called him) and my father had been friends forever, it seemed, although Uncle Courty was younger than Daddy, and they had indeed been members of the same club at Harvard.

"I'll bet you it was either Porcellian or the AD club," Kennedy said.

I smiled and said he was right. "It was the AD club." He smiled now, too, but this time it seemed to me his smile didn't look happy. I learned then that Joe Kennedy had a large repertoire of smiles.

I noted another smile a little later when the subject of his family came up. Harold and Harvey and I knew that Mrs. Kennedy hadn't been able to come on this trip because she had to have her appendix removed and thus would come over later. We had all asked the ambassador solicitously how she was doing and had been assured she was recovering rapidly. One evening Harold told the ambassador that he hoped she would be able to join him soon. The ambassador said he thought she would get over early next month, along with some of the younger children and the others would come shortly afterwards with Jack and Joe as soon as their courses at Harvard were over in the spring. None of them could get there soon enough for him, Kennedy said, smiling.

It was a soft smile and I thought one didn't have to plumb deep into Kennedy's psyche to see how sentimental he was about his family.

***

Harold's wife would get to London in early October too, he said, and Harvey's wife and their two little girls would be ready to come as soon as he found quarters for them. I chimed in to say that various members of my family would be over to see me from time to time and that several friends had threatened to descend on me wherever I lived in England.

At our dinners when we all sat together we were relaxed and informal, and we tarried over our meal. The conversation was general, with a certain amount of pleasant levity. Joe Kennedy had a ready and engaging laugh and we found amusing things to laugh about. But threaded throughout our dinners were discussions of the state of the world: the increasingly ferocious Civil War in Spain, the threats posed by fascism in Italy, Nazism in Germany—both of them major actors in Spain—and especially Hitler's reckless military appetite.

If I didn't make contributions to these discussions, I was at least fully aware of the events they were talking about. My father, a Republican on domestic issues, was also an ardent internationalist. I had often heard him say that it was ridiculous to refer to Mussolini as a buffoon, as one newspaper had. He was instead a very dangerous man, and should be regarded as such, Daddy had said. I remembered the stories about Mussolini's minister of foreign affairs boasting about how beautiful bombs looked falling on Ethiopia as the Italians invaded that country.

In a magazine back at home I had seen reproductions of that haunting painting by Picasso of the bombing of Guernica, a small town in northeastern Spain, by the German air force during the Spanish Civil War. That "gray cry of a painting," as someone had described it.

There were also allusions during our dinner conversations to the spread of Japanese military power into the east, particularly its brutal attack on China. But it was the European scene that most concerned us as we headed for England. Hitler seemed to be heating up the atmosphere to the boiling point. We knew we were in for a rough ride, and Joe Kennedy made it crystal clear that if war did break out in Europe, he hoped the US would be "included out."

* * *

I went frequently during the day to what had become one of my favorite perches on the ship, the deck on the stern, there to watch the wake we left behind. I had become fascinated by the trail of turbulence we made in the water as the bow of our great ship sliced through the ocean. After several visits there I began to see the ocean as having an extraordinary resilience of memory. The water, which only a few seconds previously had been forced into a raging wake, had re-formed itself nearly immediately back into the normal waves of peaks and crests it had been before.

One morning I was surprised to see through the porthole opposite my bed that it was snowing. I was surprised because I had never thought of snow on the ocean. After a hasty breakfast I bundled up and went to my stand on the stern deck.

The snowflakes were swirling down slowly and softly, enclosing my area of the deck with a fuzzy grayness. They felt like cool rose petals on my hands and on my cheeks. I noted that nearly the moment they fell to the deck they dissolved, leaving only a slightly wet trace of themselves. On the water they blended immediately into the ocean, and left no trace.

I watched the snow falling into the ship's wake and at first I thought I saw a slight glimmer of the snowflakes as they were being churned up in the turbulence the ship created as it cut through the water. After a few minutes, I realized that the snowflakes melded right into the wake just as they did in the undisturbed water.

The snow stopped suddenly and I considered I had the best of the day's water display and decided to go to my cabin and write some post cards before lunch. I'd write to my family and a few friends and mail them as soon as I get to London.

London, my God! I suddenly realized that we'd be in London the day after tomorrow. And I remembered that Joe Kennedy had said he hoped we would all have dinner together the next evening, the last one we would have on board. An unusual flash of sentiment on the ambassador's part, I mused, thinking that he generally seemed to wax sentimental only when mention of his children came up.

As I was leaving the deck, I saw Harvey emerge out of the mist. "I figured I'd find you up here," he said. "Harold says you hang out here sometimes." He looked at me curiously. "What have you been up to here?"

"Just admiring the ocean's amazing capacity for memory."

"That point of view makes you an anthropomorphist," he said, smiling.

"I guess so. That's what my mother always tells me." I smiled back and asked him why he was looking for me.

He explained that Ambassador Biddle wanted me to join him for lunch. The ambassador had told him that his wife Margaret had unfortunately already made a date for lunch, but that anyway they were meeting Joe Kennedy for dinner that night. He said he had wanted to corral the members of Joe's team for lunch, and get to know us all better. "Harold and I are meeting him at noon and we all hope you can be there, too." I told him I'd be delighted.

Ambassador Tony Drexel Biddle, US ambassador to Poland, was en route to London on the way to his new post in Warsaw. I knew that both Harold and Harvey admired him and considered him an eager and diligent diplomat. He had been US ambassador to Norway, considered at that time to be a fairly safe spot, but recently he had been transferred to Poland, a precarious post.

Poor Poland, Harvey had said, trapped between a Germany with a crazily ambitious Hitler and a Russia sharpening its military teeth. "A very different kettle of fish from Norway," he added.

I had gotten to know Ambassador Biddle slightly on board and found him cordial to a young person like me, and easy to talk to. He was easy on the eyes, too, as the expression goes. He would have been called handsome except for a slightly large nose, but he carried himself like a movie star and I thought he looked like an ad for sartorial splendor.

In one of our conversations I had mentioned that I knew his nephew, Angie Biddle Duke. "Oh, Angie," the ambassador said, in a despairing voice. I knew what he meant. Angie, who in addition to having inherited a bunch of Philadelphia old-line Biddle money, also had come into a lot of Duke tobacco dough and appeared to be throwing it all away as fast as possible on one foolish venture after another.

I didn't think it politic to say what I felt, but when Tony Biddle said that Angie was "sowing more wild oats than seemed absolutely necessary in order to grow up," I nodded and I suggested that Angie was bright, and added that I felt that somewhere deep down he was anxious to carve a constructive role for himself. "Exactly," his uncle said, "and when he finally grows up, just watch his smoke."

When we sat down for lunch that day, I smiled to Ambassador Biddle and, harking back to our optimistic predictions about his nephew Angie, I suggested we toast him and his future. I had not appreciated until that moment how much Angie looked like his distinguished uncle Tony, I told him. He seemed pleased by my comparison.

That was nearly the last of the lighthearted notes. It was clear as they talked that my luncheon partners wanted to seize this occasion to swap opinions about what was happening in the Europe we were going to, and for me it turned out to be history-*cum*-politics-course.

The ambassador seemed to set the scene. He started off, pointing out that, of course, we all knew there is a non-aggression pact between Poland and Germany. He cited all the agreements and pacts that Hitler had broken so far.

"I don't have much faith in that non-aggression treaty," he said, "considering Hitler's general attitude toward treaties." As he talked, he picked up a paper napkin from under a wine glass on the table. Now, slowly and deliberately, he tore the napkin into smithereens. Surveying the symbolic little shreds of paper that lay in various piles on the table, he went on. He said that his real worry was that the two most important democracies in Europe didn't seem to be aware of what was happening in their world. They seemed to be "asleep at the switch."

Both Harvey and Harold nodded, so I asked them why they agreed with that comment. For the rest of our lunch these men discussed the current attitudes of the leaders of France and England, the countries that the ambassador had obviously referred to. I felt as if I was at a ping pong game, turning my head each time to watch whoever was speaking as he sought, in effect, to answer my question.

They were highly critical of these leaders because of their appeasement of both the Nazis and the fascists for their huge—and unabashed—support of Franco in the Civil War in Spain: Nazi Germany and Fascist Italy were supplying Franco with soldiers and huge amounts of advice, arms, and matériel. Granted, Russia was supporting the elected Spanish government, but not with the same "weight and zeal, and it was after all, elected by the people of Spain," Harold commented.

As they talked I was reminded of the stories that I read in the papers back in Maryland of the German Air Force bombing in areas of Spain known to be anti-Franco. Picasso's painting of Guernica flashed across my mind again. I was surprised to learn that the role of the Germans there had triggered no flack from the leaders of France and England. I remember Harvey saying that it "looks as if the cats have got the tongues of the leaders of the great democracies of Europe." I asked why had they fallen into such a state of suspended animation. "Don't they know how dangerous the fascists and the Nazis are?"

"I think," Harvey suggested, "that they are simply tortured by history: the history of the death of so many millions of their young men in the World War. Further, the violence of trench warfare seems to have destroyed the certainties which had ruled their lives." He went on to say that that convulsive history made the present day leaders of England and France terrified that the present war in Spain would lead to another world war, and so they dare not take sides.

Then he dove into how at least one important European statesman had recently expressed his contempt, first, for this form of appeasement, and second, for a dreadful new international invasion of a defenseless country. The British Foreign Secretary, Sir Anthony Eden, was threatening to resign from Chamberlain's cabinet for its failure to condemn Germany and Italy and also in protest against Chamberlain's acceptance of Italy's conquest of Ethiopia. Harold wondered aloud how many other members of the Prime Minister's cabinet would "strike a blow for decency." Seared in the memories of the French and the British, Ambassador Biddle said, is the immutable fact that it has been such a brief time since the World War ended. He added that those memories "are so benumbingly fresh that the prospect of another war..." and he didn't bother to finish that sentence.

As I listened, I realized that I was already conscious of a sketchy history of the war. After all, my father had fought in it, a major in a machine gun battalion, although he never talked about it. Even so, through images and pictures I had seen in magazines, I was aware of the brutality of that war, the ghastly fighting in the trenches, the devastation of machine gun battles and the dreadful toll they had taken. I guessed I thought that I was generally familiar with the sweep of history that was called the Great War or sometimes the World War. But as my friends filled in toxic details in their discussions, I mentioned that the impact of how these tragedies had immobilized the British and French leaders had never occurred to me.

My friends responded by talking about the effect on the French of the shocking statistics of the Battle of Verdun. There, in the longest single battle of the war, some 400,000 French soldiers were either wounded or killed. The very word "Verdun" could still turn French blood to ice, Harold said. But even before I recovered from that shock they talked about the battle at a place called Passchendaele, until I interrupted to say I had never heard of that.

They explained to me that this took place in deep swamp country, west of Flanders, in Belgium. I was told that thousands of British and Australians and Canadians perished in what was called "the mud and the blood of Passchendaele." Tanks, newly used in this war, also sank into the mire; horses and mules got sucked in. It was a battle which had seesawed back and forth between the Allies and the Germans for weeks on end. Harold pointed out that for every inch the Allies gained, the cost was a British life. His comparison for an inch gained having cost one British life beggared my imagination. He quoted Siegfried Sassoon, the famous British poet. "I died in Hell," Sassoon had written. "They called it Passchendaele." That one word, Harold said, paralyzes the British.

Harvey went on to say that a half a million men of the Allied armies died, or were wounded, missing or captured in Passchendaele alone and a huge number of Germans were injured or killed there. "It is no wonder that this slaughter is still so fresh in the minds and the hearts of the French and the British," one of them said. "It all happened such a short time ago."

I looked grimly at my newfound friends. My God, that short time had actually been twenty years. I was twenty years old myself. I decided I wanted the word twenty to be so graphic that neither of these men, nor I myself, would ever forget that all this butchery had taken place such short a time ago. I murmured the words "twenty years" and chose the way a young child indicates its age by raising the appropriate number of fingers. I raised both hands and closed them into fists. I flicked up the fingers of each hand once, closed them, and then flicked them up again. I think my eyes must have filled and for a few seconds, I thought I was going to cry.

I guess Ambassador Biddle must have feared that same casualty because he shifted conversational gears adroitly. He said something to the effect that he didn't want to have to report to Margaret that we had spent the entire lunch upsetting the new young assistant to the press attaché. And the next thing I knew we had somehow sashayed into a conversation extolling Ignace Paderewski, the extraordinary Pole, for his prodigious talents. It turned out he was a special star in Ambassador Biddle's lexicon. We talked for a while about his musical genius, his deftness as a diplomat and his distinguished career as a statesman, which included his role as prime minister of Poland, not just once but twice.

Ambassador Biddle surprised us by telling us of another talent that Paderewski had: the amazing Pole's career as a successful vintner! About a dozen or so years ago, Paderewski had bought a 2,000-acre farm near a town in central California, the ambassador told us. The Pole planted grapes on his farm; he sold the grapes to a nearby winery, which made them into an excellent wine. Tony Biddle informed his delighted group that the farm, called Rancho san Ignacio, is still thriving and that every year Ignacio Paderewski is celebrated in the nearest community at a great wine festival.

He said he hoped we would all have the pleasure of drinking that wine some day and toasting that extraordinary Polish polymath.

Now, he said, he could report to his wife that we had ended lunch on a happy note.

Last Night on Our Trip

The minute I sat down to dinner the last night on board, I sensed that we were in for an odd evening. I don't know how I figured out so quickly that our dinner was not going to be especially lively, despite all that I had assumed beforehand. I had imagined we were all prepared for a salutation of some sort to the adventure that lay ahead for us.

I had thought we would recognize with pleasure the fellowship we had made on board. If we weren't exactly a band of brothers—and one sister—we were, willy-nilly, melded together for this uncertain experience. However, instead of being united this last evening each of us appeared to be off on a private meander. Everyone seemed preoccupied with his own concerns.

Where was the merriment I had anticipated? Where the buzz of congeniality? The only sounds I heard were the clatter of the silverware on china plates at our table, the ambient noise around us, and the happy banter and pleasantries of the people at nearby tables.

A little while later someone did say something that stirred a ripple. I don't recall who said it or even what was said, but it caused an opening and we did finally begin to chat. We started off with small talk, as we had on the occasions before when we all had dinner together, but this time it didn't sound as if it was going to evolve into real conversation or into our usual traffic in ideas. And it trailed off to thin air.

For a while I found my own mind wandering. If none of the others were affected by the significance of this particular evening, I was, damn it, I said to myself. I planned to remember this special night. I decided I would stare at these three men and fix their looks in my mind for keeps.

Here was Joe Kennedy, handsome enough, with strong features, and whatever he was thinking about now, he was wearing a slightly sympathetic expression. However, by looking at him as fixedly as I dared, I figured that he had a mercurial personality. I thought that despite the picture of sympathy he often wore, if an occasion called for it, the ambassador could look as tough as nails.

Whatever his temperament, I thought, he certainly looked younger than his forty-nine years, and his hair still had a trace of the red of his youth. I noted again those expressive blue eyes, and those super white teeth. I was already conscious of his big bag of smiles, and in my mind's eye I had devised names for some of them, but it was those teeth which made his "public smile" so attractive.

However, to me, the core of Kennedy's strong personality was none of those things. It was his extra jolt of vitality.

As I set my eyes on Harold, I hoped I wasn't squinting in an obvious giveaway. I noted for the first time that he was a little fleshy, especially around his jowls and his chin, but that didn't detract from the warmth he exuded. I could visualize him as a little boy and I figured he already had that kind, nearly sweet, look. I hoped Harold's wife was sweet because that's what he deserved. And she'd have to be bright, too, in order to keep up with Harold's broad range of interests and his nimble mind. And she'd have to have a subtle sense of humor, like his.

Harvey was balder than I had realized, I figured as I stared intently at him. His creeping hairline tended to lengthen an already long face, but I discovered there was a hint of a cleft chin and that somewhat deflected the long countenance.

I was just thinking that Harvey's streamlined look mellowed by that winning, broad smile he wore so much of the time, when I was suddenly jerked out of my miasma. I realized that either he or Harold had asked the ambassador if he could find anything in common between himself and the first US ambassador to England. Now I was fully alert and paying attention. I had come to the party.

I could see that Joe Kennedy's normal rhythm of vitality was back on beam. He laughed heartily at the question and said that he and John Adams had important things in common. "We both came from Boston and we both went to Harvard," he said. He smiled and then he added, "That's about it."

I thought he had finished with John Adams, but he went on. "And although it's been over a hundred and fifty years," Kennedy said, "since Adams was appointed to the Court of St. James's, he expressed a political point of view which I think rings true today."

Harvey asked the ambassador if he would elaborate. Kennedy said that he couldn't remember Adams's exact quote, but it was something to the effect that "people and nations are forged in the fires of adversity."

I knew, of course, that the country's fires of adversity in John Adams's time meant the revolution itself and the struggle to get the Declaration of Independence written and accepted. In Joe Kennedy's time, they had meant the years it took to recover from the worst depression the country had ever known, and the struggle to continue passage of Roosevelt's New Deal legislation.

However, I wondered if the fires of adversity to which Kennedy referred also had a special personal angle: the hostility to which he, as an Irish Catholic, had been subjected by the Brahmins of Boston. An old doggerel ran through my mind:

> And this is good old Boston,
> The home of the bean and the cod,
> Where the Lowells talk to the Cabots,
> And the Cabots talk only to God.

There was no question that from everything I had read or heard about Kennedy, he desperately wanted to have one more thing in common with John Adams: he wanted to be President of the United States.

He wanted to be the first Irish-American president. He already had a close relationship with God and now he wanted one with the Cabots. If he made it to the White House, there would be no stigma left in being a Boston Irish Catholic.

I thought about how much Joe Kennedy had riding for him in the job he was embarking on tomorrow. The way he played his cards could possibly pave the way to victory for his dream...or it could spell disaster.

After a few seconds I realized that the ambassador was talking to me. "Page," he said, in a slightly teasing voice, "I have never before heard you so quiet." We all laughed at the way he had phrased his comment. He went on, "Indeed, I don't think you have asked one question all evening."

The second remark alluded to my relentless search for information. Harold had recently scrambled a Kipling line about the person who "kept six honest serving men." He said that I was that person and these serving men had taught me all I knew. Harold had gone on to list their names, of which I could only remember "What and Why and Where and Who."

No doubt I had been abnormally quiet all evening. Now I turned to look directly at Joe Kennedy. "Well, Mr. Ambassador," I said, smiling, "I think you should be grateful for small favors." He laughed.

Clearly Kennedy was now totally engaged, and he was enjoying himself. The whole tone of the evening had changed. We were all now lighthearted and involved with each other.

The ambassador made a point of talking directly to Harold and Harvey. He thanked them both for the help they had given him in the speech he would make tomorrow on his arrival in England. It was clear he thought this speech would be of great importance. After all, it would be the first speech he would make in his new role.

Harold and Harvey smiled, pleased with the cheery words from the ambassador. Now he turned to me again and told me that he had asked Harvey to escort me to the place where I would be living in London. I thanked him profusely for his consideration and he responded with a smile.

I now had a sense that the evening, which after all, thank God, had turned out to be so different from the way it had started, was winding down.

A few seconds later the ambassador said he was about to turn in. He wished us all good luck in the exciting sojourn that lay ahead for us.

Harvey said he would like to make one comment before we all split for the night. He said there is one thing that all seasoned sailors know, or should know, and that is to Expect the Unexpected. We know the Unexpected is waiting in the wings, he went on, poised to pounce on us. In sailing it can be an errant iceberg, a sudden wild storm, anything, as long as it is Unexpected.

He paused, and in a voice edging on the dramatic, said he hoped we all could understand the significance of the Unexpected. "And, more important, I just hope that England and the other democracies in Europe are prepared for the Unexpected."

We were all standing now, poised to head for our rooms. Joe Kennedy smiled one of his best smiles and said that following up on what Harvey had just said, he wanted to repeat a Goldwynism he had made a few days ago. "In the event that England gets involved in a war," he said, "I will do everything in my power to *include the US out.*"

That idea had already been etched in my memory the first time I heard him say it. I went to sleep that night thinking about it.

Diplomatic Dilemma

If it had been bitterly cold when Ambassador Kennedy and his motley crew left the US, in contrast a sun-flecked day greeted us as we approached England. It was surprisingly cherry for an early March day there.

The ambassador, accompanied by Harold Hinton, was picked up by a tender and taken to Southampton so he could be welcomed in the style befitting a new American ambassador. Awaiting him on the dock were the Mayor of Southampton and various other dignitaries, including some from the American embassy. The counselor of the embassy, Herschel V. Johnson, a dedicated Foreign Service officer, was the leader of the embassy group.

I learned later from Harold that Herschel had been terrified that the ambassador would arrive chewing gum (he didn't). Herschel would find that worrying about Kennedy chewing gum was like straining at gnats, when he would in effect have to worry much more about swallowing camels.

Indeed the ambassador presented a diplomatic problem for the seasoned Johnson immediately. Kennedy had with him the statement which he planned to give to the press on arrival in Southampton. He showed it to Johnson.

The statement, the one for which the ambassador had thanked Harold and Harvey at dinner the evening before, was a mild but honest exposition of Joe Kennedy's ingrained isolationist views. Johnson felt awkward at trying to restrain his new boss right off the bat, but he was able to tactfully dissuade Kennedy from making that statement then, on the grounds that it didn't seem like the proper timing for such comments.

***

Once in London, it didn't need Harold Hinton's expertise to whip up the British newspapers' interest in the first Irish-American ambassador to the Court of St. James's. Joe was a natural for an uninhibited press corps. There were pictures of the dynamic Kennedy in newspapers of all political stripes, accompanied by glowing stories. And then the first time he played golf in England, he made a hole in one! The English papers ate that up. Harold was amused. "What a way to make a hit with the golf-loving British," he commented to me.

When the amazingly young-looking ambassador's wife, Rose, and seven-ninths of the Kennedy children—Joe and Jack stayed behind to finish up their college semesters as planned—appeared on the scene, the papers went into a frenzy of excitement. Pictures of this charming group, sightseeing all over London, with their broad smiles and all those gleaming teeth, were plastered in the papers.

One photographer was especially entranced by the youngest Kennedy, Teddy. He was holding his camera upside down as he took a picture of a guard at Buckingham Palace. The photographer, who had snapped the boy snapping the picture, persuaded the nanny accompanying the children to give him the film. The next day the whole front page of a London tabloid ran the picture of a guard standing on his head, giving Edward Moore Kennedy, aged eight, credit as the photographer.

***

However, early 1938 was far from beer and skittles on the international scene. Indeed the fears we had expressed en route to England about Hitler's alarming military ambition proved only too true. Our group had barely settled into its work at the big brick American embassy building that dominated Grosvenor Square—indeed we had been there less than two weeks—when disaster struck Europe. German troops invaded Austria. Hitler announced it as an *anschluss*, a "union with Germany," as if that made the invasion acceptable.

With the Nazi annexation of Austria, I was exposed for the first time to the vaunted British gift for understatement. I was living in a boarding house, called aptly enough Miss Living's, which had been recommended to me by a friend of my mother's as "safe and respectable," an unusual kind of description coming from my mother, who was given to livelier language. When Harvey had escorted me there, he carried my bags to the front door, where we were greeted by Miss Living herself. She was tall and forbidding-looking. Harvey said afterwards that she made him wince, but I learned immediately that she was actually kind and friendly.

Installed there, I figured I brought the median age of the seven or so women ensconced at Miss Living's down to about sixty. At dinner the night we heard of the German takeover of Austria, I was seated next to one of the oldest denizens of Miss Living's establishment, a wisp of a woman I reckoned to be pushing ninety. She leaned toward me and said she was shocked by the news. I told her I agreed with her wholeheartedly.

She lowered her voice. "Do you want to know what I think of Mr. Hitler?" I assured her I would like to know. She leaned close and her voice was so faint that I had to strain to hear her. "I think he is..." She put her hand over her mouth like a child does when it is about to say something naughty. I waited eagerly. She started again. "I think he is..." Now she whispered so low I could hardly hear her. "A cad," she finally said.

At Miss Living's I also learned a British expression that amused me. Beryl, the housemaid there, asked me what time I wanted to be "knocked up" in the morning. She was simply asking me what time should she awaken me for the cup of tea she would bring me.

Beryl and I became sort of pals and once she told me a wonderfully practical trick for pressing clothes, although I was never able to get it to work for me. Her husband, who was in the army, used to put his pants, properly folded, under the mattress, sleep over them at night, and in the morning put on pants that looked so well pressed they could have just come from the tailor. I tried the idea with a pleated skirt of mine and it didn't help the pleats.

***

Meanwhile, at the embassy, more of the ambassador's personal staff showed up, Edward Moore among them. Eddie was a dear gentle-appearing soul who had worked for Kennedy for years, and before that he had worked for Kennedy's father-in-law, the famous "Singing Honey" Fitzgerald, mayor of Boston. Eddie and his wife Mary were the closest non-Kennedy creatures on earth to the Kennedy family. In fact, the youngest Kennedy child, Teddy, the photographer, had been named for Eddie Moore.

Eddie's office was directly in front of the ambassador's and he generally appeared to be the ambassador's faithful old dog Tray, but if anyone wanted to see the ambassador and Eddie figured the ambassador didn't want to see that person at that time, Eddie turned himself into the proverbial junkyard dog.

Others of that disparate group that made up Kennedy's personal staff at the embassy turned up soon. Among them was Arthur Houghton, who had worked for Hollywood's Motion Picture Association when Kennedy was riding high in Hollywood. He was handsome with an open smile and wavy silver hair. He had an ample supply of jokes and he said that's why Kennedy brought him to London. "I've got to have someone to make me laugh," he'd told Houghton.

He shared an office in the embassy with yet another of Kennedy's special staff, a man named Jack Kennedy, now called "Ding Dong" so he would not be confused with the ambassador's son, Jack Kennedy. Ding Dong, who was especially friendly, had worked for Joe in some capacity at RKO Radio in Kennedy's Hollywood days. He was stocky and I thought he looked as if he could have been a prize fighter at an earlier time.

A special bell connected Arthur and Ding Dong's office to the ambassador's. When the bell rang for Arthur, he would act as if he was a fireman responding to an emergency, grab an imaginary fire helmet from off the wall, put it on his head, and shoot out of the room toward the ambassador's office.

A little later, a man named Jim Seymour appeared on the scene. He was another pal of the ambassador's from his Hollywood era. He was given a desk in Arthur and Ding Dong's office and he was only there briefly, but what Jim Seymour's role was to be remained a mystery. If he never seemed to be there when he was there, he was at least in his office when a former wife turned up, berating him in an angry voice that carried all over the embassy. My recollection is that she was demanding some back alimony payments.

Joe Kennedy, Jr. and Jack arrived in London late that spring. They were in and out of the embassy frequently, with Joe Jr. nearly always chewing gum. They were given various titles: aides to the ambassador, special assistants, roving reporters, depending on the roles to which their father assigned them.

It is little wonder that our group was known *sub rosa* by the career diplomats in the embassy as the "Grosvenor Square Irregulars." I suspect that was the most respectable moniker they gave us.

Kennedy and the State Department

When the ambassador was to make a speech, generally he would discuss the drift of what he wanted to say with Harold and Harvey and they would draft a speech. Harold batted out his copy with two fingers in a fast newspaper style. Sometimes I typed that draft up cleaner for Harold to work on. Later, when I worked on a newspaper, I learned to type even worse than Harold had!

Kennedy would then either make changes on the draft or suggest changes to the writers and Harold typed up a clean copy including those changes. And, of course, there were more changes. Anyway, when the ambassador finally got the speech he wanted, it was sent to the State Department for approval. It was the ambassador's secretary who typed up the final version, in large type, including changes the Department had indicated.

The first speech that Kennedy made in England was to a group called the Pilgrim's Club. It was an important occasion in any event, but this time it assumed a special importance because it came close on the heels of the Nazi invasion of Austria. There was a great deal of thought and time spent on the preparations of that speech.

When it was sent to the State Department the response was immediate: the tone of the speech was too isolationist and specific changes were suggested so that the speech was considerably blanded down. Kennedy told his important audience that the "US would be glad to join and encourage any nation or groups of nations in a peace program based on economic recovery, limitation of armaments, and a revival of the sanctity of international commitments." The Department had left that in.

Harold and Harvey and I often bet how much the Department would change or delete in Kennedy's speeches. We were all three surprised later when the State Department had agreed to leave in a speech the part where Kennedy warned England against her presuming US participation in European affairs. He said that the "great majority of Americans oppose any entangling alliances and that they are appalled by the prospect of war as it is now waged." In any event, our team at the embassy agreed that the ambassador was right about US public opinion at that time. That's the feeling we got from all the reports and polls we read in US papers, the American magazines we saw, and the letters we got from home.

Aside from the speeches that Harold helped to write and rewrite for the ambassador, he also wrote reports on the political scene in

England for Kennedy. These were based on scrawled notes from the ambassador, embellished by Harold, and then were sent privately to a list of about twenty of Kennedy's friends in the US. Since these did not have to be vetted by the State Department, Joe was much freer to express views not in line with the Secretary of State or even with the President, or even to express views that might be opposed to both.

Old Warrior

Some time in the late spring a beautiful young Austrian, Baroness Marietta Mengerson, fetched up at Miss Living's. She had come to England to get a "tailor made"—a suit made especially for her—and to pursue, unsuccessfully it turned out, an Englishman with whom she had fallen in love when he was in the British embassy in Vienna. She and I cottoned to each other immediately and set about finding an abode a little more suited to our adventuresome souls than our present one.

We heard of a remarkable English family that took in boarders, or paying guests—P.G.'s as the more polite term went—at their house in fashionable Cadogan Square. Within a week we had moved in with Colonel and Mrs. George Richey. Marietta and I had understood that the Richeys had come on hard times and had taken in P.G.'s to make ends meet. We decided that the house was such a white elephant for them that they had taken in P.G.'s to make the middle meet!

The house was huge. Built in 1879, it had once been described by a distinguished architect as a remarkable example of elongated elegance. It was certainly elongated. There were six stories. Someone had counted the steps between the servants' quarters in the basement and the rooms on the top floor and supposedly had come up with a number over 100. And it was elegant. There were exquisite carved decorative details all over the exterior, and the elegance was reflected in the interior with a frieze on the mantle piece in the dining room, carved banisters on the stairs and so forth.

The Richeys had filled the house with a diverting group of young people. Among them was the son of the then-British ambassador to Russia, who had just "come down" from Cambridge, a Polish woman in England to study the language, a young British Middle East expert, and a young woman studying ballet. There were also two sons in the Richey family, Paul and Michael, both in their early twenties. Marietta and I were delighted to join this merry throng.

Mrs. Richey had a warm outgoing personality. She always seemed to be in motion. And no wonder: she did the cooking and much of the housework for all of us. She had wavy dark hair, gently streaked with gray. One lock of hair fell loose from time to time and she brushed it off her face with the back of her hand in a charming gesture.

Colonel Richey was slim with sharply defined features. He was always immaculately dressed, in a handsome well-cut dark suit, which showed a little wear, a white shirt and an understated necktie. When I learned he had joined the army before he was eighteen, I figured the long life of soldiering had given him that easy, erect walk.

They were obviously a devoted couple. The family was ardently Catholic. Both the boys had gone to Downside, the Roman Catholic equivalent of Eton and Winchester and all of the other fabled so-called public schools of England rolled into one. Indeed it is sometimes referred to as a college.

Paul, the older of the two, was in the Royal Air Force. He was engaged to a peaches-and-cream English beauty, Teresa Robinson. Her father was head of the Forestry Commission, a crucial job in a country faced with the prospects of war. "Pit props" to beef up coal mines, were made of wood. Since coal was the major source of energy in an England now gearing for war, pit props were a major concern of the Forestry Commission. Teresa's brother Mickey was also in the RAF and a beloved friend of Paul's.

Paul was saved from looking like a Greek god only by virtue of a barely noticeable upturn at the end of his nose. Although he appeared unaware of his beguiling looks, he would have to be a fool not to realize how handsome he was. Just the way women stared at him should have been clue enough for him. In any event, he only had eyes for Teresa.

One characteristic of Paul's that both amused and confounded me was his smile. It was both slow and somewhat compressed. It seemed to say there was more behind it than just a smile and that he might divulge the secret—or he might not.

Michael, the younger son, on the other hand, had a broad, open smile. He too was handsome, but not in Paul's flashy way. Mike was apprenticed to multi-faceted Eric Gill, a sculptor, wood engraver, letter carver in stone and author. Gill's farm in Buckinghamshire had become the center of a movement of brilliant artists of one kind and another, who were, for the most part, Catholic. Prominent among them was David Jones, the Welsh painter and poet. T.S. Eliot had called Jones's book, *In Parenthesis*, "a work of genius." Michael

Richey developed into a talented letter carver, a brilliant editor, a writer, and an artist. One Christmas he designed a beautiful book plate for me.

Michael was far more deeply committed to his religion than Paul and had once considered becoming a monk. He was particularly close to an older half sister (Colonel Richey's daughter by his first, late wife) who was a nun, and if Mike never actually became a member of a brotherhood, he assumed some of the characteristics of a monk. At the same time, he was sophisticated and worldly. All of these characteristics jumbled together created an interesting effect.

Both Paul and Michael were keenly intelligent and each had a brisk sense of humor. They were delightful company and they both became dear friends of mine. Colonel Richey didn't wear his Catholicism as obviously as Mike. He had a more playful attitude toward it. For instance, he used to call me his favorite "Palien," a combination of pagan and alien. I was a pagan because I wasn't Catholic and I was an alien because I wasn't British. I got some kudos from him, however, because my boss, Joe Kennedy, was Catholic to the hilt. Joe Kennedy was amused when I told him that I was getting fringe benefits with my host family because of his vaunted Roman Catholicism.

***

A friend of Colonel Richey's visiting at Cadogan Square one day told me that if war broke out, Colonel Richey would go crazy not being able to be involved in it somehow. "He's already fought in five wars for England and I think that's enough," the visitor said, "but Richey won't."

"Five wars?" I said, astounded.

"And he was wounded seven times."

Later, when I had a chance, I dug out of his friend the names of Colonel Richey's wars, and nothing else made me more aware of the huge number of battles England fought in far-flung spots in her scramble to build her empire. Indeed, most of Colonel Richey's battles had been fought in exotic places I'd never heard of. I was fascinated by their names. He was in the Bechuanaland Expedition in South Africa, he was in the Mashona Rebellion and in the Boer War (that one I had heard of!). One of his seven wounds took place in an area called Water Val Drift. Then he was serving in Kitchener's Horse (shortly after he joined the army he had been in Methuen's Horse).

However, not all of his wars were in pursuit of Empire forging. He fought in what the British called the European War, or sometimes the Great War, and occasionally the World War. In 1917 he was wounded at Ypres. I don't know in what other battles he picked up the rest of his wounds, but somehow he also commanded a Brigade in Palestine. For his remarkable service he was twice awarded the DSO (Distinguished Service Order) and was three times recommended for the V.C. (the Victoria Cross), the veriest accolade of all.

He never told me any serious stories about his life in the army but once I got a frivolous one out of him. One evening I said something that triggered a memory of his when he was a young officer in South Africa.

"I found I had a lot of raw Irish soldiers under my command and I was warned that they were going to be a handful. Since I am Irish myself I knew what that portended for me," he said. "One day, early on, when I was reviewing them, I was wearing my monocle. I could tell immediately that they thought the monocle was a little eccentric, to say the least, but I didn't pay any attention."

"The next day," he went on, "I discovered that every one of my soldiers had cut the top off his tin of bully beef and had stuck it in his eye as if it was a monocle. I ignored their 'monocles' completely. As I walked past for inspection I told one soldier to shine his dratted buttons better next time; I told another to pull his damned gut in, and another to hold his bloody shoulders back. I went down the line, finding faults with about every other one. I could see they were having a hard time repressing their smiles.

"Then I walked back to my position, where I faced them all in the line. I looked at them without saying a word. I calmly flicked my monocle up in the air and caught it in the correct position in my eye."

"'All right,' I said quietly, 'Let's see you darned soldiers do that.'" He smiled his mellow smile. "They followed me 'round like pet puppy dogs from then on," he said.

Sometime after the end of the European War, Richey was sent to Albania to reorganize the gendarmerie there. One result of that sojourn is that he had to learn to speak French, the language of the few educated Albanians and of the diplomatic corps in Tirana. Adelaide already spoke French. Both of their young sons, Paul and Michael, became totally fluent in French. Later they were sent to school in Switzerland.

In the house at Cadogan Square, the Richeys had one special souvenir from their days in Tirana, an ancient dog named Jill who had been born in the American Legation there and given to the Richey boys by the American minister to Albania. Jill was showing her venerable years by white hairs, which had overtaken her original black, and by her laid-back view of life. Colonel Richey often said he was very happy now to have two Americans living with his family.

Two Wrong Ways, One Mine and One Corrigan's

Among the people I had met in England soon after my arrival was an attractive German working for a Berlin newspaper. I found Hans Georg Von S. warm and interesting with an original—if sharp—sense of humor, and we had a wonderful time together. Mrs. Richey met him once when he came to pick me up and found him "tremendously appealing." I agreed, and the more I saw of him the more appealing I found him. She suggested that he was mad for me and she wondered what I would say if he proposed marriage to me. If I said "yes" to him, would I go live with him in Germany if he got assigned back there?

Then suddenly one day I realized I had to get uninvolved with him simply because he was German. Actually, I didn't realize it suddenly, for I had been worried for weeks and the raw reality suddenly hit me: He was anti-Hitler but he was still German and I figured he would go back to Berlin someday and continue to work for his newspaper and not rock his boat with any outspoken anti-Hitler sentiments. I also felt sure that someday Germany and England would be at war and...

Reluctantly, for we had become increasingly dependent on each other, I told Hans tearfully of my problem and in view of that I thought it best that we not see each other any more. Afterwards I was immensely proud of myself that I had the wit to understand that I was on the brink of that delectable dizziness of falling hopelessly in love (falling is such an apt word in this sense) and that I had enough strength (or was it enough fear?) to pull myself safely back onto *terra firma*. At first I felt smug and then for a while I felt miserable. Once or twice I nearly called him. And then I felt entirely cured of him.

I was surprised when several months after we had last seen each other Hans called to say he had to see me, "If only for a few minutes, please, just to lay eyes on you." I was firm in telling him that I had made my decision and that I thought he had understood it. I said I didn't think it even made sense to talk to each other and I was about to tell him goodbye for keeps again when Marietta came into the room and I suddenly got a brilliant idea. I told Hans I hadn't changed my mind about us, but I asked him to come around to Cadogan Square for a drink the next evening. There was someone I wanted to introduce him to.

He wouldn't take his eyes off me that evening. I could feel them burning me and he paid no attention to Marietta then. Later I advised her to call him and just say she was happy to have met him. It worked, and then they began to see each other off and on. After a while they saw each other constantly. In a few months Marietta told me they were going to get married. I was delighted and a friend of mine told me I was a good *shadchen* (the Yiddish word for the person in the community that arranges marriages). Anyway, they went to Germany soon afterwards to get married.

***

All such personal events were taking place with the shock waves of Hitler's seizure of Austria still reverberating throughout England. Some felt that the country was drifting slowly toward disaster. Others were more fearful: they felt that England was somersaulting toward war. Hitler was rattling his saber louder and talking more of the oppression of the poor Germans in the Sudetenland part of Czechoslovakia, and of his decision for them to be brought into the Greater Reich.

Kennedy was in constant touch with Chamberlain and agreed with him that war must somehow be staved off. Kennedy was now more outspoken about the tragedy of war and the chaos, cultural and economic disasters that would follow war; he believed that the communists would be the eventual victors in Europe if there was war.

Harold's various responsibilities kept me busy and occasionally the ambassador called on me for some sort of task, but I had an odd extracurricular assignment from him for a few days in July 1938. An American pilot named Douglas Corrigan had flown nonstop from New York to Dublin in a single-engine plane without anyone being aware he had taken off; he hadn't even filled out a flight plan.

In Ireland he swore he had thought he was flying to California and thus immediately earned the nickname "Wrong Way Corrigan." At a hugely attended press conference he was asked if he could not figure out his direction by the position of the sun. The only time he saw the sun, he said, was when it was directly overhead; further, he explained, that his compass had "gone wrong."

He came to London where it was incumbent on the American ambassador to pay some attention to his famous, if bizarre, fellow countryman. I passed Kennedy in the hall as he set out to greet Corrigan. I told him I'd read that Corrigan had flown in a Curtiss Robin airplane, the same kind that my father had used for business years ago, and thus

I'd like to meet him. I couldn't believe that a plane like that could fly 3,000-plus miles across the Atlantic.

The next day Kennedy called me to his office. "You wanted to meet 'Wrong Way Corrigan,'" he said smiling. "He's yours. Take time off and show him around London. And, for God's sake, find him a chocolate bar." He paused. "A chocolate bar, with nuts in it. That's all he wants."

I met up with Corrigan that afternoon, and together we found the chocolate bar, with nuts in it. He seemed to enjoy the tours of London I gave him that day and the next. He was especially interested in the idea that my father had had a Curtiss Robin with a Challenger motor. I explained that my father had had a pilot; he wasn't a pilot himself. I told him my family would be delighted to hear from him when he got back to the US. He promised to call my family. I told him to report that I was in excellent shape, and though I missed them all terribly, I was not homesick. I said I was too busy to get homesick, and besides the family I now lived with in London was an ideal temporary substitute for my real one.

I had told my family all these things in letters but I thought they'd be amused to hear them again from "Wrong Way Corrigan." I later learned in a letter from Mother that Douglas Corrigan had called and that Daddy especially had a nice long chat with him. Corrigan told them that I was very happy and pleased that some of my family were coming to see me soon.

Shortly afterwards my sister Rosalind came to visit me. We had dinner one night with English friends of hers, went to see what the British call "pictures" in various galleries, to the theater one night, and I had a small sherry party for her in the big living room in my adopted home. (Serving only sherry, instead of cocktails, seemed to be an acceptable form of entertainment in London then).

Among the guests were, of course, the Richeys and some of my housemates and a few other friends including Jack and Kick Kennedy. Rosalind and Kick hit it off extremely well. At Kick's suggestion, I arranged that she could join us when we went to visit a friend outside London for the following weekend.

I took a few days of vacation time from the embassy and Rosalind and I went to France to a seaside village, Villerville, on the northern coast of Normandy. It was charming and unspoiled and we immediately made friends with a young French couple staying there. The Norman coast was calm and lovely and not cluttered with visitors of any kind that summer of 1938.

Rosalind sailed home soon after we returned to London, by which time I was already back at work at an embassy that had seemed reasonably calm a short while ago but which now was roiling. Hitler had announced again that the "oppression" of Germans in the Sudetenland of Czechoslovakia could no longer be tolerated. Harold was particularly occupied by the impending crisis and I was kept jumping by his hectic appointments schedule and a telephone that never stopped ringing, mostly newspaper or radio reporters wanting to know what Ambassador Kennedy was thinking.

As usual, Kennedy was pretty explicit about his point of view. He had recently made a speech at what was called the Trafalgar Day Dinner. As usual, the draft of the speech was vetted by the State Department before delivery. Joe was told his Trafalgar Day speech was "too isolationist" and that he should make some revisions. So Harold and Harvey went back to the drawing board. In any case Kennedy kept in the part where he said that democracies and dictators will "have to live in the same world, whether we like it or not." He got a lot of flak from Washington for that line and indeed his conciliatory attitude caused consternation in the embassy with the regular diplomats.

If there was going to be a war he wanted the US to be "included out," Kennedy said to his friends, as he had said on the ship coming to England.

Munich

Meanwhile Hitler was commiserating ever louder about the Germans living in the Sudetenland part of Czechoslovakia, crying crocodile tears for those poor people who didn't live in their Fatherland.

They should all be living in the Greater Reich, the Führer insisted, and that could be arranged quite simply by Germany taking over the Sudetenland. Indeed he announced that he had set a date in October for that event to take place. With his voracious lust for power and now this dire warning, many in England felt that the current situation was drifting slowly toward disaster. Others were more fearful: they felt that England was somersaulting toward war.

There had been rumors—of course, there were rumors of all sorts floating all over London most of the time but this is one I remember especially—that members of the governments of both England and France had kicked around the idea of trying to persuade Russia to help stop Hitler from invading part of Czechoslovakia. But, this idea, the rumor went, fell flat when worries surfaced about the present inadequate state of the Russian army, due to Stalin's wholesale purge of the military some years ago. And further, a few people in London and in Paris grew perturbed, remembering that after all Russia was communist, and that maybe Hitler as a fascist was the lesser of two evils.

In any event, the possibility of war became so real that the British government issued gas masks to everyone, including children. I thought that made them look like characters in a comic strip. Trenches were dug in the London parks. I watched, both sad and glad, that so many air raid shelters emerged on street corners. Machine guns were placed in Hyde Park, I was told, but the only one I saw was made of wood.

If the prospect of war breaking out in Europe sent shivers down my spine, it also frightened the United States. Shortly after Hitler announced that he had set a date in October to take over the Sudetenland, President Roosevelt sent memoranda—privately—to the leaders of Britain, France, Germany, and Czechoslovakia, urging that the crisis of Germans in the Sudetenland be solved by arbitration.

Now Chamberlain, utterly determined to avoid war, arranged a meeting with Hitler in the hope of finding some sort of arbitration or reconciliation. On September 15, 1938, they met in Hitler's mountain retreat in Berchtesgaden, but they failed to reach an agreement. Chamberlain returned to Britain with his tail between his legs.

In a few days he developed a renewed burst of zeal and flew back to Germany for another rendezvous with Hitler. This time for two long days, the men parleyed, but again to no avail. A totally disheartened Chamberlain shuffled back to London.

On September 27, Chamberlain spoke to an especially convened session of Parliament. He pointed out that it seemed incredible that the English people should be digging trenches and trying on gas masks because of a quarrel "in a far-away country between people of whom we know nothing."

The next day Prime Minister Chamberlain tried a new tack to settle this seemingly intractable problem. Now, accompanied by Eduard Daladier, prime minister of France, and Benito Mussolini, prime minister of Italy, he met with Adolf Hitler in Munich, in the German Tyrol.

There they decided on the fate of the Sudetenland. They agreed that Germany could take over that part of Czechoslovakia, with no intervention on the part of the British or the French or the Italians.

In exchange, Hitler promised that he had no more territorial demands in Europe.

Harold had picked up a tidbit of gossip that came from one of Chamberlain's assistants: There had been some delay in signing the famous document because the ink in Führer Hitler's gaudy inkwell had dried up and it took a while to find some ink. I hoped this tale was true because I guessed there weren't many other occasions for laughs at Munich, even ironic ones.

Mussolini, in what looked to me as a super flush of arrogance, signed only his last name on the Munich Agreement. For some reason Daladier signed his first name on the document as "Ed." Chamberlain and Hitler signed their full names to the Agreement.

There was no signature by a representative from Czechoslovakia, which did not surprise me. The reason for that was quite simple: there was no representative of Czechoslovakia present at the meeting during which the Munich Agreement was signed.

***

Chamberlain returned to Britain, his former gaunt appearance now replaced by one of obvious pleasure at the accomplishment of a crucial goal: avoidance of war. Indeed, as he stepped from the plane, in one hand he carried a piece of piece of paper, which he waved enthusiastically. Obviously it was the Munich Agreement itself. "There will be peace in our time," he announced to the large crowd gathered at the airport to welcome him home as a conquering hero.

In his other hand he carried his unfurled black umbrella which would henceforth be seen as the symbol of appeasement.

The next day Mrs. Richey and I discussed the huge picture in the *London Times* of Chamberlain, standing with the king and queen on their balcony at Buckingham Palace. I told her that I thought Chamberlain had worked his butt off to get this agreement and he had thus rightly earned the big smile he was wearing in the photograph. Mrs. Richey shrugged her shoulders slightly and said that she hoped that the smile wouldn't be like that of the cat in *Alice in Wonderland*.

There were, of course, a variety of responses to the Munich Agreement. For instance, within a month, Anthony Eden, the distinguished British Minister of Foreign Affairs, resigned his office in protest against it. I noted that no high-ranking French person resigned, despite that France actually had a treaty with Czechoslovakia to side with her in the event of an invasion.

Winston Churchill, who for years had been warning the English about Hitler's ambitions and was now writing a series of articles for a British newspaper, characterized the Agreement as "appeasement," a "shame," and a "betrayal." In a speech to Parliament he said that "instead of snatching the victuals from the table, the German dictator has been content to have them served to him course by course."

And, of course, "on the street" in England, there was a large inventory of invectives for Hitler and a shorter list for Mussolini. I not only heard dozens of them as I moseyed around London, but the British papers and radio delighted in writing and talking about the most colorful criticisms.

The prime ministers of the democratic countries, that is France and England, came in for their share of criticism from those who agreed with Churchill. I had discovered soon after arriving in England that the British frequently used the F-word before a derogatory adjective to add emphasis to the adjective. It seemed especially affective in excoriating the heads of the two democracies who had made the deal with Hitler. For instance, I overheard a comment on my bus made by a young man railing against the agreement. "It proves you can't trust the f....ing damn Frogs, doesn't it?" Another example was a mimeographed sheet about the Munich Agreement which circulated around London. It dragged up the old vitriol about England, "Perfidious Albion." To fully emphasize what a dastardly thing the Munich Agreement had been, the broadsheet said signing that Agreement showed what a "F....ing Perfidious Albion" we lived in.

Ambassador Kennedy, to no one's surprise, saw the Munich agreement in a positive light. He, too, believed that somehow war had to be staved off, that Chamberlain had signed an agreement which truly meant "peace for our time." Kennedy was now more outspoken about what he saw as the tragedy of war and the chaos—human, cultural, and economic—which would follow war. He was more convinced than ever that the communists could be the eventual winners if there was war in Europe. There were also many in France—some in England, I felt, but fewer than in France—who felt the same way as Kennedy.

Kennedy also knew that most Americans supported the Munich Agreement. State Department cables coming into the embassy indicated that a Gallup poll taken a short while after Munich showed that the majority of Americans approved of Chamberlain's policy of appeasement. Further, the United States financial world believed that peace would break out because of the Munich Agreement—and the price of stocks on Wall Street soared.

As I read the editorials in English papers, and in the articles in British periodicals, I realized that the meaning of the word "appeasement" depended entirely on how one judged the Munich Agreement. If, in the context that it had saved England from getting into a war with Germany, appeasement was read as a godsend: Germany had beyond doubt the biggest and best air force in the world and a large, superbly trained army, equipped with a host of heavily armored tanks.

It also had a vast navy, with shining new ships. Hitler had been especially devoted to building up German sea power, an old admiral friend of Colonel Richey, told us one evening that it was an established fact that Hitler bristled at any reminder of the Germans scuttling their entire fleet at their defeat in the Great War. And it seemed to be generally known that the German Navy now had a huge armada of submarines, poised to attack ships bringing crucial supplies to England in the event of a war.

England, on the other hand, was woefully unprepared for war, especially against a military giant like Germany. I heard a military correspondent on the radio one evening say he wondered if England even had a slingshot.

As I rolled all of those post-Munich days over in my mind, I was more confused than ever. I fell upon an idea that the whole procedure was like a minuet, with all the music already agreed to beforehand by the parties involved. We really knew that France and Britain were not going to war to stave off an invasion of Czechoslovakia, despite France's mutual defense treaty with Czechoslovakia. Both France and England were so tortured by their blood-stained history of the Great War that they were nearly immobilized, as I had learned so deeply during that lengthy discussion with Harold and Harvey and Ambassador Biddle on the ship coming to England.

I went along with the people who felt the Munich pact had made a Faustian bargain, that in reality what it had done, of course, was to agree for two countries to sell another country—a small, innocent country—down the river, in order to save their own skins and avoid war. England and France had done this in exchange for a promise from a dictator who had already proven himself to be an absolutely dependable liar. I thought back briefly to the scene of Ambassador Biddle tearing up paper napkins as his way of indicating Hitler's respect for treaties.

I wondered a great deal, often to myself and sometimes to people whose values and judgment I admired, would my country, in such a dreadful situation, ever do the same thing?

But morality aside, I certainly was grateful that England had bought time to prepare herself for the day when war would have to be fought. If that makes me a happy hypocrite, I said to myself, so be it.

My dear friend Paul Richey was glad that he and countless other Englishmen would not have to go to war in September 1938. He wrote of the "flap" (another one of those wonderfully understated British words) that had taken place in his Air Force Unit at the time of the Munich crisis "when an old-fashioned and totally unprepared RAF suddenly had to face the prospect of going straight into war with the world's biggest, strongest, and most modern air force: that of Germany."

As an example of the RAF's total unpreparedness, he said that all the officers in his squadron had "spent days in the hangars with spray guns and paint brushes helping the aircraftsmen to hide the brilliant silver of the aircraft with green and brown camouflage paint."

And to top it off, the CO of the squadron had announced to his assembled pilots that their planes didn't even have the adequate speed to attack German bombers.

In my bones I felt that the seeds for a second—and infinitely worse—European War had been planted in a town in Germany called Munich on September 28, 1938.

Kristallnacht

Scarcely a month after the signing of the Munich Agreement, the Nazis mounted a rampage against Jews in which they smashed to smithereens the windows in synagogues, and in the houses of Jews, and in their places of business. This binge of destruction came to be known as *Kristallnacht*, the Night of Broken Glass. As I heard about the savagery on the radio, I thought I could hear the dreadful sound of glass being shattered to smithereens. I began to feel that something far more fundamental than glass had been shredded on that dreadful night.

According to Nazi theory, *Kristallnacht* had been triggered by a teenaged Jewish boy's murder of a German diplomat in Paris, but the Nazis scarcely needed an excuse to further carry out ramifications of Hitler's consistent hatred of Jews.

Early on in London Harold and Harvey and I once tried to figure out Hitler's history of psychopathic venom against Jews. We decided to look at *Mein Kampf*, Hitler's autobiography, of which we read parts of a truncated English version. In the original, published in 1925, Hitler already expounded his passion against Jews and his fear that they would take over the domination of the world. He had a simple solution to that catastrophe: he believed that the Nazis should exterminate the entire Jewish population of Europe, and for starters, the extermination could start in Germany.

We didn't have to read any more. We knew the rest of the history: In 1933, he became Chancellor, and in 1935, the Reichstag passed a series of anti-Jewish laws, known as the Nuremberg Laws. These forbade sex or marriage between Jews and non-Jews. There were fierce penalties if those laws were broken. Further, laws specified that Jews could not be citizens of the Reich and could not hold public office.

And, now, of course, we were in England, and this history was happening right before our eyes. In October 1938, there was *Kristallnacht*, with its shriek of breaking glass. Following that night, we heard—but there was no way of confirming the figures—that thousands of Jews had been sent to camps in Germany where they were confined. Jewish children were expelled from German schools and thousands of Jewish businesses and properties were expropriated.

I knew, of course, that the Nazis were obsessed over drawings or paintings which did not follow what they saw as the old way respectable Germans had painted; especially the Nazis abhorred contemporary paintings created by what were referred to as "deviants." I knew this because there had been articles in England telling that the Nazis had set up an exhibit of what they called "degenerative paintings." The Nazis were obviously proud of the exhibit for they sent it to cities all over Germany and the Germans attended it in droves.

This show included paintings, sculptures, and prints by 112 artists. Among them were works by Marc Chagall, George Grosz, Ernst Ludwig, Paul Klee, and Franz Marc. All painters on the list that happened to live in Germany were immediately fired from any post they held and excoriated in the German press. I read that Hitler himself was so pleased with the exhibit that he visited it twice. Many of the artists on Hitler's hit list were not Jews but, in Nazi eyes, they were all "deviants."

Meanwhile, increasing and more threatening attacks on Jews now became so virulent that Jews were escaping from Germany whenever they could. Chamberlain and Kennedy became so horrified, that together they tried to implement a plan that would get as many Jews out of Germany as possible and send them to safety in other countries. Those of us in the embassy were delighted by this initiative. We saw it as a great humane and creative concept. It came to be called the Kennedy Plan, which made us proud, but unfortunately it never materialized.

Neither did a somewhat similar plan made by an American named George Rublee. He was head of the International Committee on Refugees, based in the US. His plan was apparently devised before Kennedy's, but about which neither Kennedy nor Chamberlain was aware. Harvey and I expressed our surprise to each other on learning that no one in the State Department had bothered to tell Kennedy, nor the British government, about the Rublee plan.

In any case neither project saw the light of day for the simple reason that not enough countries were willing to take in a sufficient number of Jews. I was ashamed of the US's role. For instance, despite the disparity in the size between England and the United States, we took in a smaller number than England did.

Even after *Kristallnacht*, even after that night of the broken glass, with its clear implications of the terror that lay ahead for the Jews, most countries would not take in many German Jews because the leaders of those countries—free countries—were fearful of the minority problems which this might create.

***

One night I heard a BBC announcer read lines from the famous German writer Thomas Mann, who had left Germany in 1933 because he was already so outraged by Hitler's destructive leadership and his announced threat to rid Europe of Jews. Mann had moved to Switzerland. The announcer read a few lines from a letter Mann had recently written to a friend.

"God help our darkened and desecrated country," the BBC man read from Mann's letter. That was part of a longer quote, but it was that phrase which had struck me to the core as the details about Jews in Germany swirled around England.

How much worse could things get for the Jews in that darkened and desecrated country?

Twenty-First Birthday

In mid-December I got a letter from my father, saying he planned to come to see me in London in January and wanted to take me to France for my twenty-first birthday. For dinner that night, he wrote me, we were to go to a famous old restaurant to which his father had taken his mother on special occasions when they were living in France. His father had studied architecture at the *Academie de Beaux Arts* in Paris. And they adored France.

Indeed, all of my family on my father's side had been passionate Francophiles. Daddy's only sibling, his sister, my beloved Aunt Rosalind, and her husband Harry Green, spent many years in an exquisite tiny village in the Pyrenees called Conques where they helped to rebuild the Romanesque cathedral of Sante Fe, which had been built in 1050. Among its relics was part of the arm of St. George—it was the one used to slay the dragon, Aunt Rosalind always used to assure me, when she told me about the relics at Conques!

The restaurant where Daddy and I would go, he wrote me, was called *La Pyramide* and was in a town called Vienne in southeastern France. I was overjoyed at the prospect of seeing him. When I told a French woman in London about my forthcoming birthday dinner, she rolled her eyes in astonishment and told me that she considered *La Pyramide* the best restaurant in France. She shook her hand as if she were shaking water off of it in that great Gallic gesture to indicate that it was very expensive.

Daddy's letter was followed a couple of days later with a letter from Mother. She said she was happy that I was going to be with Daddy for this special birthday and was only sorry she wouldn't be with me, too. She wrote that he was hugely looking forward to the trip. She told me that, as I surely knew, the US was still gripped by the Depression, and she went on to say that the plastics business had been miserable and that Daddy was working too hard. Aunt Elizabeth Kidder, Daddy's aunt, the one member of the family who had some money, had gotten the word, through the "network" (we were profuse letter-writers in our family) that everyone felt he needed a vacation. She hoped this trip, and being with me, "would perk up his spirits." His visit with me was to be Aunt Elizabeth's present to me for my twenty-first birthday. Mother's letter, as usual, was warm and loving and, as usual, the handwriting pretty nearly illegible, but this one didn't have her usual light notes in it. She added that Daddy was bringing me the birthday present from her.

In London he stayed at a small hotel not far from Cadogan Square. We had dinner with the Richeys one evening, dinner another night with the Klemmers. Harold joined us there alone, as his wife Eva was not much given to hospitality. We had lunch with other friends of mine and had tea with the Ambassador and Mrs. Kennedy. One day we had lunch with an old friend of his from Harvard, now Lord Fermoy. He had come on his title in an unusual way. Originally an American, his name had been Roach. He had changed his name into something not so inviting to ridicule—that is, had changed it to Roche—and when a cousin in England, a Lord Fermoy, died, Daddy's friend inherited the title.

Lunch with him was uneventful. He and Daddy seemed to have little in common now and indeed I found him more British than the British, but somehow lacking the British sense of humor. He also made a couple of anti-American slurs. Daddy decided to ignore them and I followed suit, of course.

***

After dinner one night, I told Daddy as casually as I could that I was sorry a good friend of mine was away. "I had wanted you to meet him and he was most anxious to meet you, but he had to be out of the country on a trip."

Daddy responded that he was sorry not to meet him. I volunteered that he worked in naval intelligence and does something called "preemptive buying," but I'm not privy to what it is he buys "preemptively." It was clear that Daddy figured out that this was someone special to me, but he never asked me further about him. I suppose he felt that if I wanted to say more, I would have done so.

Among the things I didn't tell Daddy about Noel was that he was the most attractive man I had ever met, was brilliant, extraordinarily warm, with a glowing sense of humor, and that he had the most winning green eyes I'd ever seen. They were dark emerald green, with a little amber spot, like a cat's eye.

Another thing he had was a wife. She was living in their house in Scotland. A cousin of hers was living there, taking care of her because she had some strange disease she'd had for a few years. Noel never explained it to me in detail except to say that it was not completely debilitating, but that she needed a lot of help. I guessed it was a result of some disease she'd gotten in Kenya, where they had lived for several years.

Early on in our relationship, which became intense nearly immediately, Noel and I both knew that he would never get divorced ("should never get divorced," I kept saying, and I meant it). "If she had been hale and hearty," I once said, "that would be a different story."

The most Noel ever said about them as a couple was after he and I realized we were deeply in love, that he felt he and his wife would have to go on in their "bedraggled relationship till the end of time." He looked unutterably sad as he said that. Then he added, with a mustered-up smile, "And I will be adoring you all the while."

We knew that someday I would go back to the US and after the war was over—he and I both believed Hitler would surely betray the Munich treaty—and Germany defeated, he would go back to his wife and run the little literary magazine he had managed before the war. Meanwhile, he and I spent as much time together as we possibly could.

Once he told me, in a despairing voice, that he and I were trapped in the "fatal futility of fact." Then he laughed and said he remembered that from something of Henry James he had read years ago, "and never thought I would have occasion to refer to it," and he didn't know what book it came from.

In Paris, Daddy and I saw another old friend of his, Freddie Robbins. He was a more jovial soul than the former Mr. Roach. He also harked back a long way, both to Harvard and to their Great War days in France. Freddie had fallen in love with a French woman during the war, stayed in Paris and had never gone back to the US. He was an avid collector of stamps, which he bought and sold. Now he had a precious assemblage. He and Yvette seemed to have little money, but they managed to live well and happily. The apartment they lived in was small and a little shabby but it was full of charm and loaded with wonderful provincial antiques.

Nearly every time I saw Yvette, she was wearing bedroom slippers, but she always wore pretty dresses. The night we had dinner at their apartment she slip-slopped around in her slippers; but the dinner was delicious. Fred had boasted about her cooking, justifiably, it turned out. And, after all, she was French, wasn't she?

The wine was decanted and put in a lovely old china pitcher. We drank it out of plain small glasses of lovely glass, shaped like large hens' eggs, and without stems. I was struck by their elegant simplicity. Another night they took us to dinner at a nearby bistro along with another couple. That night Yvette wore lovely delicate high-heeled shoes.

The Robbinses were genial company; Yvette spoke enough English so that we could talk and laugh together. It was clear that they were deeply devoted.

Another thing I especially remember from my few days in France was that I smelled exquisite all the time. Noel had sent to our hotel a huge bottle of perfume for my birthday present. It was *Arpege*, my favorite. He pronounced it "Our Page" and said he was going to invent a perfume called "My Page."

He liked to play games with my name. He told me once that Byron already knew how wonderful I would be and he quoted Byron to prove it: "History with her volumes vast, hath but one Page." Indeed, he was a Byron buff and once gave me a first edition of that long sad poem, *Mazeppa*. A tragic tale, he said, but he was happy to have been able to find any first edition of a Byron book for me.

In Paris my inclination was to put a drop or two of perfume behind each ear. It made me feel close to Noel. However, it seemed to envelop me and anyone nearby. Daddy finally persuaded me to desist, so I used it sparingly.

Daddy and I went to the Louvre, of course. Then and there I decided that the French should send the *Victory of Samothrace* back to the little island whence she came. They could have a perfect copy of her made for the Louvre. Even if she didn't have a head, I thought she looked unhappy where she was. We went to a couple of other museums and galleries, including a little-known one such as La Marmottan, where some years ago a reporter looked at a Monet there and said it wasn't a painting. It was an "impression" and the name was born! We walked in the Luxembourg garden and we ate deliciously in small noisy restaurants.

One day Daddy rented a car and driver. He wanted to see if he could find any of the scenes of the battles he and the thousands of other Americans had been in during the Great War. There seemed to be no evidence in Paris in the winter of 1939 that the probability of another war lurked around the corner. I didn't see there anything comparable to the preparations already underway in London, and as far as I could tell there was no rationing. When Daddy initiated questions to the Robbins and their friends we met at dinner with them about the threat of war, they all seemed to feel that it would blow over. Freddie said, "blood on the killing fields of France is scarcely dry but in the unlikely event there is war again, the Maginot Line will be our savior."

Our driver, named Eduardo, who wore black leather gloves for the entire trip, and Daddy and I set off for an area which had been known as the St. Mihiel Salient and where Daddy had been in early 1918. He hoped to find a ravine, a hillside, or a forest that triggered a memory. Freddie and Eduardo, too, who spoke pretty good English, had told us this would be a footless mission, that there would be nothing recognizable to Daddy. All the countryside had been built up so much that there would be nothing that would wake a valid memory. Indeed, Freddie declined to join us on the venture.

It was drizzling when we started out and soon it was raining in earnest. As we approached the area we were headed for I found Daddy both quiet and dispirited at his recollections of the war. And nowhere did my father find a spot that summoned up the twenty-year-old ghost he had both wanted, and feared, to see. Instead what we saw were the signs for one memorial after another to the Americans who were buried there. Eduardo wanted us to stop and see the memorials but Daddy, to my relief, said that we should just drive on. We passed two more large memorials to *Amercaines*, and indeed, one monument dedicated to the American troops which had "distinguished them-selves" there in 1918. And we saw at least two more each with signs indicating large numbers of Americans buried there.

My God, I thought, the slaughter of Americans was unbeliev-able. And shortly after that we passed a large cemetery with a marker that said it was dedicated to "unknown soldiers." And I realized that we hadn't even seen the memorials to the thousands and thousands of French, or any to the British or to the other nationalities who had fought in that war.

Our original plan had been to go to Reims for lunch and then drive around past some more countryside, but I knew we would see evidence of more American graveyards and Daddy would not find what I was calling to myself that "jolting memory" for which he was looking. I said I felt tired and feigned a yawn or two and suggested that after we had lunch we head slowly back to Paris. To my surprise, Daddy agreed with me.

Eduardo, who knew Reims well, suggested a little café for Daddy and me, which had a good view of the town. Eduardo would go to a place for lunch where he knew he could get a special Alsatian beer he liked. At lunch Daddy and I looked out of a window at the lovely Gothic cathedral through a scrim of rain. He mentioned that his rec-ollection was that the cathedral had been nearly destroyed sometime in the fighting before his battalion got to France, but that it looked now as it must have looked when it was built sometime in the thir-teenth century.

Back in the car, Eduardo said he had heard that a rich American had given the money to have the cathedral rebuilt after it had been damaged so badly in 1917 and that the reconstruction had just been finished. We all agreed that it was a generous gift of the American and that the cathedral looked glorious now.

We decided we would get off the main drag to Paris whenever it struck our fancy. On one of those little jaunts we came across acres and acres of vineyards and knew that most of the grapes, which would appear in the late spring, would end up in the famous wine of the countryside, the only wine in the world that can claim the name *Champagne*. We drove on that road, admiring the countryside until we felt we should get back on the Paris road.

In another small road excursion off the main drag, we came across a barren field where there was a big white marker with black letters. The letters were small so we got out to read them. All it said was *Ici fut la ville de Fleury*. It didn't take any imagination to conjure up the little village which had been wiped off the face of the earth by war. Daddy seemed devastated by the scene. We were quiet for the rest of the drive back to Paris.

At dinner that night Daddy said he found it impossible to believe that humans were considering doing such things to each other all over again, and yet I knew from many of his conversations with me and with other people we had seen in London, that he felt war was inevitable and that he believed the sooner the US joined the allies when war did break out, the better it would be. He seemed to know inherently that Hitler would trigger the worst war the world had ever known.

***

Two days later Eduardo, wearing presumably the same black leather gloves, drove us to Vienne for my birthday dinner. In contrast to the weather on our other jaunt, the countryside this day seemed to throb with winter sunshine. Somewhere en route Daddy produced the present for me that Mother had sent by him. As I peeled off the wrapping paper, I yelped out that I recognized it: an elegant little black velvet evening bag with which I was very familiar. I knew it was especially precious to Nannie, and I was deeply touched that she was giving it to me. It had been an object of admiration in our family because of its beauty and originality. The bag was attached to a carved silver frame, and the figures on the frame are from the Arabian tale of Aladdin and his magic lamp. There is Aladdin in his oriental trousers, and indeed there are two lamps, as well as a lion and some other unrecognizable animals. The purse was also treasured by our family because it was Dutch and had been given by a Dutch cousin to my father's mother, Nona (as we grandchildren called her). She had, in turn, passed it on to Nannie. And now Nannie was passing this rare evening bag on to me.

If it had been an object of admiration, it had also been the source of some amusement in my family, for smack in the center of the bag is a silver escutcheon, on which is engraved what we have always assumed to be the Huidekoper crest. We had thought that the pretensions of aristocracy, and its accoutrements, such as crests, didn't fit in with the middle-class background of our family in Holland. And certainly not with those members of the family who had emigrated to the US in the early 1800s, representing the Holland Land Company and settling as pioneers in Western Pennsylvania. I told Daddy then that I had always liked this forbear's description of his surprise on his arrival in New York to find that everyone he met, including African Americans, spoke low Dutch. Further, he was "shocked to find cows and hogs on the loose," wandering around in the city.

I told Daddy again how happy I was to be the proud possessor of this lovely present and we had a little laugh over the fancy crest, but I did remind him of an article in *The New Yorker* of years ago which had made gentle fun of some of the Dutch families in the US who think they bear fancy old Dutch names. The article said that with the exception of the Huidekopers and perhaps one or two others, there is no American family which bears an aristocratic Dutch name. If we'd laughed at that article we were also briefly a little puffed with pride with it as well. So, I suggested it is okay for us to have a crest, if only on an evening bag.

Daddy commented then that he hoped I'd find an opportunity to get together with some of our Dutch cousins while I was so close to Holland. I promised I would. Older members of our family had kept in close touch with cousins in Holland over these many years, and I wanted to also.

***

The bright light that had accompanied us from Paris on the way to my twenty-first birthday celebration started to fade into dusk as we fell into the Rhone Valley. In the far distance I could see the Alps topped with snow which was turning a shade of pink in the sunset. I announced that I thought I could see Hannibal and his elephants, but neither Daddy nor Eduardo shared my view. I suggested that perhaps my eyes were sharper than theirs.

We got to the small hotel where we were to stay in time for us to shower and get dressed for dinner. I had borrowed an elegant dark red dress from my ballet-dancer housemate. There was no full-length mirror in my room, but when Daddy came to my room to pick me up for dinner he told me I looked "wonderful," so I settled for that. I know I smelled wonderful.

The waiters made a nice, not-too-extravagant fuss over us. I guess when Daddy made the reservation he had told them it was my birthday. The lamb we had was delectable, well laced with garlic and crushed, fresh mint. There were tiny potatoes roasted along with the lamb. We had fat, white asparagus and a salad in which I could not recognize any leaf. I drank a lot of hearty red wine and I got tearful when I was presented with an apricot soufflé with a lit candle in the center of it. Daddy looked surprised when I ordered a *calva* for each of us after dinner. He was surprised that I was I was familiar enough with calvados to know its nickname and amused when I told him that I had told a French friend of mine in London that the same drink was known in the US as "Ole Mule Kick" and had tried to transliterate that into French.

The waiter, however, suggested that since we were in a famous apricot-growing part of France, maybe instead of a calvados we would like to try an apricot brandy. We did and I told Daddy that now we knew what the gods called nectar.

The weather again was harmonious for our drive back to Paris. I don't know if we purposefully avoided any references to the likelihood of war but it never came up in our conversations. Daddy told me more about his mother, whom we children called Nona. All his life he called her Mater, the Latin for mother, which sounds formal but they obviously adored each other and had an easy, open relationship. Although I scarcely knew Grandmother Nona, I had felt close to her. I had never even known that grandfather, Daddy's father, also Prescott Huidekoper, who had become a successful architect in Worcester, Massachusetts, where they lived. He died at some ridiculously young age—I think he was in his early fifties—during a flu epidemic that killed many people in the US sometime before the even more disastrous one which followed the Great War. Daddy was at Harvard at the time of his father's death.

We had an uneventful drive home and spent most of it talking about family. I wanted to hear much more about Nannie and Rosalind and Nancy and my younger brother Huidy, away at the same boarding school Daddy had gone to in Milton, Massachusetts. And I told him I had some trinkets which I'd give to him to take to darling Nannie when he left.

We just enjoyed talking about a lot of things. I remembered en route that when I was younger Daddy had taught me a poem by

Robert Louis Stevenson. "The world is so full of a number of things. I think we should all be as happy as kings," it went. It was back in those days when kings were thought to be happy. And, actually, the things which my father had in mind in reciting the poem were things which the moth and the rust cannot corrupt.

Heartbreaking News from Home

The following spring a personal tragedy of monstrous proportions fell on me. I was awoken early the morning of March 2 by Mrs. Richey, who told me I should come right away with her to her bedroom. She threw my wrapper around my shoulders, took me by the arm, and guided me into her room. Colonel Richey was sitting on the side of the bed and motioned for me to sit down beside him. He put his arm around me. Mrs. Richey picked up the phone.

"Rosalind wants to talk to you," she said. "She has sad news for you. Terrible news." She handed me the telephone.

"Ros," I shouted, "what is it?"

"Daddy is dead."

"Dead?" I said. "Dead? What do you mean? I don't believe it," She was crying but I could feel her trying to catch her breath to talk to me.

"Dead by his own hand," she said. She started to say something else but I interrupted her saying, "No, No, No."

She went on in a low monotone. "He went to his office on Sunday and he shot himself."

"I don't believe it," I said, and as I broke down, I was able to ask how Mother was.

"She is as brave as you would expect," Rosalind said softly.

***

I handed the phone over to Mrs. Richey since I was unable to talk anymore.

"Rosalind," she said, "Page will call you back in a little while." She paused. And with tears in her voice she said, "Please give my love to your mother."

I staggered into my bedroom. One of the windows there faced due west and I seemed to have spent a long time staring out of that window, figuring out somehow that if I looked hard enough I could look across the whole of England, across the Atlantic Ocean to see my family in

Maryland. I started thinking about going home. Are there passenger planes flying to the US? If so, when do they depart and from where? Or should I go by ship, and so forth, and decided then that I was now capable of talking again. I'd telephone; I felt I'd be all right on the phone now. But just before I called, Mrs. Richey came in, and hugged me. She didn't say a word but she made me feel a tiny jot braver.

I made my voice strong when I talked to my darling Nannie. Practically the first thing she said to me was that everyone knew that this would be doubly tragic for me, being so far away, but, she said, she wanted me to stay where I was and keep on with my work. I told her that I was coming home. I was going to start making plans immediately to get home as soon as I could, by plane if possible, if not by boat. I told her not to set a date for a memorial service until I knew what was the earliest I could get home.

She told me to wait a minute, "There's someone here who wants to talk to you." She put our beloved old friend Jim Carey, also our family lawyer, on the phone. He was sweet and stern at the same time, "Everyone here feels it is better if you just keep on with your life there."

I talked to Rosalind again and to brother Huidy. Some teacher at his school had driven him home as soon as he heard the news. They both said I should stay in England. Nancy had not yet arrived at the house but she called me a little later, and also urged me to stay there. "There is nothing you can do here, and besides, I know that Daddy would want you to keep on there."

I said I would have to think about it. I went back to my room, beyond tears, emotionally stripped and desperately tired. After a while I called back and Nancy answered the phone. I told her I would stay in London. She promised me she would call me right after the memorial service, which was going to be in a small old stone chapel in the nearby countryside and tell me all about it. She also said she and her husband Cokie were coming to see me in August. She told me that a friend of theirs was renting a castle.

"A castle?" I asked.

"A castle in Scotland," she explained. "Yes, a castle in Scotland for the grouse season and they want you to join us, so please plan to take a holiday in mid-August."

I found for the first time that day that I could nearly smile. The very idea of me going to Scotland for the "season" and shooting grouse! Then I lapsed into tears again.

I talked to Mother again and this time she sounded less valiant. I tried to make my voice sound very strong but the minute we said goodbye to each other I collapsed all over again. The Richeys enclosed me in their warmth and sympathy, especially in the day or two I stayed home from work. Everyone in the embassy was kind and expressed sympathy, except for those who find it impossible to articulate a word about death. The ambassador and Mrs. Kennedy sent me a big box of flowers. Kick came to see me and was very sweet.

My family, of course, told me in detail all about the memorial service, the lovely plain flowers, and the number of old friends who had been there. Daddy had wanted to be cremated and his ashes strewn in the Susquehanna River. Jim Carey reminded me that he and his wife still had their old house on a bluff overlooking the Susquehanna. I remembered the house was called Octarara and that it was as beautiful as its name. "We'll wait till you come home, of course," he said on the phone.

Everyone in the family sounded brave and I figured if they could handle broken hearts that way, I should be able to as well.

Try as he might, not even Noel was of much help to me. I seemed to have an overwhelming need to be alone. I hurt his feelings, I realized afterwards, when I wouldn't let him be with me as much as he wanted. Anyway, he knew, of course, that I hewed to no orthodox religion. I had told him sometime not long after we met that I was looking for "the god that tempers the wind to the shorn lamb." I had learned that that god exists only in some old French proverb, and it appears in Laurence Sterne's *A Sentimental Journey*. I suggested to Noel that of the countless religious constructs humans have invented there are many all powerful gods but none of them have protected the "shorn lamb" from floods, or plagues, or earthquakes, the bitterest winds or any of the other destructive elements, or from wars, I added.

Noel responded that in one instance, at least, I had the bard on my side of the argument and when I looked perplexed, he said that in King Lear, Gloucester says that gods wage wars for their own amusement. "As flies to wanton boys are we to the gods. They kill us for their sport."

Colonel and Mrs. Richey, who clung more loyally to their faith than anyone I knew, did not offer to introduce me to their priest because they knew I was not practicing any particular brand of religion, obviously not theirs. They gave me a world of consolation with no tinge of religion.

Joe Kennedy, in a warm gesture, asked me if I thought it would be of any help for me to see a priest whom he particularly admired. A good friend of mine, a handsome young Jew, a member of the Montefiore family, offered to take me to meet his rabbi if I thought it would be healing for me. I also knew Protestants, too, but declined the offer of one such friend to meet her minister, as I had declined the offers of my other friends.

I knew I was on my own on this most lonely of paths and that I had to find my spiritual bearings myself. Thinking that work might help, I went back to my job at the embassy, and although it was an exceptionally busy period, the concept that working hard was a panacea for a shattered heart turned out, in my case, at least, to be a myth.

It was nearly a week after I had learned of the tragedy, with nearly daily telephone calls to my mourning family at home, that I knew what I needed was to go somewhere by myself for a while, preferably on some "desolate, wind-swept space." I don't know where I got that description but I felt in my aching bones (yes, even my bones were aching from shock) that that was where I would find solace. That is, I thought, if it is solace I was seeking. Or is it just acceptance of the irrevocable reality that I was searching for? Or was it the answer to the fundamental question about life and death?

I looked at the map of England and decided to go to a northwestern area of the country which would look over a wind swept Atlantic Ocean toward the United States. I took a bus to a small town called Tintagel in Cornwall because I had found an advertisement which said that prevailing winds flew in from the Atlantic there. The ad also pointed out that Tintagel was a special attraction for visitors because of the castle there which legend said was the birthplace of King Arthur, which was of no interest to me but it was a lodestone for myriads of trippers, I found. It was those "moist western winds" coming in from the Atlantic, which the ad mentioned, that appealed to me. I thought winds coming from the west, from my own part of the world, might help and that moist ones might mingle with my tears.

Actually it turned out that there weren't many tears for me in that little village. I seem to have exhausted the supply, but there were paths which led to huge rock formations where I could get the draughts of wind over the water that I sought. I rambled over those hills and I rambled over the happy years I had spent with my father, and those thoughts, of course, concluded with his tragic death, and that was too deep for tears anyway.

I thought back especially to the first time he must have seen me, January 15, 1918. Daddy was a young officer in training at Camp Lee, near Richmond, scheduled at any moment to go to France where he would be in charge of a machine gun battalion. He and Mother, with their two young daughters, Rosalind and Nancy, had taken a small house in Richmond so they could be close together while he was still there and also to await the imminent birth of their third child.

Late the night of January 14, Daddy rushed Mother to the Richmond hospital and some few hours later, I was born. My imagination harked back to that day and suggested to me that both Mother and Daddy must have desperately wanted that baby to be a boy. With two beautiful girls already, and with the father headed any minute to the hell of war in the trenches of France, surely both of these parents must have longed for a boy.

If they did feel that way, I never saw a scintilla of evidence of it. Indeed they were always the most adoring parents, and even when Daddy came home, safe and sound from the war and sometime afterwards they did have a baby boy, I always thought that I was always my father's favorite child. I think all four of us children each thought that we were Mother's favorite.

There, on the top of those eternal high rock formations in England, I reflected on these emotions and realized how grateful I was to have had those extra wonderful warm days with Daddy when he came to take me to France for my twenty-first birthday. And I wondered if there was anything on Earth I could have done to stave off his tragic death, that is, of course, if I had had any idea of the depth of his depression.

I knew there was nothing I could have done, and that made me even sadder.

On my way back to London, I knew I had set off trying to cope with a death I had found impossible to believe. I returned having accepted the catastrophic reality of Daddy's death and the consciousness that I would mourn it forever. I had a tailor sew a black band on my fawn-colored polo coat, an old-fashioned custom that simply denotes the wearer is mourning the loss of someone especially dear. Friends who didn't know of my father's death would ask me who I was in mourning for and it gave me a chance to talk about my father.

Spring 1939

In England in the spring of 1939 the sense of impending crisis was nearly palpable. Gas masks were issued to everyone and I thought they made kids look like characters in the funny strips. Hitler was talking about the poor Germans living in the rest of Czechoslovakia and of how he should save them by taking over the rest of the country. Shrill editorials urged more speed in building up armaments; shelters blossomed on more street corners; barrage balloons were anchored over London to interfere with low-flying enemy aircraft. The very atmosphere seemed combustible.

Then the Nazis lit the match. In the Munich Agreement Chamberlain and Daladier had agreed to turn over the Sudetenland part of Czechoslovakia to Germany in exchange for Hitler's promise not to make any more demands on Czech territory. Now Hitler symbolically incinerated the Agreement: In mid-March the armored vanguard of the Third Reich blasted its way into the rest of Czechoslovakia. It was followed by hundreds more tanks. That very evening Hitler himself marched brazenly into Prague.

Only seven months after he had signed the Munich pact he had racked up another bloodless victory: he had been able to incorporate all of Czechoslovakia into the Third Reich.

Now the feeling in England was that Europe was tumbling uncontrollably toward war. Kennedy, in both private comments and in public statements, stressed his hope that whatever happened, the US would stick to its own knitting and keep out of Europe's business.

Even so, Kennedy knew that if and when war came, England would be hugely dependent on military equipment from the US He therefore sent Harvey Klemmer around the major western ports of England to analyze their capacity for the unloading of heavy equipment. Harvey suggested some ports needed beefing up; Kennedy passed this on to the pertinent British official.

It was that Nazi assault, Hitler's ruthless sweep into Czechoslovakia, that became the crystallizing moment for Prime Minister Chamberlain. He warned that if Germany attacked Poland, England would come to Poland's aid. The French government followed suit: it announced that if Germany attacked Poland, France, too, would come to Poland's aid. I remembered the newspaper reporter who had wondered whether either of those countries had enough sling shots for war.

If I was totally concentrated on the war, newspapers from the US in early May diverted my attention completely. The great American contralto, Marian Anderson, had been expected to sing the Easter Concert in Constitution Hall in Washington, but the organization which owned Constitution Hall, the Daughters of the American Republic, the DAR, suddenly scuttled the idea. Miss Anderson was an African American and thus the DAR would not allow her to sing there.

It didn't matter, as the papers I saw pointed out, that Marian Anderson had sung to acclaimed audiences all over the US and in many of the famous halls in Europe.

Eleanor Roosevelt immediately swung into action at this outrageous insult to the exalted singer and indeed to all of our black citizens. We read with joy now in the British papers that President Roosevelt announced that Miss Marian Anderson would be singing the Easter Concert on the steps of the Lincoln Memorial.

Seventy five thousand lucky people heard her sing there; among them were members of the Supreme Court, Congress, and of the Roosevelt Cabinet. Many thousands more people, radio columnists estimated, heard her on their radios.

Harold and Harvey and I and several friends celebrated this happy occasion by going out to an elegant spot for dinner. There we toasted Miss Anderson to the gills; we also drank to FDR, too, remembering he had addressed the DAR some years back by greeting them, saying, "Hello, fellow immigrants."

***

One day later that spring Harold said that he wanted to take the Rats Club out to lunch. He and Harvey and I constituted the whole membership of the Royal Order of the Rats Club (RORC). This distinguished organization had come about soon after we had arrived in England, when we three had lunch at a pub near the embassy which boasted a huge choice of English and Irish cheeses. I had sampled a great variety of those cheeses and either Harvey or Harold said I must be a little rat to be so crazy about so much cheese. RORC developed from such an indifferent comment as that and occasionally the Club got together for lunch, especially when we had choice tidbits of embassy or political gossip to chew on. The mood on such occasions was lighthearted.

This time, though, the mood, set by Harold, was serious. We soon learned why. He was going to leave the embassy and go back to Washington to resume his career as a political reporter on the *New York Times*. Harold didn't explain what was behind this decision in detail (anxious to get back, he said), but it had been increasingly clear to me that he and the ambassador hadn't struck up a great bond of friendship. It wasn't that Harold disagreed with Joe Kennedy's analysis of the international scene. (Harold did disagree, but only in private.) It was just that their styles were at polar opposites.

I remember one little example which had taken place a few days before. A friend of Harold's in the Foreign Office had been asked by a *London Times* reporter to characterize the official view of the current tension between Germany and Britain. He had responded, "We view the situation with equanimity." That expression had become a source of amused banter between Harold and me. Every situation that arose, Harold and I viewed with equanimity.

The ambassador had come into our office that day while Harold was talking on the phone. Harold smoked through a short black cigarette holder with a filter that he changed frequently. I knew instinctively that Joe Kennedy looked upon a cigarette holder as effete, although that is not a word Joe would have used. Anyway when he came into our office, Harold was holding his cigarette in its holder in one hand and the phone in the other.

Harold had not seen the ambassador come in and continued his conversation. "So, I'm sure," Harold said, smiling, "that you view the situation with equanimity." Whatever the response of the person on the other end of the phone, it made Harold laugh.

That was the end of the telephone conversation. Harold now noticed the ambassador's presence, greeted him, and offered him a chair. They talked about whatever it was that had brought Joe into the office. But I had a terrible feeling that it was also the end of the relationship between Harold and Joe Kennedy.

Harvey and I were deeply distressed at the prospect of Harold's departure. And so were many of the regular diplomats in the embassy. They had all admired Harold. When Harold announced that he was leaving the ambassador told me that the woman in charge of the file office had said she needed another hand and wondered if I could be transferred to a position there. She had told him that she thought I'd be a great asset. Joe asked me how I felt about that and I said it sounded interesting.

I knew that many of the files were full of fascinating and also frightening material. Dealing with them would open up a broader world for me. It was also one of the busiest spots in the embassy, which I would like. There always seemed to be a stream of people coming in to get files or to return them. As well as them were the code clerks, who had to go through our room in order to get to and from code room. All incoming and outgoing mail was funneled through the file room. The daily dose of analyses of anything about Germany meant numbers of cables and memos, all of which had to be filed (filed twice, actually, once by subject and once by date). In a way it seemed to me to be the heart of the embassy operations.

I was stimulated by my new job, but I missed Harold's humor, his incisive take on the European dilemma, and his deep empathy for the British people and for the ordeal he felt surely lay ahead for them. Further, he and I shared a firm conviction that whatever happened England would prevail. I wished that the ambassador wasn't so frozen in his feeling that the British could not hold out against Hitler. I now decided that on the occasions when I had a chance to chat with the ambassador, I would put in my measly tuppence to try to persuade him to moderate his isolationist stance. When in the lion's den, I'll have to figure some tactful way to broach the subject, lest the lion bite my head off.

A Holiday Interrupted

I was due a week's holiday and I had looked forward to spending it with my sister Nancy and her husband, Cokie. They would be staying with their friend in Scotland, who had kindly invited me there, too. However, peace seemed so fragile to me and I knew how busy the embassy would be this summer, especially the file section, so I hesitated about going off on a holiday at this juncture. Nancy would come to see me in London instead. However, the ambassador told me to go and visit with my sister, forget about any impending war and have a good time. "And bring me back some grouse," he added.

It was the first time Nancy and I had seen each other since Daddy's death and we fell into each other's arms. I was happy I had decided to come to be with her.

The spiffy English and the zealous shooting folk of other countries take this grouse hunting season so seriously that it's opening on August 12 is known to all of them as the "Glorious Twelfth." However not being a shooting type, I opted instead either to walk through the beautiful countryside, or go on a tasting tour of the close-by Scotch distilleries. Or alternately I went salmon "killing," as salmon fishing is called in Scotland, with the "ghillies" (the guides). On the fishing occasions, I wore a pleated wool skirt I had bought in London, which sported a pattern never before seen in Scotland. When the ghillies, wearing their wonderful plaid kilts, asked me in their thick Scottish brogue, the name of my plaid, I responded in the thickest Scottish cadence I could muster, and smiling, said it was "the plaid of the Clan

McHuidekoper." Several times they commented on how much they liked the plaid of the Clan McHuidekoper. We clearly had a jolly time together.

***

I had been in Scotland four days when I got a call from Harvey Klemmer telling me the situation was deteriorating rapidly and the ambassador said I had to cancel the rest of my holiday and should get myself back to work immediately. Harvey didn't say that I should "get the hell back to the embassy" but his voice seemed to imply that. He told me that the ambassador had picked up a rumor that the Russians and Germans were planning to sign a non-aggression treaty, which meant, of course, that now Hitler could invade Poland without any interference from the Russians. Harvey didn't have to tell me not to pass on that rumor to anyone in my group up there.

He knew that I was good at keeping rumors to myself, but on the train going back to London, I kept thinking of all the dreadful words with which I could savage Hitler. I knew that Muslims could buy stones to throw at the devil and I figured that would be more satisfactory. I had telephoned Noel before I left Scotland, and he was there to meet me. Just seeing him revived my spirits, but I was still frazzled by that rumor.

At work the next day the lines of miserable German refugees around the embassy desperately hoping to get visas to the United States seemed infinitely longer than they had before I'd left. I bowed my head in a kind of shame at being so fortunate as to be an American as I wove my way through the refugees to get to the entrance of the building.

I happened to be in Kennedy's office later that day when James "Scotty" Reston of the *New York Times* came in. Scotty and I greeted each other affably and then I started to leave but the ambassador asked me to stay and pointed to a chair and indicated I should sit there. Then he turned his attention to Scotty and said he had asked him to come to see him because he wanted to say that American newspaper men and other American men in England should send their families home. And he though that Scotty could get that word around.

Joe went on to say that even as imminent as war seemed to be, he still clung to a hope that some kind of a bargain could be made to prevent any impending disaster. He did not mention the possibility of a non-aggression treaty. Anyway, he said, he made no bones about where he stood. "I am for appeasement 100 percent," he said, "and if 1,000 percent is more than 100 percent, I'm for it 1,000 percent." Scotty did not send his family home then. I don't know if he got the word around.

***

On August 23, Molotov and Ribbentrop signed a non-aggression treaty on behalf of their two countries. President Roosevelt saw this as so ominous that he sent cables to the leaders of Germany, Russia, Italy, and Poland urging negotiation, arbitration, or even conciliation to avoid war. Reading copies of the cables in the embassy, I prayed that these men would go for one of Roosevelt's recommendations. It seemed to me that they shared Kennedy's concept, couched in more delicate words, but still it was "don't go to war."

As it turned out Roosevelt's pleas fell on deaf ears. On September 1, Hitler's tanks roared into Poland.

The Rubicon had been crossed. Nazi bombers headed for Warsaw.

***

In the confusion of the cataclysmic news, it wasn't surprising that I had forgotten that weeks before, long before I had gone to Scotland, I had promised a good friend I would have dinner with him on September 1. In the early afternoon I got a call from Frank Kent, Jr., a reporter for the *Baltimore Sun* in London, whom I'd gotten to know well, reminding me of our long-standing dinner date. "I may not be your most glamorous admirer," Frank said, "but I bet this will be a date you will never forget."

We talked briefly and probably incoherently about the impact of the day's event, which we both knew meant "war." He said he'd already filed his story about the reaction in England and he'd come around to Cadogan Square at seven to pick me up.

Later I got a call from a glamorous Russian friend of mine, Alla Balash, who said she was so shocked and agonized by the news that she could not bear to be alone that evening. She didn't care what I was doing, she said, I had to include her. I told her to come and join me and an old friend for dinner. "Turn up at Cadogan Square around seven," I said. She sighed with relief, told me I was a "something" in Russian. I took it to be a compliment.

Then I began to wonder how two such different types would get along. Alla was ravishingly beautiful. A movie director had thought so, too. She had a bit role, that of a glorious young woman, in the movie *Mayerling*—all of my friends who had bit roles in movies seem to have been in *Mayerling*. She earned a living now, but barely, by selling little paintings she had made of vaguely remembered Russian landscapes. Anyway, she talked in a low voice with a purring accent, and she had a fine sense of frivolity. Frank, on the other hand, was very earnest, solid, and conventional. He didn't lack a sense of humor, but it was pretty down-to-earth.

I need not have worried how they would get along. In mid-September, wreathed in happy smiles, they told me they were going to be married, but not before I had to respond to a cable I got from Frank R. Kent, Sr., a well-known political columnist on the *Baltimore Sun*.

The cable simply said, "Who is this adventuress that you introduced Frank to and that he wants to marry?"

Part Two

Sugar Candy

"We have not journeyed all the way across the centuries, across the mountains, across the prairies, because we are made of sugar candy."

–WINSTON CHURCHILL

Let Slip the Dogs of War

On the surface nothing seemed out of the ordinary at the American embassy September 3, two days after Hitler had invaded Poland. The usual long line of refugees from Nazi Germany was not there, but that was not surprising. It was Sunday and the consulate was closed.

It was a sunny day, with a high cloudless sky, and there was a gentle breeze. I could even see shadows of the barrage balloons on the ground. On my way to the embassy I had thought it was obscene of the weather to be so soft and beautiful. Better a biting, cruel wind in these circumstances.

Instead it was so warm that the embassy doors were flung open. In those days there were no security officers. There was only the regular tall, thin doorman. He broke off his conversation with Dodsworth, the messenger boy, and managed to greet me with his usual cheery "'Ello, Miss 'Idekoper," but I thought he looked even more stunned than most of the people I had passed on the street that morning. Then I remembered he had a son of call-up age.

On the way to the second floor, where the embassy offices were located, I figured I must be one of the few people there today. Of course, anyone with the slightest bit of rank was in the Houses of Parliament, awaiting the speech of Prime Minister Chamberlain in which he would announce that England had declared war on Germany. As the lowest person on Ambassador Joe Kennedy's personal staff, I naturally had not expected to be among those in the great hall where the tragic Prime Minister would speak. Despite my deep affection for the English family with which I lived and their entreaties to listen to

59

the speech on the radio with them, somehow I wanted to be in the American embassy for this momentous occasion.

It was nearly eleven, the time Chamberlain was due to speak. I walked quickly to the room where the Reuters news ticker would be carrying the speech. For a brief moment, I found myself wondering if Chamberlain would have his umbrella with him and smiled at my nonsensical idea.

At a few minutes past eleven the ticker started to print out the Prime Minister's opening words, which laid out the background that led to this dreadful day. He said that everything he worked for, hoped for, and believed in had "crashed in ruins." Suddenly the ticker shifted from the Houses of Parliament to a snooker game in south Kent. There will always be an England, I decided as I read the scores of the various snooker games. Then I realized there was a mechanical lag and the ticker had to wait to print out another chunk of Chamberlain's speech.

I was still waiting for the machine to catch up with the prime minister's speech when Dodsworth came in and handed me three envelopes. "Delivered by," he explained in an excited voice, "by a special messenger." They were addressed to the ambassador and bore the imprint of the Foreign Office. I knew, of course, that they were official, rather than personal, and presumed they had to do with the outbreak of war.

I thanked Dodsworth and headed for my office. I placed the envelopes on my desk, and slowly, deliberately, I picked up the top one and slit it open with my little brass stiletto. The letter was on heavy, vellum paper, and was the creamy color of the elegant Georgian houses in Belgravia. It was folded twice and when I opened it and first looked at it, I thought it was an invitation. The main body of the letter was engraved in an elegant Spenserian script. I shook my head in disbelief.

"His Most Excellent Majesty George the Sixth, by the Grace of God, of Great Britain, Ireland, and of the British Dominions beyond the Seas, King, Defender of the Faith, Emperor of India," the printed body of the letter read, "is constrained to announce that a state of war exists with..." Here the printed part of the letter ended. Following that, filled in by hand, in pen, also in the same elegant script, was the word "Germany." On the line below, also handwritten, was "the third day of September, 1939."

I held the letter for a long time before I laid it down. I pressed out the two creases the folds had made and stared at it for a few minutes.

I opened the second envelope even more slowly than the first, but before I had the letter fully out of the envelope I could see that this one bore no resemblance to an invitation. It was neatly and unashamedly typed, in a handsome bold typeface. In essence it was a request that the United States represent Great Britain's interests in Germany and those countries under German occupation for the duration of the war. I put that letter under the first one on my desk.

The third letter was based on the assumption that the US would agree to the request to represent Great Britain's interests. A correct assumption, of course, it turned out. The letter got right down to the nitty-gritty. It explained that a small British circus was stranded in Prague and needed the good offices of the US to help the troupe get back to England. The circus consisted of a husband and wife and a couple of acrobats (if the little circus had any animals, they were never mentioned). It appeared that the couple owned and ran the show. Sort of a mom-and-pop operation, I thought, as I placed that letter on the bottom of the little pile.

I sat absolutely still for a few moments and then I ran my hand over the top letter, as if, with a gesture like that, I could wipe out the news it announced. I smiled grimly at the engraved text and its handwritten additions and suddenly thought of Mark Twain. Someday they will give a war and no one will come, he had said.

I left the letters on the desk and headed for home, on my usual bus, but this day there were very few passengers and I noted that most of us were carrying our gas masks.

I was close to Cadogan Square, across the street from the house where I lived, when air raid sirens went off. I do not know why I decided to go into the ornate Square, for there was no air raid shelter there, nor indeed do I know how I got in there because I did not have a key to the Square. There was only one for each household that surrounded the Square.

Anyway, I found myself inside. I ran for the closest bench, tearing my gas mask out of its bag as I ran; I sat down, shoving the mask over my face, when I discovered that I was crying. I didn't know how breathing into the mask would work along with tears but I didn't have time to find out. Within seconds the "all clear" siren blared out. I removed the mask, wiped my face off, ran my comb through my hair, and by the time I got home and greeted the Richeys, and learned that a false alarm had set off the sirens, I had managed to smile.

Mrs. Richey gave me a hug and said she hoped I would be staying home for dinner that night. Paul and Mike would be there and so would Teresa, Paul's beautiful girl.

Of course, I'll be here: I wouldn't miss it for anything, I told her. I knew that she figured this was probably Paul's last dinner at home before his squadron was sent to France. (She was right. Paul left for France a few days later.)

Mike announced at dinner that he had gotten assigned to a mine-sweeper. He had made it plain months ago that he was a conscientious objector. His grandfather had been a soldier and his father had fought in five wars for England, but both Colonel and Mrs. Richey accepted Mike's decision with grace (on the surface anyway). Minesweeping was a particularly dangerous occupation, which was why, I knew, Mike had chosen it.

Now the war had come thuddingly close to my dear English family, but like them, I felt I had to hide my fears under a bushel basket.

Anyway, now Paul's planes were better equipped to take on the German bombers than they had been a year ago. In his brilliant book, *Fighter Pilot*, Paul later wrote of the period after Munich. "Fortunately for us, for England, and for the world, Mr. Chamberlain had managed to stave off the war for a year." That vital year gave the RAF time to complete re-equipment of the regular fighter squadrons with modern Hurricane and Spitfire fighters, and Paul, among others, was profoundly grateful.

The Wheel of Fortune

Nancy and Cokie had originally planned to sail back to the US on a British liner, the *Athenia*, which was to sail from Ireland on September 3, but a generous offer on their part diverted that plan.

Our hostess at the castle in Scotland had brought with her from her home in Virginia a young Scottish couple who worked for her there. It seemed to be a golden opportunity all around; they could help her in territory unfamiliar to her and at the same time the young couple could hang out with family and friends in Scotland who they hadn't seen for a few years. They had brought with them dozens of pictures of their little three-year-old girl to show everyone. She had been left in Virginia with close friends of theirs. They sent her a postcard every day, and had bought a bunch of Scottish clothes and toys to take to her.

However, now that war had broken out, there was another side to this golden opportunity. The young man, still a citizen of England, was the right age to be called up to serve in the British armed forces. Most of his relatives and pals in Scotland near his age had already gotten the obligatory invitation and it soon became apparent to him that if he stayed longer—their tickets back to the US were for the middle of September—he, too, could end up in uniform. It wasn't that he wasn't patriotic for England, he said, but their child was an

American, and besides he felt more like an American now that he had been living there for so many years. Indeed both he and his wife were planning to become American citizens soon after they got back home in Virginia.

Anyway, Nancy and Cokie were thoughtful enough to say they would give their tickets on the *Athenia* to the young couple since their ship was sailing so much earlier than the one the Scottish couple had tickets for. The young couple was effusive in their thanks. They cabled the friends their little daughter was visiting, apprising them of their new date of homecoming and saying they were wildly excited to be returning so much sooner than planned. They would be sailing on the *Athenia* September the third.

A few hours after the ship, clearly a passenger ship, left its port, it was torpedoed by a German submarine. Among the 112 people who were killed in that dreadful attack on a civilian ship were thirty Americans.

The people who were rescued, many of whom had spent the night struggling in life boats, were taken to Glasgow. Ambassador Kennedy dispatched his son Jack to Glasgow to do whatever he could for the survivors.

The young Scottish couple was not among the survivors. They were lost forever.

***

Several days later, Nancy and Cokie were able to get tickets home for themselves on a recently inaugurated trans-Atlantic airline flying from Europe to America. They flew home from Portugal on one of the earliest flights of what was known as the *Yankee Clipper*.

The last thing Nancy said to me as we bid each other "goodbye" was that she was going immediately to see the little girl in Virginia whose parents had been casualties on the first day of the war.

London at War

The early months of the war were called the Bore War (a play on words, of course, on the Boer War) or that period was called the *sitzkrieg* (for the Germans a "sit war") but it wasn't dull for everyone. It wasn't dull for Noel, who had to travel a lot, especially to Scandinavia, I guessed.

It hadn't been dull for Squadron Number One in France either. Paul's squadron was based near France's German border with the responsibility of protecting all British units in France from an attack. He and his fellow pilots had been very active.

He was able to get leave to come home over Christmas to marry Teresa. By then Paul's plane had already been shot at by British anti-aircraft, mistaking his plane for a German one, and attacked by French fighter pilots, making the same mistake. His squadron had shot down four German planes. One of the German pilots survived and the British pilots figured the German had "put up such a good fight," Paul said, "that we determined to entertain him in our mess." They drank a lot together, swapped reminiscences, and the British proposed a toast "to all pilots."

So except for air battles that had taken place over France, there was little action around the Western front. The British could still joke about the Siegfried Line (the defensive line in Germany along the French border, which was finished in 1938), and there was a song which started off, "We're going to hang out the washing on the Siegfried Line." Another song, which showed the lightheartedness of the British at that time, was a song sung to the tune of a Disney hit, "Whistle while you work, Hitler is a jerk. Hitler's barmy and so's his army; whistle while you work."

London didn't seem dull either with all the preparations for war; indeed the artifacts of war dominated the city. The parks bristled with anti-aircraft guns, nestled in trenches with sandbags around them. Many of the exquisite black wrought iron fences around buildings in London had been torn down; the iron was more valuable as war material. There were seemingly endless streams of lorries either camouflaged or painted a muddy shade of green, and every day I discovered a new air raid shelter marker with its big black arrow pointing in the direction of a safe haven.

I constantly saw soldiers marching down the street, some of them looking like choir boys and all looking heartbreakingly vulnerable. And I saw WRENS (Women's Royal Naval Service) frequently, scores of them marching along, swinging their arms, trying not to smile at the onlookers who were smiling and waving to them.

There was no way you could escape the icons of war or the impact of war itself for long. Sometimes the wheel of fortune seemed extra cruel. Noel and I met a German refugee, Max, at a party of an artist we knew. A Jew, Max had gotten out of Germany in the nick of time. He had been warned by a friend that the Nazis were now rounding up Jews in his immediate neighborhood, and his friend helped him to escape. Somehow he had gotten to England. In London the British had given him a ration card, but he had no money. We found out that he was surviving mainly on peanuts and raisins, so Noel and I often invited Max to dinner.

We had an amusing time together as our new friend tried to describe his abstract sculptures to us, in German, of course, and Noel, who had spent several summers in Germany as a teenager and picked up a smattering of German, would translate what Max said. Occasionally Max drew a version of one of his sculptures on a paper napkin when we had taken him to dinner in a restaurant.

We talked one evening about the Nazi exhibit of "degenerate artists." Max explained that, of course, he was not distinguished enough to be exhibited there, but he had gone to see it and said it was the most wonderful collection of paintings that he could dream of. Noel and I smiled with him and I told him his English was getting better.

Anyway, he called me one day and his English was now good enough for me to understand that he had just learned the British were sending a boatload of German refugees to Australia for safety and he was to be among them. He said he would send me a card soon after he got there and he added that someday he would name a piece of his sculpture after me. I think he understood me when I told him how touched I was by that idea.

About a week after that, Noel told me that he had learned that the ship Max had been on was hit by a torpedo from a German submarine. There was not a single survivor. Noel and I drank sad toasts to his memory, and I shed bitter tears at the sad irony of his death.

One Sunday a few days later I was strolling with Noel after a leisurely lunch in a Chelsea pub. I mentioned that among the things in London that lifted my heart in these dreadful days were the flowers bursting in the window boxes which decorated so many of the houses there. I was rattling on about the colors—red, pink, blue, purple, yellow, gold, orange, "and all shades thereof," I said. "The window boxes just seem to explode with happiness and bravery," I said. "To compensate, I guess," I added.

Noel looked at me sadly. "Not all of them explode with happiness," he said. I asked him what he meant. He said he would show me. He took me by the hand. We walked to the end of that street and turned a corner. In the middle of that block he stopped. We looked at the house in front of us. There were two boxes of flowers, one under each window on either side of the door. The flowers in those window boxes were different from any I'd seen before: tulips of such a dark purple that they seemed black; there was something that looked like a miniature peony that was ebony; some dark-colored pansies; and a mass of other somber plants, the whole effect unrelieved by a hint of a bright flower or even a white one.

"The young woman who lives in that house had been married only a short time to a pilot on an aircraft carrier. The carrier was the *Courageous*."

I knew that the *Courageous* had been torpedoed with a huge loss of life. "Her husband was among those killed," Noel explained. "She says that her flowers will forever be in mourning for him."

Later that evening, I wondered what those grieving window boxes would look like at night if they had a light shone on them, but of course the blackout was total lest a light give hints to enemy planes. And there were plenty of air raid wardens around to ensure that no chink of light escaped into the dark.

"Night time here really is as dark as Erebus," I wrote my mother, borrowing a word from her rich vocabulary. Erebus, she had once explained to me, is the dark underground cave in Greek mythology that leads to Hades. It wasn't as if there was just an absence of light, it was as if everything with which you were familiar had been inked out.

I sometimes figured that if we lived forever in a blacked-out world, we would develop sonar equipment like bats to help us find our way around. In London, light itself seemed to take on an animate life; you had to force it back in, so to speak, or it would try to escape when you opened a door. I felt that it would actually try to insinuate itself into the dark.

On the other hand, the light that greeted you when you came in out of the dark took on a luxurious, sensuous quality. For me the biggest contrast between the light and the dark was passage into a London nightclub, the likes of which had remained very popular during the war. The one I knew best, the Four Hundred, had two layers of entrance, so to speak. From the opaque atmosphere of the street, you opened a door and were then ensconced in a little area of redundant pitch dark. You felt your way to a pair of heavy dark curtains which you slipped through as fast as possible. These opened up to the glaring light of the nightclub. The blare of the music added to the brightness and had a sizzle which contrasted hugely with the demonic quality of the blackened street.

An attractive American, Gertrude Niessen, with a husky, dusky voice, sang at the Four Hundred for a while. I had gotten to know her slightly through a good friend of mine, Virginia Jersey, wife of Lord "Grandi" Jersey. Virginia had been a famous actress in the US; as Virginia Cherrill, she was the lovely blind girl who was befriended by Charlie Chaplin in the movie "City Lights." Virginia had invited me to lunch a couple of times along with Gertrude Niessen, who seemed as dynamic in a restaurant as she did in the night club. In the evenings she packed admirers in at the Four Hundred.

One nearly forgot about the war when she was singing. Noel and I especially liked to hear her sing *Oh, Johnny*. She just seemed to blaze away any sense of sadness in that room when she sang about how Johnny could love. Several times there we had a chance to chat with her and tell her what brightness she brought to a dark world.

There were, of course, attempts to make nighttime walking less hazardous. There were great white swathes painted on the trunks of trees, on telephone poles, and other upright obstacles to help one notice them in the dark, but even so, walking in the black velvet night always seemed dangerous.

A few of the officers at the embassy, most of whom had sent wives and children home, moved closer to the embassy in order to be able to go to and fro more easily during the night. The embassy was nearly as busy at night now as it was in the daytime. Naturally there was much more cable traffic than there had been before the war. It seemed as if the ambassador sent multiple dispatches a day now. Further, US embassies and legations in occupied Czechoslovakia and Poland were sending their messages through the London embassy for transmission on to Washington. That meant, of course, that there was much more reporting sent by pouch—the bag for diplomatic dispatches—of what was going on in wartime Europe than there had been.

The file room, which was where material for the pouch was collected and stamped, seemed hectic all the time now. There were three stamps for mail going in the pouch, all different colors; one was for general mail, the second was for mail to the State Department, and one for mail important enough or sufficiently secret to be registered. Since it was always easier for me to have a tag word to help me remember something, it was easy for me to remember that the "red" stamp is for documents or mail that had to be "*red*gistered." I don't remember now how I figured out the other two.

Harvey was now writing the ambassador's speeches. Both in his speeches and in his general demeanor, Kennedy was viewing the situation with anything but equanimity. Just before war broke out he had gone to see the US ambassador to France, Bill Bullitt. Kennedy came back from Paris more discouraged than ever. Harvey reported to me in one of his secret-sharing sessions that Bullitt had told Kennedy that the Germans would go through the Maginot Line like shit through a duck. I didn't find the analogy very delicate but it certainly was graphic.

Aside from the dramatic increase in the volume of paper going through the embassy, and the large number of Americans who came to the embassy for help in getting home, there was another obvious change from the pre-war days. There were no Kennedy children drifting in and out to see their father. I hadn't realized until then how odd it was to look up and not see one or the other of them coming through. Joe had sent Rose and all the children, except Rosemary, home sometime after the outbreak of war.

Ever aware of the vagaries of fate, he had arranged that they travel in batches on different ships. Rosemary stayed in Britain because she was happy working with children in a convent outside of London, Eddie Moore told me. Joe visited her often and she came to stay with him in his house in the country frequently, Eddie said.

The *sitzkrieg* brought to mind the title of Erich Maria Remarque's book about the war in 1918, *All Quiet on the Western Front.* Joe Kennedy thought that this present quiet offered the crucial moment before the fighting erupted into all-out war, the vital time for the belligerent countries to come to some sort of a rapprochement. He felt that this was the last chance for such an initiative.

Many slings and arrows were flung at Kennedy publicly and privately for this point of view, but he wasn't the only American who opted for negotiations that would avoid the otherwise inevitable bloodletting. President Roosevelt sent Under Secretary of State, Summer Welles, and a number of assistants to Rome, Berlin, Paris, and London to see if the leaders would consider negotiations to end the present hostilities and agree to establish a European peace—a peace that would be both just and permanent, they said.

Most of the officers in the embassy felt that this idea was a nonstarter. They turned out to be right.

The would-be negotiators left England to go back to Washington, crestfallen and empty-handed just as spring was about to break over Europe.

Europe in the Spring

The spring that unfolded in England in 1940 was one of the loveliest that the British had seen in years, and everyone welcomed it especially joyously, for it followed the coldest winter since the last century. Noel had taken me one evening in February to show me a phenomenon that he said I was never likely to see again: the moon reflected in the ice which now covered the Thames. The Thames had last frozen over in 1888.

Now the daffodils were out and they seemed more golden than ever. The sweet-smelling dog roses and lilies of the valley were in full bloom. The trees in Cadogan Square, which I could see from my bedroom window, were already various shades of green, including one that I call baby green, which is to dark green what baby blue is to dark blue. The spring seemed so magical and delusive that on waking one morning under its spell, for a moment, I nearly forgot that there was a war on.

Apparently it was a beautiful spring across the Channel, too. The tulips and other early flowers in Holland had never been more brilliant, according to a letter I got from my Dutch cousin, Truss van Eighen, toward the end of April. I had visited her family in late spring the year before and her garden seemed enchanting then. She said it was infinitely more beautiful this spring.

But not all of Europe shared that glorious spring. T.S. Eliot said that April is the cruelest month, and it must have seemed so to Denmark and Norway for it was then that the Nazi armies suddenly swept in and devoured them. The attacks on Scandinavia stunned the British. This new example of Hitler's further outrageous betrayal of the Munich pact brought calls in England for Chamberlain to resign, which he now felt compelled to do. The tenacious bulldog, Winston Churchill, First Lord of the Admiralty, was invited by the King to put together a new government. Churchill formed a coalition which now included the Labor party. The British reacted with a burst of hope in the new leadership which was sorely tested immediately.

Churchill's government had barely taken office when the Nazis attacked and overran in amazingly rapid succession Luxembourg, Holland, and Belgium. Now the blitzkrieg was on in spades, with panzers bucketing along toward a France that seemed to have little will to fight.

In his first statement as Prime Minister, just three days after the Nazi assault on the Low Countries, Churchill, never one to mince words, told his countrymen that he had "nothing to offer but blood, toil, sweat, and tears."

My immediate response to the agonizing descriptions on the radio of the force and speed of the Nazi attack made me think of a poem (or at least part of it) that we had learned in early school years and which I hadn't thought of once since then until now: "The Assyrians came down like a wolf on the fold, its cohorts were gleaming in purple and gold." I seemed to be able to hear the screaming dive bombers and the crunching panzers, coming down like a wolf on the fold.

Now these panzers were moving so furiously through the Low Countries, racing "between the lilac and the roses," as H.G. Wells put it, that sometimes they were fifty miles ahead of their infantry. Planes preceded the armored vehicles, dropping in parachutists to destroy bridges and disrupt communications in any way they could.

On May 12, we learned that scores of German tanks and armored jeeps had crossed the border into France. People on the streets in London registered their horror at this turn of events by an uncanny silence. Even the bus I regularly took to work, usually full of chattering riders, held little conversation. There were none of the cockney accents I had become so used to; no Indian sing-song English, that I had a hard time understanding. There was none of the usual chit-chat between certain English people pronouncing "jove" as in "by jove" to sound as if it should be spelled "jauve." There was even no one trying to engage the driver in conversation.

It was as if the fate that the French faced now that the Nazis had actually invaded her was so appalling as to be literally unspeakable.

Paul Shot Down

Prior to the invasion of the Low Countries, Paul Richey and his famous squadron Number One, stationed in France, had been successful in shooting down a substantial number of German planes with minimal loss to themselves. Twice Paul's planes had been so badly damaged in combat that he was forced to bail out. Each time he had been able to maneuver his parachute sufficiently well so that he at least landed safely. Neither time had he been seriously injured and each time he had been picked up and taken care of by French people.

A few days after the invasion of the Low Countries, the Richeys learned that this time in his attempt to attack a German bomber, Paul had not been so lucky. His plane was honeycombed with bullet holes and cannon shells, his propeller shot to pieces, and he was badly wounded. Somehow, "with a shower of blood" down his right side, Paul had been able to land his battered crate.

He had collapsed on the ground where he was found sometime later by French soldiers who nearly shot him, thinking he was German. A French officer finally appeared on the scene. "Oh, *mon pauvre*," the officer said when he realized the badly wounded young pilot was not German. Paul was put on a makeshift stretcher, placed in a truck, and taken to a hospital, which, it turned out, was in the process of being evacuated due to German bombing. The truck driver aimed for another hospital which he couldn't find. Paul finally convinced him to take him to the American hospital in Paris.

That was the last news the Richeys got for a long time. The style with which they went through their ordeal, waiting for news of Paul in what I called the limbo period, became for me another symbol of British courage.

They went about their business as usual. Colonel Richey, always dressed as if going on a stroll down Bond Street, sat at his desk writing to everyone he knew, and some people he didn't know, searching for more news of Paul and of a useful role he himself could play in the war. Mrs. Richey was eternally busy at running a full house.

They both smiled freely, kept up their end of the conversations without being obvious or heavy-handed. They seemed to have stripped away all except the most fundamental values. They saw life now in a different dimension. Nothing unimportant was important to them or ever would be again. Their response became an epiphany for me—for the rest of my life, I like to believe.

***

Mrs. Richey never lost her capacity to think in imaginative terms of someone else's needs, even during that period, which I knew to be agonizing for her. For example, she knew that the family I was going to visit one weekend during the limbo period, had a young son. She pointed out to me that since I had been out for so many dinners that she had never come close to using up my rations: four ounces of butter and twelve of sugar per week. The amount of meat allowed was so minimal, I have forgotten it.

"I'll give you some of the sugar and butter that's due you. Take it to your friends. They can make candy or cookies or something for the boy."

My hostess (her husband, very lame, was working in a factory near Liverpool that packed parachutes and was living with a cousin near the factory) was delighted with my present. She baked dozens of cookies while insisting I sit in the lovely garden and drink Pimm's cups, a marvelous brew with a sliver of cucumber stuck in a concoction of some fruit juices and a dollop of a special brand of gin.

The next evening our hostess invited a neighbor, whose husband was in special intelligence stationed in Cairo, over for drinks. George, the ten year old son who had been the happy beneficiary of a lot of cookies, was pressed into service by his mother to run to the kitchen to get a shawl for the visiting neighbor or on other such errands. He approached these chores with little enthusiasm—indeed with obvious distaste. Once when he was out of hearing range, his mother asked, "How old are they when they develop some kind of manners? Do they ever learn to be polite?"

"For God's sake, don't worry about his being polite," the neighbor insisted. "And certainly make sure he is not ever too polite. That can get someone in a lot of trouble." She sounded so earnest that we felt compelled to ask her what she meant.

Her twenty-year-old son was in the Navy. His ship—they were somewhere in the English Channel, she explained—had either been bombed or hit with a torpedo. He never knew which but he found himself in the drink, which was quite rough. However he wasn't hurt and he had his life jacket on. After swirling around in the water, he could finally see a coastline in the distance. He felt he could make it to that shore despite that he had no idea what country he was looking at. Unfortunately, he thought, it couldn't be France. He was sure he had not been that close to France when his boat had gone down. Our visitor was telling us this in a steady voice, as if she was watching it take place.

Her son figured that in any event he had to get out of the rough sea. And he knew that he would have to take his chances as to which country he was headed for.

She talked on in her even voice, pausing once or twice to take a sip of her drink. Our hostess and I listened, rapt, sipping along with the guest.

As he crawled up the beach, she continued, he learned to his vast relief from a fisherman who came to his assistance that at least he hadn't fetched up in Germany. He learned to his further relief that he was in Holland. The fisherman passed him on to a nearby farmer and practically immediately he was shunted to the Dutch underground. He was outfitted in the ordinary clothes of a Dutch peasant and was hidden in a small village until the underground figured an escape route for him.

On his way from the village to his next destination he and his guide had to travel through a large, crowded railroad station, boiling with Nazi soldiers. He was hustled along by his guide. He speeded up, as he was directed, and in doing so he bumped into an old Dutch woman.

He hit her so hard she nearly lost her balance. "Excuse me," he called out, as he swept past her.

Every German soldier in the station looked in the direction of the English-speaking voice. Her son moved along, terrified, the neighbor told us. Now she paused for a few moments, as if to share this fearful occasion more fully with us.

I, for one, was on tenterhooks until she went on. She picked up her story in an excited voice. All of a sudden, the station was full of Dutch voices saying, "Excuse me, excuse me," in fake English accents, she told us. The station was ringing with Dutch men and women calling out, "Excuse me, excuse me"—and occasionally a child's voice would pipe through saying, "Excuse me." She smiled happily. The German soldiers were bewildered. And furious, she added. They looked around wildly but there was nothing they could do.

I sat back in my chair now and felt my muscles relax when she finished. Now I was able to take still another sip of my Pimm's. Actually that sip was more like a gulp, I thought, a gulp of relief.

"Don't ever bring a child up to be too polite," she cautioned us, now laughing. Anyway, she told us, although she could not know the exact route, somehow her son had been spirited out of Holland and gotten back to England. Probably through Spain, she guessed. She had never asked him, on purpose, and wouldn't until after the war was over, she told us.

Anyway, he was back home again and was now being assigned to another ship somewhere in the Atlantic now. "Practicing being rude," she added. On my train back to London I had a joyous time mulling over that young man's escape from the Nazis in Holland.

***

Finally, after those agonizing days of not knowing whether Paul was alive or dead, the Richeys heard that he was more or less okay. A French surgeon at the American Hospital in Paris had removed the bullet from his throat and, after a series of operations, patched him up so well that he would be able to leave the hospital in a few weeks. It turned out that Paul had been shot in the side of the neck just short of the carotid artery. "A little more to one side, a fraction of a millimeter would have been enough, and I would have bled to death from my carotid within five minutes," Paul later described his wound. That's when I learned that the word to "garrote" came from "carotid." I had heard harrowing tales that sometimes, in the Spanish Civil War, a man would escape death by grabbing his captor around the neck and pressing so hard on the carotid artery that he killed him.

By now the Germans were sweeping through France. "The shadow of the German army was already spreading over Paris," Paul said later. A few days after he was released from the hospital he went back to thank his doctor once more and to tell him goodbye. Together they went to the rooftop of the hospital to look off in the near distance for signs of the approaching Germans. Many of the casualties brought into the hospital had reported the Germans were shooting at ambulances even though the Red Cross was clearly visible. Paul's doctor commented that he was glad they had painted out the big Red Cross on the roof of this hospital.

On June 10, when Paul was to leave Paris to try to track down his squadron, the last thing he did was to buy a hat for Teresa. His squadron had been moved to several different airfields since he had been there, but he finally found it. Obviously in his condition he was of no use to his group, so he was told to get back to England as soon as he could, and however he could. On June 13, he was lucky enough to bum a ride back to England on a mail plane, carrying the hat box with him.

***

His confused and complex reaction to being back in England surprised him. On that flight home, he wrote, he had had an incredible capacity for sleep since his wounding. "And I slept now. I woke over the Channel Islands. They were bathed in sunlight and stood out very clearly in a smooth sea. Soon we were crossing the Dorset coast, and as I looked down on the calm and peaceful English countryside, the smoke curling, not from bombed villages, but from lazy little cottage chimneys, I saw a game of cricket in progress on a village pitch. After the poor war-torn France I had just seen, I was seized with a sudden disgust and revulsion at this smug insular contentedness and frivolity that England seemed to be enjoying behind her sea-barrier. I thought a few bombs would wake those cricketers up, and that they wouldn't be long in coming, either.

"As we glided down on to Herndon aerodrome my feelings were so mixed that I had difficulty in controlling them. I suppose it was a culmination of emotion that brought the tears to my eyes—something to do with the things I had done and seen, perhaps, with the friends I had left behind, and the almost unbelievable fact that I was home."

Before Paul's squadron left France, it would have destroyed 155 enemy aircraft. Paul himself was credited with nine. Three British pilots were counted as missing, presumed dead, two wounded, and one taken as a prisoner of war.

***

I don't know under what category the Royal Air Force listed the death of one pilot killed in France. Maybe Paul could have suggested a category.

He wrote of a day in early June in Paris sometime shortly after his release from the hospital when he got in a car and wandered a little outside of the city. He stopped when he saw a Hurricane roaring down and "beating up" on a British airfield squadron southwest of the city.

"Beating up" was a procedure obviously popular with expert British pilots in France. It consisted of extremely dangerous, wild maneuvers over a friendly airport to give everyone on the ground the kind of thrill you get when you are scared out of your wits with fear that the pilot is carrying things too far and will be killed. I suppose it offered some kind of psychic release to pilots constantly risking their lives in battle. Or perhaps it was their way to celebrate the sheer joy of being alive.

One "beat-up" Paul described, with a little poetic license, was such a success that it had "blown the paint off a few boats in the harbor."

Toward the finish of the beat-up Paul saw that day in France, soon after he had left the hospital, the pilot "did a couple of flick-rolls in succession at 200 feet and foolishly attempted a third with insufficient speed," Paul wrote. "Naturally it spun out. It straightened out promptly enough, but of course had no height and went in."

Paul was shocked to learn that the ill-fated pilot was an old wartime friend from a different squadron whom Paul had actually run across the night before in Paris. He had been sitting at a pavement table with friends, on leave for a couple of days. Paul discovered, in talking to the friend he ran across, that his friend had shot down seventeen German planes. "I noticed, but without surprise in the circumstance," Paul wrote later, "that he seemed nervous and preoccupied and kept breaking matches savagely in one hand while he glowered into the middle-distance. Like the rest of us, he'd had enough for a bit."

There were all manners of ways that one could be a victim of the war without being on a battlefield, I thought when I heard this sad story of Paul's friend. Indeed, I thought, my father too, had been the victim of war.

Kennedy and his Children

Joe Kennedy was gloomier than ever at the tragic events unfolding across the Channel and although it was at his insistence that his family had gone back to the US, he missed Rose and the children hugely.

There was no doubt that the softest spot in Kennedy's heart was for his family, and he had a special affinity with his two older sons and his daughter, Kick. Once home now, Joe Jr. was at Harvard Law School and Jack was at Harvard as an undergraduate. Kick had tried, unsuccessfully, to get into Sarah Lawrence College; instead she was now at a junior college. I got an occasional card from her, and it was clear she was homesick for England.

Joe felt their absences keenly. When he had the family with him in England, as ambassador, he knew he was in the catbird seat to give his two older sons chances to gain the broadest political, economic, and cultural education possible. He could offer Kick a world of excitement on the social scene.

Joe Jr. and Jack were both attractive, each in his own way, I felt in the few times I saw them. In the brief periods they were in London they were big hits on the chic dance circuit, but those diversions were simply a way station for them. They were ambitious and longing to try their wings.

Joe seemed mature for his years, I thought. He was sure of himself, and appeared fully conscious that he already cut a handsome young-man-of-the-world figure. He smiled a lot but wasn't given to laughing much.

Jack, on the other hand, still seemed to have some puppy boyishness. And he was thin, nearly to the point of being scrawny. He sometimes wore clothes that seemed too big for him and often wore a smile that also seemed too big. He liked to laugh. He laughed at other people's jokes, I noted, but he really preferred laughing at his own, which generally had a touch of irony. I thought this was interesting because he also seemed to have a quiet kind of sweetness. The brothers seemed to me to be totally opposites, with little in common, except that they were both ambitious and each wanted to cut a big swathe in the world.

Father Joe did everything possible to create opportunities for his sons to fuel their ambitions and to expand their horizons. He had already seen to it that they studied at the London School of Economics, a bastion of socialist theory. Joe wanted them to go there on the grounds that they already had a heavy dose of capitalist and conservative economics and he thought it important to be exposed to all points of view.

He sought out circumstances—or invented them—that would launch Joe Jr. and Jack off on trips covering nearly all of Europe and further. The ambassador would conjure up newspaper assignments for them to explore a certain area or would simply send them off as his aides to make reports to him on the condition and circumstances of the various countries they visited. These adventuresome journeys offered young Joe and Jack a formidable intellectual challenge and developed in them a heightened capacity for observation and for analysis which Father Joe felt would be useful to them in whatever they did in the future.

He was immensely proud of the reports he got back from his sons, especially a comprehensive one from Joe Jr., who had gone to Spain to write about the Civil War there. After three years and a million dead, the war was winding down. It had far-reaching ramifications: over 40,000 foreigners including those Americans in the Lincoln Brigade had volunteered to join the Loyalists. Only 1,000 foreigners had volunteered to join the Franco forces. Russian military experts advised the Loyalist forces; Franco's army not only had military advisors from Italy and Germany, but military equipment as well.

Since I had first learned about the Civil War in Spain, back when I was living in Maryland, I had plumped for the Loyalists. Now in the spring of 1939, when the imminent conquest of Madrid by Franco's army would ring the death knell for democracy, I was among the many concerned onlookers who viewed this tragic war as the dress rehearsal for an inevitable war to come between fascist and democratic countries. Actually, since I was so absorbed with the death of my beloved father, I didn't realize the Loyalists had been defeated at the end of March in 1939 until well after it had happened.

Dodging the crossfire in Madrid, Joe Jr. wrote his reports on the last days of the war in a series of letters addressed to his father. Joe Kennedy found these letters so interesting and so vivid that he read parts of them to Chamberlain and various other men and women at informal dinners and gatherings. He wanted everyone to have the opportunity to hear or read these reports on Spain. Why not a book, he thought? He gave Harvey Klemmer a copy of the letters with the charge to turn them into a book. "You'll make enough money to send your girls through college," he added. Further, he said that Joe made reference to Spanish politicos whose names might not mean anything to many readers; Harvey could identify them to everyone's edification.

Somehow that suggestion to Harvey to polish young Joe's letters from Spain—and for which Poppa Joe would have paid Harvey well—was forgotten and the letters fell between the cracks. That is, it was forgotten until much later.

Now every focus was on the sense of impending crisis in England after Hitler took over all of Czechoslovakia and followed it with his invasion of the Low Countries.

Kennedy, in both private comments and in public statements, continued to stress his hope that the US would stick to its own knitting and keep out of Europe's business, but he also saw that wars offered opportunities for the young Kennedy men to see war close up and learn from the experience. Joe Jr. had filled that role in Spain, and father Kennedy arranged for Jack to get an assignment with an American news service to cover the scene in war-torn Czechoslovakia. Through various devices, and to the vast annoyance of the US embassy people in Berlin, who were stuck with making the arrangements, Jack managed to get into Czechoslovakia under Nazi domination. There he wrote a series of comprehensive articles on the occupation of that beleaguered country.

They really did test their wings, the young Kennedys! Joe Jr. spent some time working in the US embassy in Paris. Between them they toured most of Eastern Europe, the Balkans, Turkey, and Palestine. On nearly all of these jaunts, they wrote articles or reports for their father. He was immensely pleased with their analyses and he talked about them with obvious pride.

***

What Joe had to offer his adored (and adoring) daughter Kick was not the opportunity to stimulate her intellectual curiosity or to broaden her political horizon. Those weren't Kick's cups of tea. What he was able to offer her instead was a big theater in which her social talents could be on full display. She was a success in the debutante circuit in London and in the grand houses in the lush countryside where her friends played over the weekends. Slick magazines carried photographs of her in the expensive, rather demure dresses that she and her mother had bought for her in Paris. One magazine named her "the debutante of the year."

Kick made no pretense of being intellectual but she had a special charm of her own. She could be too gabby at times; surprisingly she was also a good listener. She was notably candid: indeed her frankness occasionally slipped into tactlessness. But no one seemed to pay much attention to those social impieties. She had a pretty, alert face, surrounded by thick red-blond hair. She appealed to the young men she met and she also had a gaggle of new girl friends. The parents of her friends liked her, too. Indeed, she got along with all ages.

There were other young women, English women in the same orbit, more worldly than Kick or more polished, some with more sex appeal. But they weren't the success she was. She had one gift they didn't have—couldn't have—and she played it to the hilt.

It was her frank, unalloyed Americanness.

Joe was immensely proud of Kick, of her many friends and admirers, and of the way she conducted her life. He also recognized that she too was ambitious, and why not? What the hell, she was a Kennedy, wasn't she?

Bobby, seventh child and special pet of his mother, and Teddy, the youngest of the tribe, always good-natured and smiling, were both far too young to take advantage of the golden opportunities of their father's position. And this was true also of the younger girls in the family. A gay and giddy social whirl was not yet for them.

I noticed that when Joe talked about young Joe or Jack or Kick (or indeed any of his children), his smile was different from any other Joe Kennedy smile. It was gentler and more subdued. In any case it wasn't the kind of smile where his teeth showed. There was such a sense of mellowness in that smile that it almost seemed sad.

Anyway, the dance music went round and round and the parties that Kick had liked so much played on in London, as did parties for all ages and types, despite the Nazi's greased lightning sweep across much of Europe.

By now Hitler had broken not only the Treaty of Versailles and the Covenants of the League of Nations but the Munich Pact as well, to say nothing of the human toll his war had taken.

I now remembered one other Hitlerism from my brief exposure to his own autobiography. In *Mein Kampf,* Hitler had written that to win the easiest victories, use "terror and force." That seemed to be a pretty elemental military exposition and it certainly had worked for him so far, in spades. Indeed, it seemed to me that much of Europe, across the Channel from England, lay in shreds due to his terror and force.

For the Duration

The wildly successful German onslaught on the Low Countries increased the fear in Britain of an attack on England itself. And there was little left in England to avert such a calamity. As everyone knew, including the Nazis most of all, the majority of Britain's trained soldiers and their support equipment were in France, and so were the most experienced pilots and most advanced planes.

And if fear of an invasion on a mammoth scale scared some people, so did the prospect of individual Nazi paratroopers being secretly dropped into England. They had been very useful in the Low Countries, creating havoc and paving the way for advancing Nazi troops. An English friend told me that she was certain she had seen a paratrooper disguised as a nun in her village near London. Now whenever a nun came into my view I looked carefully at her feet to see if she (or could it be he?) was wearing German paratrooper boots.

Once when I visited Harvey and his wife Josie and their little girls in their cottage in the country, Josie told me they were now even afraid of the gypsies who sometimes camped in a field nearby. She laughed when she said that before the war she had been warned by neighbors to watch her girls carefully because the gypsies might steal children, darken their skin with walnut stain, and then disappear with them. Josie told me that now there were neighbors who thought that maybe German paratroopers were being dropped in parts of England disguised as gypsies, so she was warned about the gypsies again.

Josie and the girls went back to the US in late May. She called before she left to say it wasn't the threat of fake gypsies that was making her leave. Harvey was insisting on it. She asked me if I planned to stick it out. I assured her I did and said that I knew the British would win in the end. "As long as they have the Channel and Churchill and the Courage of the British they will never give up." That was my party line all the time, those three Cs, and I believed it absolutely. Whatever the Nazis did, the British would never surrender.

I only lost faith once, and that was in a nightmare, so I don't think it counts, but it was so weird and realistic that I woke up still clammy and frightened. I was in Sussex. I seemed to be by myself, admiring the lovely chalk downs. I heard sheep bells, and lambs bleating for their mothers. Now I saw a great bunch of ewes and their lambs, all with narrow black faces and black legs which was odd since I knew that those kind of sheep come from a totally different part of England. Along with the sheep bells and the lambs crying, there were some other strange noises. I put my hands over my ears to drown out the cacophony. Suddenly the sheep peeled off their wool covering and I saw they were Nazi soldiers, armed to the teeth. I started cursing them and the Nazis yelled that cursing would get me nowhere.

"We have taken over all of England," they said in English. "You will just find more of us wherever you go." While I was running I put my hands over my eyes as if by not seeing them, they would disappear, but instead I could hear them coming closer and closer. I tried to scream but couldn't and I ran and ran. I was still running when I woke up, sweating and terrified. Fortunately, I recovered my perspective after I had been awake awhile.

Later that day an expression now much in vogue came to mind, "for the duration." It meant that while the British might go through hell now, they knew it was temporary. When the war ended, with Britain victorious, of course, all the things that they had to disrupt or that got disrupted during the war would be put back in place again.

I had heard that the Queen, the epitome of bravery herself, had commissioned one of England's great artists to make a series of detailed drawings of Windsor Palace and its surroundings. This was done so that if the Palace was destroyed by German bombs, photographs plus those excellent drawings would make it possible to rebuild the palace and its surroundings exactly like they were before the war.

The crown jewels had been sent to some secret place a long way from London, to be retrieved after the war, I was told, and to adorn royalty on the appropriate occasions forever thereafter. I had learned on my most recent visit to the National Gallery that many of my favorite paintings were no longer there. The most valuable had been sent off for safekeeping (one rumor had it that they were in hiding in Wales). Temporarily, of course! Some of the animals in the London zoo had been sent off to visit kinfolk in zoos distant from London, to return as soon as the war was over. (Poisonous animals, such as some snakes and so forth, were put to death. This was for keeps, however, not just for the duration.)

Another wartime decision was to silence the famous bells of the churches of London for the duration. It was feared that

German planes could possibly orient themselves by the sound of a particular bell.

I learned, however, that there was no ban on singing about them, and the children of a friend of mine taught me the song:

> *Oranges and lemons,*
> *Say the bells of St. Clement's!*
> *When will you pay me?*
> *Say the bells of Old Bailey.*
> *When I grow rich,*
> *Say the bells of Shoreditch.*

For some reason I never heard the words to Bow Bells, the most illustrious of all. They are the bells of St. Mary-le-Bow in Cheapside of London, or as the area was sometimes called, Cockneydom. Unless you were born within their hearing, you were not considered a Cockney. Now with Bow Bells quelled, I wondered, how do Cockney babies become Cockney?

Although there was the rule that bells wouldn't be rung during the war there was also what I saw as a contradictory one: the bells of England were to be rung as loud as possible if England was invaded. I was sure that would never happen, but I knew those bells would ring to the high heavens when the war was over and Britain victorious. I figured you just had to know the context in which they were rung!

Many patients had been evacuated from London hospitals and sent to distant accommodations. Large numbers of the "stately homes" of England were already set up as temporary field stations for the wounded from the expected bombing raids.

The British knew that these were all transient arrangements. Everything would be put back in place once the war ended. This was all "for the duration." But the most common application of that term was used especially for the most precious of all: the children. Thousands were being sent out of London to visit relatives, if possible, or to other accommodating homes in faraway spots in England. Many children were being sent to the US and Canada "for the duration."

***

I saw many vivid examples of that one evening in a station in London where I had gone to meet Noel on his way back from Scotland. His train, it turned out, was going to arrive late, so I had a fine opportunity to study the flock of children gathered there to be sent away while the war was going on. The children and their parents seemed to me to be playing a game I invented on the spot and simply called, "The British Game: For the Duration."

I envisioned it as a board game in which steps toward a goal could be won, or lost, by the behavior of the participants. If both parent and child could smother the inevitable fear or anxiety behind a mask of bravado, their counter in the game would advance twenty steps. The threat of a tear sends the counter back eight steps. If a tear actually materializes, that's back eleven steps. Artificial banter, to avoid the sting of separation, gives five steps forward. Fathers and sons punching each other (as a means of indicating deep affection) get six steps forward. Mothers and daughters carrying on totally irrelevant conversations in order to avoid relevant conversations gain nine steps forward.

I heard one exquisite little English voice say to his mother in a loud complaining manner, "Nigel is lucky: he's not to be shipped out to stay with a dreary old aunt. He gets to stay in London. He'll be able to hear all the bombs, maybe even see some." I didn't know how to score that on my board game. Indeed I could not figure out in my game how to get the players back to the place on the board marked "home." About then I heard that the train Noel was on was due in a couple of minutes. As I was heading toward the arrival gate I ran across an old friend whom I'd not seen for a while. We greeted and I asked him how his wife was.

"Oh, she's still stuck off in the country, poor dear, trying to run a kindergarten for all the extra children in the village." He looked at me quite sadly. "I'm afraid she is having a rather dusty war."

***

Then because it was un-British to complain he recovered quickly and gave me his nice toothy smile. "Course, it's only for the duration," he said.

Embassy Characters

One day in May, Joe Kennedy told me that Mary and Eddie Moore were going to have dinner with him at the embassy residence—at Prince's Gate—that evening and asked me if I would like to come, too. He said maybe I could add some cheer to overcome the pall that left us so depressed about events across the Channel. I told him I didn't know about the cheer bit but I'd be delighted to come to dinner. He'd have his chauffeur pick me up and the Moores could drive me home.

When I got to the huge residence at Prince's Center, the ambassador said Eddie had called and told him they'd be late, but anyway he had a funny story to tell me. He asked me if I remembered the suggestion I had made to him to keep him from blowing his top at any remark the slightest bit critical of the US.

I said of course I did. My advice to him was to look at the person who might be foolish enough to even consider such a thing in the ambassador's presence. He should then try to imagine what that person looked like as a baby. I had told him to try it. "You'll find it works every time," I had said. "You can't get mad then."

He started to laugh and asked me to guess who he had tried to imagine as a baby a few days ago. I shook my head to indicate I couldn't guess. He said he had seen a certain person at a luncheon last week. "I know he's furious with me because of how I feel about the US role, and he'd like to say so publicly but he doesn't want to risk offending Washington and certainly not the President. This man is perfectly polite but I can sense his anger at me. The fact is, I am still representing the point of view of the American people who do not want the US to get involved in the war. It's not my country he would like to criticize. It's me, and I must not get annoyed with him. I admire him immensely and I think he likes me but he doesn't approve of my attitude toward the war. I suddenly realized that I should take your advice and try to visualize what the Prime Minister looked like..."

I finished his sentence for him, "What Churchill looked like as a baby." We were both laughing when the Moores arrived and there was no further discussion of Anglo-American relations at that point.

Conversation at dinner was largely about the devastation of the Low Countries and the terrifying Nazi attacks on the civilian population. Then we got off onto something else but I remember especially at that dinner being struck once again by the closeness between Joe and the Moores. Once at dinner Eddie said something to Joe Kennedy that I could not hear clearly. Then I heard Eddie say, "Everything is all set. We've got nice staterooms and it'll be a fine trip."

Joe turned to me to explain that Rosemary was going back to the US with Eddie and Mary. "They're going back the end of the month." I had heard Joe talk about all of the children except Rosemary and I'd scarcely ever heard him talk about her before.

It was broadly known that Rosemary was intellectually disabled, but her problem was not a subject of general conversation.

She had a full face, with lovely eyes; her features gave her a sensuous look, utterly unlike any of the other Kennedy girls. At the same time, in contrast to the sensuous look, she had a still expression. I had tried to greet her extra warmly the few times I had seen her and got an uninflected response.

I felt compelled to make some comment in response to Joe's remark that Rosemary was going home. "How great," I said, looking at him. "Now you'll have all your children together under one sky again." He smiled and I figured that was the end of that conversation for now.

***

We were quiet for a few minutes. Then I turned to Mary and asked her why she never came around the embassy more often. "Don't you want to see what kinds of nefarious things we are up to?"

She said that Eddie was a good reporter about what's going on there. She seemed to think for a second, then she added, "But he never tells me much about the other people in the embassy. He tells me about the ambassador and you and Harvey and Arthur, and of course about Ding Dong, but there must be other people there that I never hear about."

Joe looked at me and said I probably had interesting comments about some embassy people, "including me," he added, laughing. He said he had warned me I had to sing for my supper, so I better have some amusing tales to tell.

I found myself being inveigled into talking about a few of the characters in the embassy. I described especially one of the women in the file room, Miss J., a sweet, frail-looking woman with gray hair, who was competent, bright, and kind. I mentioned also that she goes out of her way to be helpful to me.

"Anyway," I went on, "she often has to give files to officers in the embassy, which turns out to be awkward because she is terrified of men and, as we know, all of the officers are men. To see her try to hand over a file to a man, who waits with outstretched hands to receive it makes the procedure look like some sort of bird anti-mating dance. She approaches the man, and then she backs away. His instinct then is to take a small step toward her, to get the file, which is a mistake because she backs away a little further. The man then stands still and she moves slowly and hesitatingly toward him, holding the file out at arm's length. He reaches for it without moving toward her and grabs the file. And she flees."

Eddie laughed at my description and said that he has been caught in that dance. The Ambassador, who, naturally, always had someone else get files for him, made Eddie promise to let Miss J. give him a file sometime.

They wanted me to go on, so I described a couple of other people. When I'd finished, Mary asked me were there any bachelors in the embassy. I knew she meant bachelors of interest to me or vice versa.

I told her about the only two I knew. One was Alan Steyne, who had been working in the Commercial service housed on the first floor of the embassy building. Joe had found Alan very well-informed on economic issues and had had him elevated to the diplomatic corps, "thus making," I said, raising a glass in a pretend toast to Joe, "Alan Steyne the first Jew in the Foreign Service of the United States."

I went on to say that Alan and I were good friends and had done some sightseeing in London a couple of times and had dinner together once or twice. "He is pleasant enough but too damned earnest for me, so I can't say I'm interested in him," I said. And then quickly added, "And nor is he interested in me, which is fine with both of us."

Mary asked about the other bachelor. "The only other one near my age, since I see what you are hinting at, is a code clerk, Tyler Kent." I pointed out that he always wore wonderful-looking suits that seem to be tailor made or "bespoke," as the expression goes. "That's the main thing I notice about him. I see him often when he goes through the file room, which he has to do to get to the code room."

"What does he have to offer other than his fancy suits?" she asked me.

"I scarcely know him so I was surprised when one day out of the blue he invited me to go sailing the following weekend with him and some friends. I made up some excuse to refuse because I just don't take to him."

I went on to say that he seemed like a nice clean-cut American boy, probably from the Midwest. "He's okay-looking but I imagine he's pretty dull," I suggested. Then I apologized about being so negative about him since I didn't know him at all.

Just before the Moores and I left, the ambassador told me I had done a "fine job of singing for my supper." He said he didn't see any more laughs ahead for a long time, what with the Nazis moving so fast they have now bottled up thousands and thousands of British troops. The situation looks absolutely desperate, he said.

A few days later I was in Eddie's office, shooting the breeze with him and worrying with him, as I and everyone else in England, about what would happen to the British soldiers now that the Germans were sweeping into France. All of a sudden he changed the subject. "Do you know what Rosemary's problem is?" he asked me. I was startled but I answered quietly that I did not know.

Eddie told me that when she was very young she had been on a big family picnic at the beach where she had eaten too much lobster meat. She had severe convulsions after that and she had never gotten over them. That's what has made her a little mentally challenged.

I think I just said something bright like, "Oh," and I was thinking, "Nice try, Eddie," and I still have no idea why he told me that story.

Anyway, it was clear that he and Mary were extremely fond of Rosemary. I'd heard that her siblings, too, were always very sweet and patient with her. Her brothers, Ding Dong and Arthur Houghton, often danced with her at parties, but it was the Moores who seemed to be her special pals.

As I left Eddie's office I told him that I hoped I hadn't seemed too critical of Tyler Kent at dinner a few nights ago, especially since I really didn't know him.

Dunkirk: Between the Devil & the NOT Deep Blue Sea

Having conquered the Low Countries weeks ago and having already established a foothold in France itself, the forbidding Nazi war machine now concentrated on attacking the British in France. By late May the Germans had driven the British to the water's edge at the beaches of Dunkirk, a French town on the North Sea. There the British, along with some French troops, were literally trapped between the devil and the blue sea. The devil was mainly the *Stuka* dive bombers—which aside from being so swift and deadly, were equipped with ear-splitting sirens when they dove—and the blue sea, which was any thing but deep at Dunkirk. Indeed the British Navy was blocked from getting in to rescue its troops at Dunkirk because the sea was so shallow there. The ambassador, after a visit to the Foreign Office, sent a cable saying the situation looked "very grim."

As this terrifying scenario developed all of us in the embassy were in a constant state of anxiety over the fate of the ensnared soldiers. The British that I passed on the street looked pale and horror-struck. At dinner at the Richeys' house, we seemed to find only superficial subjects to discuss in order to avoid the reality across the Channel.

There seemed to be no alternative to total defeat for the British unless there was some magic way to rescue those troops huddled on the beaches of Dunkirk. And magic was in short supply for the British that spring. Everyone knew that rescue was a near-impossible operation. Ships simply could not get into Dunkirk due to the shallow water.

Additionally there were solid rumors about fierce divisions in the British cabinet: Some members felt that the situation was so obviously hopeless that the British should negotiate now with the Germans; this was the time to make the best deal possible. A few days beforehand, the King, in a broadcast to all his people, had called for a day of prayer against the enemies of his nation. I wondered to my friend Noel whether Churchill, who was not exactly head of the Office of Circumlocution, would speak frankly about the problems, and still insist the British forge ahead and do the best they could.

In unvarnished language in a special address to his cabinet—which leaked immediately—Churchill said that due to the impossibly shallow harbor at Dunkirk, the British would be lucky to save some 40,000 troops at Dunkirk, that the Luftwaffe was disarmingly strong, that the French were about to give up the ghost, that sometime after Dunkirk the Nazis would try to invade Britain.

He ended his speech by presenting a haunting contingency: "If this long island story of ours is to end at last, let it end only when each one of us lies choking in his own blood upon the ground."

But still he won his argument that there would be no bargaining with the enemy. At his insistence, the evacuation was started and it went appallingly slowly—to nobody's surprise. We heard that the experts guessed that they might be able to rescue as many as 45,000 troops, and even those at a huge cost, because the Germans were fiercely bombing British ships, the beaches, and even soldiers already in the water.

The procedure was called Operation Dynamo, but the name didn't seem very appropriate to start with, Colonel Richey suggested to me.

Facing formidable attacks—mainly swarms of Stukas—the British Navy managed to rescue some men from the beaches, but compared to the number stranded, the number was pitifully small. It was a cruel situation. The harbor was just too shallow to let the anxiously awaiting Navy ships in. Fate seemed even more cruel than it had been to Tantalus, I thought. I further thought, if ever a word had a logical derivation, it was *tantalize*.

The Mosquito Fleet

Now all of a sudden the British government put out an urgent call for small boats of every kind, from all over England, to join the Navy fleet in this crucial enterprise. The small boats could navigate in shallow water, load up the troops and carry them to the larger ships out in the deeper water, and those ships would bring the beleaguered troops home.

Over that week of the rescue operation, 600 civilian boats, according to the newspapers and the constant radio accounts, fishing boats, motor yachts, and at least one ferry, made their way to Dunkirk. "The unforgotten and un-Homeric" ships of the Dunkirk evacuation, as Philip Guedalla the British poet wrote, were the "*Mary Jane* and *Peggy IV, Folkstone Belle, Boy Billy*, and *Ethel Maud, Lady Haig*, and *Skylark*, the little ships of England brought the army home." I fell in love with all the skippers of the little boats. They repeated their routine of loading up a bunch of troops, transporting them to the big ships awaiting them, which then took the soldiers to England; then the little boats hurried back to the shallow Dunkirk harbor, loaded up another batch of soldiers, and carried them to the big boats. They kept up this routine for days and days and nights and nights. Chugging their way into history, Churchill called them the "Mosquito Armada."

Indeed, the Navy and those unprepossessing ships helped to save more than 300,000 British and French troops from Dunkirk. At a nearby port another 4,000 troops were rescued. Further, hundreds of Polish, Dutch, and Belgian soldiers were among those rescued by that brave little fleet and carried to the waiting big ships.

The RAF tried desperately to keep the large and hugely aggressive Luftwaffe at bay as much as possible. Nazi planes attacked from the land and from the sea, but as Churchill pointed out later, the "kill-ratio of the RAF" was amazing. I learned that the last battle Paul's old squadron would fight in France was to help cover the evacuation of those troops from Dunkirk.

It was a deliriously exciting moment for everyone in England. I was thrilled to the core by the audacity and the success of the rescue. I got carried away by the drama, and like nearly everyone else treated it as if it had been a rousing victory for the allies.

I thought that Churchill sounded like the bard himself speaking in the House of Commons during the Dunkirk rescue: "We shall not flag or fail," he assured the world. "We shall fight in France, we shall fight on the seas and oceans, we shall fight with growing confidence and growing strength in the air, we shall defend our island, whatever the cost may be. We shall fight on the beaches, we shall fight on the landing grounds, we shall fight in the fields and in the streets, we shall fight in the hills; we shall never surrender."

A few days later I learned that after that speech Churchill had added to a person sitting next to him, "and we will hit them over the heads with beer bottles, which is all we have really got." There was more truth than poetry in Churchill's aside after his magnificent speech, obviously unaware that his mike was still on.

***

For all the apparent glory of the Dunkirk operation, the soldiers were able to bring with them from France only their rifles. Hundreds of tanks, thousands of other vehicles, including motorcycles, tens of thousands of machine guns, ammunition and untold numbers of other armaments had to be left behind. Further, the stories of the human tragedy, such as the troops no one was able to rescue, were not announced immediately to the people of Britain: for instance, at another port in France, 6,000 men of the famous 51st Highland Division were taken prisoner by the Germans.

I learned later to my deep sadness that two men that I knew well didn't get back from the Dunkirk beaches. Among my friends who had survived that particular hell, one had taken a bullet in his leg which had gotten infected, and later he had to have his leg amputated. Another friend looked so different from his previous self—as if he was seeing ghosts—that I scarcely recognized him. Further I spent many hours that spring writing letters of condolence to the heartbroken families of friends who had been killed in fighting in the Low Countries or during the evacuation from Dunkirk.

As soon as the Germans had crossed the border into France, brave Mussolini, known to many in Britain as the "Sawdust Caesar," declared war on England. That night windows were broken in a few Italian restaurants, including Noel's and my favorite one. Now another brave character, American poet Ezra Pound, left France, where he had lived for years, and went to Italy to spout propaganda for the Italian fascists.

Yet another American turncoat, an Irish-American named William Joyce, broadcast wild anti-British fables from Germany. He was known throughout England as Lord Haw-Haw and his stories were so patently phony that he supplied an element of humor to our evenings at the Richeys listening to the radio for news.

Before actually announcing the day's news every evening, the BBC now went through a ritual. First, it played the British national anthem, which was then followed by the anthems (or part of them) of the countries which had been invaded by the Germans or the Italians and now had representation in London: Czechoslovakia, Norway, Denmark, Holland, Luxembourg, Belgium, Poland, and Ethiopia. The last had been the first country to fall to the Fascists, having been conquered by Italy in 1935. The former emperor of Ethiopia, Haile Selassie, had been living in London ever since he was forced from his own country. His home now was Brown's Hotel, a stylish conglomeration of houses just off Berkeley Square, where affluent friends sometimes took me to lunch or dinner. I saw the former emperor on several of those occasions, a small frail figure in a long white robe, with a beautiful dark mottled face.

France's national anthem was not yet on the BBC Program, but I felt sure we'd be hearing *Le Marseillaise* on that program soon. There was, of course, always scuttlebutt rumbling around London during the war, and a bit that I heard at that time was that Churchill had flown secretly to Paris to try to persuade the French to fight on as long as possible. He was rumored to have said he was going to France "to stop the rot" he saw pervading that country. Indeed the French had already been talking "armistice," and some were horrified when Churchill had suggested they should fight on "in the ruins" of Paris, if and when the Germans got there.

***

Fortunately, by now, a major change had been taking place in the US attitude toward helping the British. The determination of the British in the Dunkirk rescue and their heightened need at this point had surely been factors in Americans' new appraisal of the war. Harvey and I, who now comprised the totality of RORC now that Harold had left, took off for a special Club lunch to celebrate when we got word that our President had been able to persuade Congress to modify the Neutrality Act's embargo so that vastly more military supplies could be sent to belligerents (read: the British). Now surplus and outmoded but still functioning stocks of arms, munitions, and aircraft would be coming to Britain. The bills authorizing this had passed in Congress despite being vociferously opposed by some members of that body, as well as some national organizations, mostly right wing, around the country. The most fiercely isolationist among the latter was called America First.

Isolationism however was not confined to the right; indeed the US Socialist Party, meeting in Convention in the early spring of 1940, according to a clipping Mother sent me, called the British and French "aggressors in an imperial war."

I knew that if my father was still alive, Republican as he was, he would have been ardent in his support of Roosevelt's efforts to give as much help to England as possible. And he would have been happy over the results of Roosevelt's leadership. After all, the majority of Republicans and Democrats in Congress were now supporting Roosevelt's increased domestic military spending as well as aid to Britain, but it was also clarion clear from everything that we in the embassy read and heard that most Americans still were absolutely opposed to direct US involvement in this war.

Kennedy spoke often about how happy he was that the US was going to send more military equipment to England. He also talked frequently about the bravery of the British. But he always had to add in his general opinion about the war; he followed up such remarks by confirming his continued support of the majority of Americans who didn't want the US to be dragged into this conflict. Arsenal, yes, but active engagement, no!

Thank God for Churchill

Though I could laugh at a joke about Churchill, with his baby face, as I did that evening with Joe Kennedy when the Moores and I had dinner at his house, I shared with my dear friend Noel an extravagant admiration for the Prime Minister. Noel and I had fallen in love months ago and we spent nearly all our evenings together when he was not off on a secret mission of what was known as "preemptive buying." Where he went and what he bought, I was not privileged to know.

An uncle of Noel's had been a friend of Churchill's and was elected to Parliament the same year, in the early part of the century. I was hugely interested in hearing stories about his background from Noel. Churchill had already made a reputation for himself as an intrepid war correspondent for a British newspaper. Following his newspaper career he fought in the Northwest Frontier province of India. At that time, Noel pointed out, Victoria had been Queen of Great Britain and Ireland and Empress of India. Churchill was in a cavalry charge in the Sudan the next year, and later was taken a prisoner during the Boer War.

He was elected to Parliament as a Conservative, but four years later he joined the Liberal Party. Noel's uncle had always been a staunch Liberal, so he was delighted to welcome Winston to his party, but somehow he knew that Churchill would go back to being a Conservative. (It took him twenty years to do so.) Regardless of his party he was always in the thick of political action, of one kind or another, sometimes supporting archly conservative causes and at other times, remarkably liberal ones. In any case, the Tories always mistrusted him because he was "too radical," Noel said, for he had favored National Health and had once tried to abolish the House of Lords!

Churchill had certainly taken the full measure of Hitler early on. The newspapers had made countless comments on his extraordinarily prescient book, *While England Slept*. There he had written that "Dictators ride to and fro upon tigers which they dare not dismount. And the tigers are getting hungry." The wonderful resolute Anglo-Saxon language that was his hallmark now was already evident in the speeches he made in the middle thirties warning about the threat Hitler posed.

I was amused when Noel told me that Churchill credited his mastery of language to his having been such a poor student that he repeated classes in the lowest form of Harrow, his earliest school. "There," Churchill had said, "I gained an immense advantage over the cleverer boys. I got into my bones the essential structure of the ordinary British sentences." Now, as prime minister, his speeches were so forceful that a newspaper columnist called them "part of the arsenal" of Great Britain.

But the awe in which he was held did not damp down tales about his drinking. Joe Kennedy, a teetotaler himself (although he had made a nice chunk of money selling whiskey in the US after the prohibition act was repealed) was among those who personally expressed surprise at Churchill's excessive drinking. Noel told me that a friend of his family, an admiral, was among those many people he knew that worried about the amount of booze Churchill was able to put away daily; scotch, champagne, and brandy were among his favorite beverages. Water was not. There was a story that when Churchill was offered water at a dinner party, he put his hand over the glass to indicate that he did not want water. "Fishes fuck in it," he was alleged to have said, though that quote has been attributed to W.C. Fields and countless other famous drunks.

I told Noel to go back to his friends who didn't approve of Churchill's alcoholic consumption, and tell them what Lincoln said when someone complained that his General Ulysses S. Grant was drinking excessively. Lincoln said to find out what brand the general was drinking and see immediately that all the other generals in the Union army were given barrels of it.

Churchill's son Randolph also had a fondness for alcohol. But mainly he had the reputation of being exceptionally obstreperous, and tales about him and his antics floated around London. One was of the evening a while back when Randolph and his father were dining at the Carlton Club in London. Randolph was annoying everyone at the dinner table by telling how he would have run the war if he had been in charge of the British troops in France, one such tale went. To demonstrate, he pushed the knife to one end of his "battleground," and identified that as the Siegfried Line, and placed a fork not far away and said that would be the Maginot Line. He pushed salt cellars and said they were the British and French troops. He placed all the spoons opposite them and said these were Germans and, talking loudly, saying if he had been the commanding general, he would have called for all the air cover we had, including ordering all of the RAF fighter planes out of Britain and sending them over to France. He picked up a roll off his butter plate, called it the RAF. He kept waving the roll around over the German troops.

He droned on and on. It was clear that many of the people at the table had seen a like performance before, and for those that hadn't it was already too much. One man kept saying, "Fine, Randolph, fine," as a way of trying to get him to stop. A couple of people left the table but Randolph kept on moving his soldiers and fleet of planes—his dinner roll—round and round.

Finally, his father too had run out of patience. "Randolph," Winston Churchill said in a loud voice. "Randolph," he repeated, "Lie down."

***

Once I told Noel sometimes this great feeling of heartfelt veneration I had for Churchill's faith in the British wells up so strongly in me that it brought me to the verge of tears.

I told Noel another reason I admired the man was because it is so obvious that he adores his Clemmie. "It breaks me up to hear about him singing 'Oh, my darling Clementine' to her." I suppose I must have read somewhere that Chamberlain had a wife too, but if so, I didn't remember ever having seen her first name in newspapers. And I couldn't imagine Neville Chamberlain ever singing a song to her, even if the song celebrated her name.

"Anyway, Noel, hat's off to Chamberlain now," I said, for it was generally known that Chamberlain had most strongly supported Churchill's position during the precarious Dunkirk rescue that there would be no negotiations with the Nazis.

Noel put his hand up like a British bobby stopping traffic. "For God's sake let's stop this frivolous conversation, and let's talk about something serious. Let's talk about you and me."

"Second" World War

Harvey Klemmer, Ding Dong, and I spent a weekend in May at the ambassador's house in the country. When he invited me he asked if I would like to bring a friend. I thanked him but said that I was happy to come along with Harvey and Ding Dong. I knew that Noel had to be out of the country over that weekend, or else I would have been in town with him. Driving down with my "stable mates," as I referred to anyone on the ambassador's staff, I chuckled to myself thinking what a crazy mixed-up group we'd have made if Noel had been present.

After dinner Friday evening, Joe said to me that he bet I didn't often talk to my mother on the telephone. I said it is so bloody expensive, that I only called on special occasions. We write to each other frequently, however, I told him.

"Please call her from here," Joe said, "any time you'd like and talk to her as long as you want to." I thanked him, of course, and told him I'd certainly take advantage of his kind offer.

Joe looked at me with a kind of wistful smile and said he would give anything on earth to be able to talk to his mother, who had died many years ago. I don't remember how we got from there to talking generally about his children but he said something to the effect that if he died that evening, each of his nine children would inherit a million dollars. "And none of them would have a life anything like as exciting as I've had," he added.

The next day he asked me if I had called my mother. I thanked him again and said we had a wonderful, and very long, warm conversation. Additionally, my brother had come down from Harvard to celebrate his nineteenth birthday with Mother, so I had a chance to have a happy chat with him, too. Joe said he was delighted.

***

Joe and I went riding after breakfast Saturday. He kept a couple of horses there, although I looked upon them as nags. I didn't think Joe knew anything about horses but I enjoyed riding with him anyway. Riding along he told me that two more guests were coming for the night, Clare Luce and a friend of hers. Clare, he explained, had just come from Paris and been on a trip through the Low Countries to see how all those miserable people were faring in the wake of the Nazi devastation. She was planning to write a book about the war.

"I think you and Clare will like each other," Joe said. I felt immensely flattered. She was a successful playwright, the author of countless magazine articles, and also the wife of the *Life* and *Time* publisher, Henry Luce. Joe said that he was going to take the three of us to Cliveden, the home of Lord and Lady Astor, for tea the next day. Lady Astor had asked him to come and when he said he had guests, she had said, "bring 'em, of course." I guessed Harvey and Ding Dong were to be left to their own devices.

Clare and her friend Charlotte Brown arrived in time for cocktails before dinner. Clare was open and friendly, although she seemed extremely tired. Despite that when she smiled, I thought she looked even prettier than in her photographs and she had the only really pearly white teeth I'd ever seen. It turned out her friend was from Cooperstown, New York, where I had good friends whom I had visited years ago. It was a small town and she knew them well. We fell into easy conversation.

During dinner we asked Clare to tell us about her recent travels. She described the lost, disoriented people in the Low Countries and in France who had been caught in the path of the Nazis. She talked slowly, in a soft voice, and with suppressed emotion. Only once, she said, did Nazi soldiers stop the small car that she and her driver were in. The soldiers were rigidly polite to her and did not interfere with her travels. She saw lots of other Nazi soldiers driving along in their Jeeps, but no one bothered her.

On the roads there was the endless line of miserable refugees, some on ancient bicycles but most were walking, "Rather limping painfully along," she said. "Mostly I saw old women and old men and lots of children. I rarely saw a smile, even from a child. None had anything to smile about, I knew, and they all looked pale and wan." She had seen whole families in small wagons drawn by horses and the horses looked exhausted, too. Indeed she saw some that had collapsed still in the shafts of the wagons or carts.

Along the roadside, she said, there were many dead farm animals; cows and horses, with bloated bellies, killed in the cross fire, she guessed. "There were scores of deserted farms, with withering crops rotting around them. There was destruction and devastation every-where," she said in a low voice. "And always the German soldiers, riding in the middle of the road, in their jeeps and..." She explained that she never saw tanks, that is German tanks, anywhere. They obvi-ously were much further along, now on their way to take over France. She did see a number of twisted hunks of metal, which had once been British tanks, obviously destroyed by the Germans. There was no indi-cation that there were still bodies in them, she said. "Although, of course, if there were," she continued, "they would be inside the tanks so we would never have seen them."

Now she was speaking in what seemed like a hoarse voice. "Although we saw a few dead people in the countryside quite a dis-tance from the road; my driver and I figured they were civilians, as they were not in uniforms. He and I expressed our surprise, happily on both our parts, not to have seen bodies of soldiers. We guessed that whichever poor fighting men had been killed along this roadside had been buried by the retreating civilians. We were grateful for that," she commented.

Clare paused in her descriptions when Kennedy was called to the phone by someone from the embassy, and resumed when he came back, but only briefly. It had obviously been a grueling trip and now she seemed limp with exhaustion. She ended her conversation by tell-ing us in a nearly inaudible voice that she was going to write a book about her experiences, and was planning to call it simply "Europe in the Spring."

The next morning Joe told us that he was going to beg off from the tea. He said he had already called Lady Astor to tell her, but she was looking forward to seeing the three of us anyway. He was sorry but some business had come up and he was expecting someone from the embassy to come to talk to him about it. His driver would be happy to drive Clare and Charlotte and me to an interesting inn nearby for lunch, he suggested, and then do a little swing around a lovely part of England until it was time to go to Cliveden.

We set off in the early afternoon, had a long lunch at a simple, pleas-ant inn and then were driven through verdant, peaceful countryside. Clare remarked that the war looked a million planets away from where we were. For a moment, I thought she was going to cry at the contrast.

On the way we chatted about our tea-time hostess. We knew that Nancy Astor was considered an eccentric in a country famous for them, although she was not British-born. (She came from Virginia.) She had the distinction of being the first woman elected to Parliament

in England, where she played a controversial role. We decided that
Lady Astor was one of the three American women who had made
a dent, good or bad, in recent British history. The other two were
Wallis Warfield Simpson and Jenny Jerome Churchill, the mother of
Winston Churchill.

Nancy Astor had been among those who had supported
Chamberlain in his Munich decision and those who agreed with her
were said to be part of the "Cliveden Set." Since Joe Kennedy was
among her friends, the London gossip columnists saw him as a card-
carrying member of that "Set." It obviously never had a formal structure and it included a number of well-known British politicians and
writers, among them the distinguished Lord Halifax, and others of
the same conservative coloration.

***

It was a clear, mostly sunny day and the first view we got of Cliveden
was of a large house set in a great swath of golden green drifting
down to the Thames. Lady Astor was at the door to greet us when we
arrived. She had a smile that came and went pretty quickly as if on an
elastic band, but I thought she seemed very handsome.

Clare's description over tea and scones of her journey through the
war-torn Low Countries and France was even more graphic and sadder than it had been the night before. I felt it seemed clearer, too, how
much she had been seared by the experience. She also talked more
about how superficial so many people in Paris seemed. Lady Astor
made her promise she'd send her a copy of the book as soon as it was
published.

To lighten the conversation now Lady Astor turned to me and
mentioned that her son Bill had a house very near the American
embassy. I told her I knew that because Bill had been kind enough to
have a luncheon at his house for me shortly after I arrived in England.
He had been goaded into it, I said, by my dear polo-playing brother-
in-law, Cokie Rathborne, who was an old friend of Bill's. I told Lady
Astor I also knew another of her attractive sons, Jake. He was in the
army; all of the Astor sons were in the armed services. She said Jake
liked Americans immensely, and that he was a great friend of Kick
Kennedy's. We talked about what a delightful person Kick was. Lady
Astor was clearly very fond of her.

After tea our hostess gave us a guided tour of part of the big elegant house, of which I remember very little. There is some story, by
an American writer, I think, about two women who travel through

France and Italy and England and remember nothing about their journey except the hotels in which they stayed. I am just the opposite. I was lucky enough to visit or even stay in a couple of the "stately" homes of England, of which I remember practically nothing. But I can tell you who else was there, what the paintings were like, pretty much what we talked about, and even maybe the names of the dogs.

I remember staying in a wonderfully elegant house, belonging to a Duke, a cousin of Noel's. It was awash a with ancestors from hundreds of years back, in great gilded frames, dripping from the walls, masses of servants and every evidence of plenty of moola; yet when I left to go back to London the butler presented me with a bill for a shilling or two to pay for a call I'd made to London. I wondered if the same system was practiced at Cliveden.

Lady Astor told us that there were already plans for Cliveden to be set up as a sort of auxiliary hospital for wounded soldiers and sailors. "As it had been, in the First World War," she said. I noted she emphasized the word "first."

Driving back to the ambassador's house, I told Clare and Charlotte that I'd not before heard the 1914–1918 war referred to as the "First" World War. "If that was the First, then, ergo, we are now in the Second World War!" I moaned.

"Poor world," I said. "Poor world." I said it even more sadly the second time.

The Code Clerk

On the Monday, May 20, after that weekend at the ambassador's, I noted that the "well-dressed" code clerk, Tyler Kent, wasn't at work. He didn't turn up the next day, nor the next day after that, nor the next. Indeed he never came back to work. Everyone in the embassy was naturally curious about his absence but we were cautioned not to discuss it.

A couple of days later an American newspaper friend of mine took me aside at a party. "I hear that someone in the embassy has been nabbed by MI5," he said, "and now he's in the poky. So what's cookin'?" he asked me.

I told him that honestly I didn't know anything about it, which was true at that time. But later I learned the story: my usual source of all the embassy skinny had told me in absolute confidence, what had happened. I kept it confidential until the whole tale broke and I often wondered if Joe Kennedy remembered my analysis of Tyler Kent as a "nice, clean-cut American boy." Anyway, he never teased me about it and, as it turned out, I was wrong on every count about the code clerk, except that I hadn't liked him.

Tyler Kent, it developed, was picked up by British intelligence as a spy. I later learned that it was this shocking news from an embassy official about Tyler Kent that had called the ambassador to the phone the first night Clare Luce was there. Over the phone Kennedy had directed a cable be sent to the State Department saying that he was immediately revoking Kent's diplomatic immunity so Kent became the responsibility of the British. It was an appointment to meet with embassy officials and British intelligent representatives the following day which had kept Kennedy from going to Cliveden that afternoon for tea.

The code clerk, it turned out, had been making copies of confidential cables he was sending to the State Department. These included especially highly secret correspondence between President Roosevelt and Prime Minister Winston Churchill which the code clerk had been passing on to certain friends, mainly British fascists, who would pass them on to the Nazis.

A series of secret letters between the two leaders had been initiated months ago by President Roosevelt when Churchill was First Lord of the Admiralty. These had been sent and were received on our cables. Exchanges of this nature at that time were extraordinary because of the unequal positions of the two men when they started this exchange: one a President and the other a member of the cabinet of the other country. Previously Churchill had signed himself "Naval Person." Now that he was Prime Minister he simply signed himself "Former Naval Person." I was amused at Churchill's sense of fun when I first learned about the new designation he had given himself.

Although Kent turned copies of these letters over to those who spied for Germany, what he had in mind, I learned later, as the final disposition of the correspondence was its release in the US. He felt that this frank, uninhibited exchange would prove that Churchill was conniving to get the US into the war and that Roosevelt was helping him toward that end. Kent, at his chimerical best, thought that if the correspondence was given to America First (the extreme anti-interventionist group in the US) and thence to members of Congress, that it might lead to the impeachment of FDR. Kent figured that these exchanges could be read as collusion between the two leaders to bring the US into the war. Kent was correct to the extent that Churchill was trying everything on God's parched earth to get the

US into the war. Roosevelt, on the other hand, was trying to accommodate him in every way possible, except by actually going to war. So Kent was wrong about the President, but Kent didn't seem hipped on accuracy.

Aside from the damage done to the British by the distribution to its enemies of the correspondence between Roosevelt and Churchill, Kent had compromised the most secret and secure method of communication in the US intelligence system. Our entire code structure was now worthless and had to be completely overhauled.

Among the copies and photos of embassy documents found in Kent's rooms after he was picked up by the British were a huge number of embassy documents other than the Roosevelt-Churchill cables. Indeed it took sixty-seven pages to list them all. His address books contained names and addresses of a swarm of women, many of whom were already under surveillance by British Secret Service agents.

Kent never seemed to lack for female friends in London. Indeed, he had such a visitor when he was nabbed. She was wearing the top of his pajamas. Kent was wearing the bottom. Also found in Kent's flat, according to my friend Harvey, again letting me in on secrets of a special order, was a Japanese Joy Box. When Harvey told me that, my only response was, "Hmmmm?" At least, I suspected, that had nothing to do with spying.

***

The last message that Tyler Kent encoded and copied at the American embassy was from Former Naval Person to President Roosevelt. It was written as France had been invaded and was tottering to her fall. It consisted of two long paragraphs, the latter of which reads:

> "Our intention is, whatever happens, to fight on to the end in this Island and, provided we can get the help for which we ask, we hope to run them very close in the air battles in view of individual superiority. Members of the present administration would likely go down during this process should it result adversely, but in no conceivable circumstance will we consent to surrender. If members of the present administration were finished and others came in to parlay amid the ruins, you must not be blind to the fact that the sole remaining bargaining counter with Germany would be the fleet, and if this country was left by the United States to its fate, no one would have the right to blame those then responsible if they

made the best terms they could for the surviving inhabitants. Excuse me, Mr. President, for putting this nightmare bluntly. Evidently I could not answer for my successors who in utter despair and helplessness might well have to accommodate themselves to the German will. However, there is happily no need at present to dwell on such ideas. Once more thanking you for your good will."

A handwritten copy of this cable, in Kent's writing, was found in his room when the British picked him up. There was a savage irony in this tale, I thought, for this poignant cable, with all its extraordinary implications, was not actually sent to Roosevelt. Churchill had gotten wind of Kent's suspected "status" and did not want that cable to get into the enemy's hands. He immediately got in touch with the US embassy officer on duty that night, an officer named Rudy Schoenfeld, who recalled the cable literally minutes before Kent was to send it on its way. So Kent never had a chance to distribute it to his network of fellow spies.

When I first saw the words in that cable, I tried to imagine what it must have cost Churchill to bring himself to draw a picture of England defeated and compelled to bargain over the value of her fleet. I figured it must have been one of those rare moments when Churchill's "black dog" had gotten the best of him. And then I had another idea: maybe it wasn't black dog, but instead a kind of gentle blackmail. Churchill was marvelously canny; he figured he would scare Roosevelt so much about the possibility of defeat for England, that the President would somehow manage to get Congress to agree to send to England the crucial ships it needed so desperately.

Was Kennedy Taken Into Camp?

That night at dinner when I told Mary Moore about some of the embassy characters, Joe Kennedy was joking when he suggested that he also might be one of the people I could talk about. The odd thing was that about a week later I found myself talking about him at great length.

I was often asked by British friends or even acquaintances why Joe Kennedy was such an isolationist. The tone in which that was asked made it seem that the word "damned" was meant to precede "isolationist" or even precede "Joe Kennedy." I generally explained with a slight smile that Joe Kennedy was the old-fashioned type.

"He was just following the advice of President Jefferson, who in his inaugural speech warned the US against entangling alliances," I said, and added that Kennedy believed the role of the US was to be the arsenal of democracy, and to avoid those "entangling alliances." The US should supply the sinews of war, but stay out of it, was his point of view. And actually it was also the attitude of the majority of the people in the US. I personally felt differently, I'd explain, but I was asked about Ambassador Kennedy, not about what I thought.

Noel and I rarely talked "shop." It seemed we always had so much else to talk about. Anyway, he couldn't talk about his work and I didn't talk about my job very much. However, one rainy night late in May, in a little Italian restaurant in Soho, the kind where the candle is stuffed into the neck of a raffia-covered wine bottle, Noel said he'd like to learn a little more about Kennedy's outlook.

"From the horse's mouth," he added. "I'd really like to know what you think makes Kennedy tick."

For instance, Noel said, he had read a while ago that some Americans had wondered how a red-headed Irishman could be taken into camp by an isolationist group in England. He wondered if I thought that had happened. Was he "taken into camp?"

"Hell, no," I said. And this was the one time when I talked about Kennedy at length. He was an isolationist long before he set foot on the ship that brought him to England, I pointed out. He even had to be restrained from making an isolationist speech on the day of his arrival.

Once here I think he just naturally gravitated to the people he met who felt that war should be avoided. The Astors, for instance, and their friends who used to be frequent guests at Cliveden, I explained. These many friends included Chamberlain, whom Kennedy warmly admired, and whose judgment he trusted.

Then I went on to tell Noel that when people thought Kennedy was a Johnny-come-lately isolationist, it reminded me of a joke.

"A guy is brought up before the judge and accused of having set his mattress on fire," I start. "The judge asks him if this is true. The accused keeps denying that he had set any mattress on fire. The judge continues to ask him the same question and the accused continues to insist that he had not set the mattress on fire."

"Sir," he finally says to the judge, "I assure you I didn't set the mattress on fire."

I explain that the man paused. And I paused, too, now smiling. I go on. "The mattress was already on fire when I got into the bed."

Noel smiled, poured me some more wine, and said he didn't see what I was driving at. I said that my analogy was that Joe Kennedy was already an isolationist when he got into that bed in England. Noel was just determined not to laugh at my joke.

He went on to say he guessed he could understand how an American could be an isolationist, but then he asked did Kennedy really have to be so "bloody pessimistic" and have to be such a "gloomy gus?"

I tried to explain that Kennedy honestly believed that the British could not hold out against the Germans. Hitler has been preparing for war for years, on land, at sea and in the air and when Kennedy talked to Lindbergh and read his analysis of the Luftwaffe and the German capacity for producing planes, Kennedy was even more convinced that the Germans couldn't be stopped.

Now I repeated what Noel had often heard me say before, "I am sure as long as we have Churchill, the Channel and the Courage of the British, England will hold out." I paused. "Kennedy is just plain wrong," I said.

We clinked our glasses to my little speech. Now encouraged by Noel, I went on. "Although Kennedy has often said he admired the guts of the British, I don't think he has any real comprehension of the special quality of British resolution and bravery. Maybe," I suggested, "he hasn't read enough Shakespeare."

I told Noel that a friend in the embassy and I had decided that Joe Kennedy took all the facts and cranked them in that abacus he has in his bright head and with all the facts programmed in, the abacus told him Britain would be defeated. We felt Kennedy didn't deal with intangibles nor with abstractions, but if they could be fed into the abacus too, the answer that came out could be very different.

I quoted a definition of an ambassador that I had read: an honest man sent to lie abroad for the good of his country. Whatever Kennedy is, I suggested, he doesn't fit that definition. He insists on telling the truth as he sees it and at this point the majority of people in the US do not want to go to war, according to all recent polls.

Kennedy has devolved from isolationist to pessimist, I suggested and that he was paying a dear price for this latest stance. There's no question but newspapers in England, as you know, are highly critical of him.

Before Mrs. Kennedy left to go home she and the ambassador, once so very popular here, were now invited less and less to dinners and other social shindigs. One time when he came back from a trip home, Kennedy said he felt like "an outcast here in England." Clearly, from reports from the US, the President was getting more annoyed with him, too, so Kennedy was now odd man out on both sides of the Atlantic.

I told Noel that a little while ago a very dear British friend of mine told me that the two yellow races of the world would end up fighting each other. I asked him what he meant and he said that he meant the Japanese and the Americans. I was too shocked to even answer him and later he apologized profusely. He really was mortified that he has said such a thing but I had a terrible, gnawing feeling that hostility to Joe Kennedy in England, though unwarranted because he expressed the feelings of the country he represented, had triggered such vile sentiments.

Kennedy certainly knew he had ruined whatever chances he might ever have had for the presidency. Indeed he may already have been thinking that if he can't make it, by God, young Joe can. "Joe Jr. has been elected a delegate to the Democratic convention to take place this summer, so he is already dipping his toes into the political waters," I pointed out to Noel. "He's astute, well-informed, and out-going and could make a great 'pol.' I guess it is unnecessary to add that he is ambitious."

Noel nodded at me every now and then as I held forth. I noticed that he had nearly finished his dinner and I had scarcely touched mine.

"I've got yet another opinion, too. I'm full of opinions tonight, aren't I?" He nodded yes and smiled.

"And since you asked me, I'll tell you more. Shortly before Kick Kennedy was to go, reluctantly, back to the US, she stopped in the embassy to see her father about something and to tell me goodbye. I happened to be in Harvey Klemmer's office and she sought me out there. When she left Harvey and I talked about what a lively, smiling girl she is and we agreed it was no wonder that she had been such a hit on the social scene in London."

After she left I mentioned to Harvey that I was suddenly struck by an odd juxtaposition I saw between Kick's status at the moment and that of her father. It almost seemed that the brighter Kick's star shone, the dimmer her father's star seemed to be. "Obviously, I didn't mean to imply any cause and effect. It had just happened that way," I said.

I went back to Noel's apartment with him after we had finished dinner. There we didn't talk anymore about Joe Kennedy, but when Noel was driving me home late that night I said I hadn't meant to be disloyal to my ambassador; I was just answering Noel's question about what I felt made him tick.

Part Three

Ask the Infantry and Ask the Dead

*"Never think that war, no matter how necessary nor how justified, is
not a crime. Ask the infantry and ask the dead."*

–ERNEST HEMINGWAY

The Ambassador Remembers a Promise

From all the news we could glean from the newspapers and the radio,
and it was confirmed in all the cable traffic, the German troops were
swinging along through the French countryside, pointed like an
arrow toward Paris. There were no British troops left there to try to
stop them and the French seemed to have lost their zeal for fighting.

Churchill had said after the famous rescues at Dunkirk that "wars
are not won by evacuations." Now, with the certainty that Hitler
would try to invade England, the British Expeditionary Force, the
core of the most experienced British army personnel, was based mostly
in the south of England. Along with the BEF, were the most seasoned Dutch, Belgian, and Polish troops who had also been rescued
at Dunkirk.

To this formidable array it was soon added a volunteer force of
nearly a million men. They would be trained to deal with random
Nazis who might get through the barricades. They would be on special lookout for German parachutists, who had done such devastating
damage in Belgium and Holland, and were already sneaking their way
deep into France.

But none of these preparations could stop the German air
force from trying to destroy as much of the crucial infrastructure of
England as it possibly could. The protection of England's military
installations, ports, and factories depended entirely on the courage
and skill of the Royal Air Force. And it was no secret to any one that
the number of planes in the RAF were vastly outnumbered by those
in the Luftwaffe. The rumors that floated in the ominous ether over
London seemed to say that after Nazis hit Paris, France would fold.

There seemed to be little hope that she would put up much of a fight if her capital was invaded.

And that would be the signal for the Germans to start bombing the bejesus out of England, as Harvey suggested. Colonel and Mrs. Richey also felt the bombing would start soon after France threw in the towel and they again urged me to become more familiar with all the air raid shelters in my orbit. I promised I would as soon as the first goosestep hit Paris.

Once in early June the ambassador asked me if I'd like to spend a weekend in the country. Since Noel was off on one of his mysterious official jaunts, I said I would be delighted and I drove down to the ambassador's Saturday morning with Arthur Houghton, who was always good company.

It turned out that a tall, gangly, black-haired Irish friend of Joe's, Pat Murphy, was also staying at the ambassador's country house. At first I thought he was a vaudeville character since he seemed such a stereotypical Irishman. He dominated most of the dinnertime conversation and delighted us most of the time.

At breakfast Sunday morning, just before I was to go back to London, Joe announced that he had something to tell me. He admitted it was going to be something I probably did not want to hear and he was taking the coward's way out and telling me when he had other people on deck who would support him. Thus, he said, I would have less chance of persuading him to change his mind. I looked over at the other people, Pat Murphy and Arthur Houghton. Their faces were blanks.

Joe reminded me that he had promised my father he would send me home if any situation looked dangerous for me. Consequently, he said, he was now compelled to honor the promise he had made to my father. The experts, including especially Winston Churchill, he said, believe that the bombing of England—ruthless, fierce, endless bombing—would probably begin soon.

I stared at him and let him go on. He said, of course, as we were aware, that his family was back in the US. Harvey Klemmer's wife and their two little girls were there. He mentioned other embassy people who had sent wives and children home and said, that he was going to ask all embassy and consulate officers to send their wives and children home, if they had not already done so.

When he paused for a moment I excused myself and left the table. I said I'd be back in a few minutes. I went out and stood on the steps that lead to a garden. I was utterly torn. Of course I wanted to go home to be with my family. I hadn't seen my beloved mother in over two years. On the other hand, I felt certain the US was going to get in the war. My brother Huidy would be among those coming over to England in the US army, I knew, and I'd be here to greet him. Also I didn't want to feel that I was leaving. I couldn't let myself say "like a rat leaving a sinking ship." I smiled at the "rat" bit because of our Royal Order of Rats Club and I certainly didn't even think "sinking ship."

After a few minutes, I went back to the breakfast table. The men were self-consciously talking about something entirely different. Even Pat Murphy didn't say anything funny.

I asked the ambassador if I could have some hot coffee, please? "Mine has gotten cold," I said, as if it was his fault.

I didn't bring the subject of my departure up again. I knew that Kennedy meant what he had said.

Tim Clayton and Phil Craig, two brilliant English writers, wrote a book based on their hugely admired BBC TV series. It is called *Finest Hour*. I had gotten to know them early on when I was in London and they knew about how much I loved their city. In their book they wrote about my reluctance to leave England at this time. I felt like a Londoner, they said, and that I wanted to share in whatever the city was about to go through. They wrote that I "tried to imagine the sky over Grosvenor Square dotted with bombers, like the drawings in some of the papers, and all of the grand old houses in ruins." Knowing of the bombing that surely lies ahead, "she wonders if her friends will be dead." I always tried to avoid falling into the depths of envisaging a British defeat, but those sensitive writers must have gotten into my soul for they said that I wondered if my friends would be arrested.

Then they went on to say, "She was going to take one of the treasured places on one of the last boats going out, and she didn't even want to go." They sure had that right on the button, I thought when I read that.

When I got back to Cadogan Square that afternoon I started making my plans for going home. I was now wildly excited at the prospect of seeing my family again. At first I didn't cry over the prospect of leaving Noel and the Richeys and one or two other dear friends until they started giving me presents. Teresa gave me an exquisite little silver tray and someone gave me a small cut glass flask. These seemed to be loving gifts of sympathy for me because I had to leave England, and to leave at that point! Noel always gave me books and perfume. A few days before I was to leave he gave me a lovely edition of Ernest Dowson's poems.

Mike Richey turned up to tell me goodbye. His mine sweeper had been hit by a German bomber. As the ship was sinking, most of the crew was able to escape safely with life preservers. Some, however, had been strafed while struggling to stay afloat. I guessed that Mike was no longer a conscientious objector. Anyway, he joined the Navy where he could put his passion for navigation to good use. Paul appeared looking remarkably well considering how badly he'd been wounded. He was back with his old squadron now, but to his disgust, was assigned to duty other than flying, at least for the time being.

On June 10, Mussolini, known to many of us a Sawdust Caesar, declared war on England and France. This meant, of course, that Hitler had command of the Italian fleet, on top of his own excellent fleet with its sleek new submarines.

This new turn of events made Joe Kennedy more despairing than ever about the state of the war. Even so, when I told him goodbye I repeated my party line, that England would prevail because of the courage of the British, and because of Churchill and the Channel, although I admitted that the Channel was shrinking all the time. When we talked about the war, Joe smiled at me for my implacable, and to him, misguided, faith in the lasting power of the British against the juggernaut of the Nazis, which they had been building for years.

He said he knew that I was leaving behind some dear friends. I said that I was. He seemed to know, although it was something I had never discussed with him, that I had been engaged in an intense love affair. He was wearing his social smile when we first started talking, then his smile grew warmer and sweeter. He was genuinely sorry to see me go, and apologized at having to make me leave.

***

Noel and I had both realized, of course, that we would have to leave each other sometime. We had talked with unutterable sadness once that we could never have an "afterward." We knew that my going meant a clean and permanent break for us, but having known this didn't seem to smooth the passage for us. We saw each other as much as possible before I had to leave, but I had told him I didn't want him to come to see me off at the station, which would be the first lap of my outward-bound journey. I had to tell him goodbye when we were alone.

Somehow we had made a sort of pact to "cut clean," as I put it, with apologies for the awkward term. I thought it was an American wrestling term. We decided we would not write each other love letters, which, over a period of time would become irrelevant. "Or even tawdry," I suggested, and then we fell into a bout of laughter since we both thought the word seemed so odd (and he had once explained its origin to me). We rationed ourselves to one long letter at the end of the year so we could at least learn what was going on in each other's life. "And the one," Noel insisted, "that we can write to each other sometime soon after we have parted."

Neither of us had any hope that we could stick to this kind of regimen in letter writing but it seemed to make us feel that we were being brave, or at least I think that's the way I looked at it.

After dinner at his apartment the night before I was to leave, he put some of our favorite records on his old player and we danced for a long, slow time. We drank a lot of wine and tears were streaming down my face when we realized it was getting light and I had to get back to Cadogan Square in order to leave it. We both managed to smile when I was getting dressed and I realized I had put my dress on backwards and had to take it off again to put it on right.

Driving me to the Richeys, he said he was going to make a Byronic-like plea to me. We left each other as he was saying, "Maid of my life, 'ere we part, Give, oh, give me back my heart."

On the High Seas

A good friend, Leslie Benson, an American married to a distinguished Londoner, Rex Benson, who was slated to be the British military attaché to the United States, was also sailing on the USS *Manhattan*. Leslie and her two little boys and the driver she had hired to take us to our ship were awaiting me in a town somewhere north of London. I was to meet them there and since American ships could not land in belligerent ports, the driver would take us to Cobh, Ireland, where we would board our ship. I had told Leslie that I'd be happy to help her look after her kids on our journey.

After she had settled them in the US, she planned to go right back to London and then return to Washington with Rex. They would find a house in Washington, retrieve their little boys, and Rex would start his assignment as the British military attaché to the United States.

Colonel Richey took me to the station, put me on the train and found me a seat. He gave me a warm hug, and we both came close to tears when he headed off the train. From my window seat, I waved my jazzy white cotton gloves, with their pretty hand-stitching, which I was holding in my hands. I clutched them tightly as I signaled my goodbye. The train pulled out and we could no longer see each other, but I waved my gloves for a few more minutes anyway.

I smiled to myself as I thought of the beginning of a story I had read years ago about a person who is on a train just as it is leaving the station. This man also uses his gloves to wave a last goodbye to the friend who has come to see him off. In the story, however, the departing man drops one of his gloves. The minute he realizes that, he tosses the remaining glove, as quickly as he can, back as close as possible to the lost glove.

Now as I sat back in my seat and carefully put both of my gloves safely in my purse, I remembered again how struck I had been by that story because it tells so much about that man. First, he is elegant; the story established that his gloves are of fine leather. He thinks extraordinarily quickly, and he is thoughtful (he realizes that a glove is no good to anyone without its mate). And, I figured also, he must be a good pitcher if he could throw the second glove close enough to the first so that someone would find a pair. And I wished I could find again the story that starts off with that illuminating little episode.

For days I had been torn between my sadness at leaving the England that I love and the joy of seeing my mother and the rest of my family that I love. And now my excitement at going home overtook me. I noted that I was smiling for the second time that day. Before I realized it, I was at the little station where I was to meet Leslie, her boys, and the driver who was to take us to our ship.

Leslie's two little boys were going to stay in "Amedica," as they pronounced it, for the duration. Our group arrived in Cobh shortly after midday. From there we would embark on the USS *Manhattan*.

The *Manhattan* had two nicknames in England; one reflected the anti-American point of view of some there. If it was mean, it at least had a touch of humor, I thought. It was called the USS *Gone with the Wind*.

The other name aptly described the situation we'd find on board: the huge number of babies and young children being sent to the US and Canada for the duration. Its name referred to the essential accoutrements of babies and thus was called the USS *Diaper*.

Leslie took the boys into the hotel where we were to have lunch. I told her I'd join them in a few minutes and headed for the hotel garden to stroll around a bit beforehand. The only other people in the garden were the drivers who had brought the US-bound people to Ireland. They were relaxing before their return to England. I could hear the buzz of their chatter and I smiled especially when I heard a cockney word or two. One of the men had a radio which he held up to his ear.

For a few moments I forgot the war, the ship, and everything except that this day, June 14, was the anniversary of my mother and father's wedding. When I got home I'd tell Mother I was thinking of that wedding while I was in a lovely garden in Ireland on her wedding anniversary. And of course, I was thinking of my father, and figuring that this anniversary must be especially moving for my mother. She would be celebrating this occasion alone—that is, without her beloved husband. It was the first such anniversary since Daddy's death.

All of a sudden my sentimental reflection was shattered. The man with the radio yelled, "Cor blimey, the 'Uns have reached Paris. They're in Paris now."

I let out some sort of a moaning sound and put my hand over my mouth to stifle another one. I finally turned to the man who had the radio. "Can you tell if there is any fighting? What are you hearing?" I asked frantically.

"No, Miss," he said in a pale voice. "Seems like the 'Uns are just marching in unmolested like." I thanked him and slowly made my way into the hotel. Once inside I sat down on the first chair I came across. If Paris has fallen, all of France will be next. I sat awkwardly on a chair in a hotel in Cobh, Ireland, mumbling to myself, "England's alone." The words kept running through my mind like a piece of film that is stuck and goes round and round. The tape seemed to get caught in its sprocket. It was long minutes before I remembered that I was to have met Leslie and the boys quite a while ago. Walking fast now, on the way to join them, I continued to mutter under my breath the phrase, "England's alone."

Word of the invasion of Paris had gotten around the hotel dining room by the time I found Leslie and her sons. To have known that the German occupation of Paris was nearly a foregone conclusion had not cushioned the shock of those of us that met and commiserated in the dining room. We all agreed that if Paris had fallen, a fellow diner said, then it must follow as the night the day—as if the metaphor was original—that all of France would give up shortly.

I didn't hear anyone say out loud "and not a shot was fired against the conquering army," but I heard it unsaid all the same. I was finally able to say, "It's England alone" out loud. People looked at me as if I'd uttered a blasphemy.

It was a dismal bunch that climbed aboard the *Manhattan*. Even the gaiety and noise of the children wasn't able to penetrate the gloom.

The first person I saw on the ship that I knew, except for Leslie and our boys, was Sally Reston, wife of *New York Times* London correspondent, Scotty, and their young son. We greeted each other warmly but Sally had her eye glued to the dock where Scotty was wildly waving goodbye to them. She waved back just as wildly. As the ship pulled out he was still there waving. He started to run along the dock more or less parallel with the moving ship. He and Sally were still waving to each other.

He kept on running until he was very close to the edge of the dock. I was afraid he would just keep going until he ran out of dock and would fall into the water. To my relief he stopped, just in time. As the ship pulled away the figure on the dock got smaller and smaller but it was still waving.

The boat was so full of children going to a safe haven that room had to be made in odd places to accommodate them. The swimming pool had been drained and was now filled with dozens of cots, small cots, of course. Somehow the cots in the deep end seemed the most pitiful. There were also scores of little life preservers stored in corners about the deck. As I stared at them, I shivered at the thought of a disaster that would call for their use.

Cabins and staterooms too were overflowing. Leslie and I knew we'd be squeezed in close quarters. Indeed she and I and the kids and a Canadian woman with a little girl slept in a cabin originally meant for three. In the daytime we could pile the cots on top of each other so we had some, if limited, move-around room.

Leslie's former husband, Condé Nast, the famous American publisher, had offered to harbor her children when she returned to London and then she would pick them up when she and Rex came to Washington.

I thought to myself that Condé Nast was certainly generous to offer to take care of his former wife's children by her present husband and after a few hours on board I knew he would have his hands full. I hoped he could solve a problem with the boys that neither Leslie nor I could.

Apparently the children had spent all the time with their nanny and Leslie had probably seen them only at afternoon tea. Anyway, she had never herself plunked them on the potty seat because obviously she didn't know the key word for that essential procedure. We could never figure it out from the boys themselves. She and I spent much of the time on that Atlantic crossing trying to catch them at the crucial moment beforehand, so to speak. Or failing that, washing out elegant little English linen pants, with lots of big pearl buttons, during the few times when the water on our ship was running at more than a trickle.

Otherwise, we had a good time with our little boys and they were happy and easy to amuse. Our not knowing that key word was not their fault.

There seemed to be ten children to every adult, but many of the adults set to gallantly to try to help. A couple of days out we joined up with a group of women, most of whom also had young children in tow, and worked out a deal whereby we could share the job of looking after the kids and at the same time offer the children new playmates.

When I wasn't on duty at the makeshift daycare center I found a spot where I could read. I was more than halfway through *The Great Gatsby* and since I couldn't read in bed at night (I didn't want to put a light on and risk waking up any one of my five roommates) I was delighted to have a little time during the day to read.

I finally got to the sad ending of that brilliant book but was hugely surprised by a paragraph near the end. Nothing that Nick Caraway, the narrator-spectator, had said before had indicated the depth of his sentimental feeling about America and its history. However, on his last night on Long Island, he looks out over the Sound, and his eloquent musings hit such an emotional chord in me, returning to America, that I memorized some of the lines. While they were still fresh in my mind I went up on deck and made for the bow and looked across the vast expanse of water toward America.

As Nick is looking at the Sound, he says that he gradually became aware of the old island (meaning Long Island) "that flowered once for Dutch sailors' eyes," and I picked up the rest of Nick's words and repeated them into the winds. "For a transitory enchanted moment man must have held his breath in the presence of this continent...face-to-face for the last time in history with something commensurate to his capacity for wonder."

I fell to meditating about Nick's idea, and although bewitched by his description, I figured it wasn't the last time in history where there was something commensurate with his take on man's capacity for wonder. My mind raced back to the England I had just left. It didn't take any stretch of imagination to visualize the devastation that would surely be wrought on England by the Luftwaffe nor the fortitude it would take for the British to withstand it.

Some decades from now, I asked myself, will people look back and see that British courage as something commensurate with our capacity for wonder?

***

My copy of *The Great Gatsby* came to what Leslie considered a disastrous condition. I had left it in our cabin one morning when I went out for a brief walk and came back to find that our boys had scrawled all over some pages with the very fat, lush crayons which I brought on the trip as a present for them. One page was nearly completely covered in black squiggles, for instance. Leslie was horrified but I assured her that it was, after all, only an inexpensive paperback copy. She still looked distressed. I told her that, in fact, one page looked exactly like what Laurence Sterne had done with his novel *Tristram Shandy*: He had occasionally had entire pages simply blacked over (and others left blank). Other pages the boys had decorated with an array of mottled colors. I assured Leslie that those pages, too, looked as if they could have been in *Tristram Shandy*. She still looked unhappy at the improvised art work in my book. I tried to reassure her by saying that I was sure Scott Fitzgerald would be flattered to be mentioned in the same context as the great writer of *Tristram Shandy*. She didn't appear to be much of a *Shandy* fan, but she at least she now seemed reconciled to the crayon work.

In the evenings when our boys and the little Canadian girl were asleep, Leslie and I dragged two chairs out of our stateroom and sat near our door. Leslie was especially graceful and could lean back easily, with the front legs of her chair off the floor and her feet on one of its rungs. I had to work on the balance several times before I felt at home in that cavalier pose.

We took turns going to the bar to get drinks as we sat there expressing our frustration at not being able to hear any news. Our ship was neither receiving nor sending out signals for fear of attracting German submarines. The last news we had heard had been from radios just before we boarded the ship was about the surrender of Paris.

I confessed to Leslie an odd feeling I had felt in London. I was certainly not delusional enough to think I had any control over events, but it was as if by simply knowing what was happening I was playing some kind of a role. She laughed and said she thought our greatest problem now was not having a clue as to what was going on. For instance, what was happening to the French Navy? Over the evenings we played out several scenarios.

Will French officers race their vessels to neutral ports, or at least to places where the Germans can't get them? Will they have to scuttle their own ships so the Germans won't have a chance to get their paws on them?

Leslie and I frazzled several nights away on the fate of the French fleet. As we headed back to our stateroom one night, I asked dreadful questions. "Is it possible the French Navy will go over to the Nazis? Would the British have to destroy French ships, and kill French sailors in the process in order to prevent such a disaster?"

***

Generally the combination of my weariness at helping chase two (or more) children around, Leslie's and my ranging conversations that kept us up late into the night, and the lion's purr of the ship's engines put me to sleep nearly immediately, despite our Canadian roommate's snoring.

One night however, I fell to thinking, randomly and profusely. And no matter how I tried to turn the spigot off, the thoughts came tumbling out. So I fell back on an old trick of mine as in an inducement to sleep: to name all of the negative words I can think of in alphabetical order. Words such as animosity, blister, calamity, etc.... I went through the alphabet with them and then I started on the words with good connotations (angels, boys, champagne, and such words), got through that and felt a little sleepier. I always liked to end this nonsensical exercise with the good words.

The next to last thing I thought of was Leslie telling me that she bet the minute the war was over—and England victorious, of course—I'd be hot-footing it back to England. Then as I was nearly asleep, I seemed to be in London. I heard great bells ringing out joyously from all over London, and I knew everything would be all right. I started to sing in my usual tuneless voice ever so quietly so as not to awaken anyone, "oranges and lemons, sing the bells of St. Clement's, the bells of St. Clement's, the bells of St. Clement's" until I fell into a glorious sleep.

Another night I started off with a happy dream that turned into a nightmare. The war was over. I was back in London joyously, but I could not find Noel. I looked and I looked, despite all the promises we had made that when we parted that we had parted forever, I telephoned all the people we knew in common. I remembered the telephone number of the office where he had worked. I went to the old building where his apartment was and "Wonderful Wanda," as I called the super, had turned into a grumpy old man who had never heard of Noel. I went to all the familiar spots, the places we had been to in London and the few we had been to outside of London: restaurants, little galleries, parks and so forth.

I was never able to find him, and it was dawn before I fell asleep.

Home Again: Happy and Sad

I had met Arthur Krock, the head of the Washington bureau of the *New York Times*, and one of the most distinguished, if conservative, political columnists in the country, when he was visiting Joe Kennedy in London shortly after the star-crossed Munich meetings. Arthur was accompanied to London by his charming friend, Martha Blair. I learned through the embassy gossip vine that Arthur's wife had been ill and hospitalized for years and that he and Martha had been together for a long time.

At some point Arthur asked me what I thought was going to happen next, that is, in the wake of the Munich Pact. I remember only that I said that the British look upon Munich as if it was an act taking place in the theatre, and now the asbestos curtain has come down (in Britain the asbestos curtain acts as a firewall between the audience and the actors and is dropped at the end of a play). The audience, I said, will forget about the play for a while, but it doesn't mean the drama is really over.

Far from being over, I suggested, the drama will be replayed soon again but with a far more terrifying next act. For some reason, Arthur had liked my take on the situation. Indeed, he said, he was amused by that analogy. He mentioned that he had liked other comments I had made about the English and the general political atmosphere. He thought I should be writing and he would be delighted to help me find a job on a newspaper, if I was interested. He asked me to please call him if I was ever in Washington.

***

Back in the US, in late June of 1940, I definitely planned to call Arthur Krock at some point because I knew I would be in desperate need of a job. But all I wanted to do now was to get caught up with my family. I went immediately to my beloved mother, who was living with her mother at Long Branch.

On Daddy's death Nannie had sold the house we had outside of Baltimore and moved to Long Branch, which she had left over thirty years ago as a bride. It was at her mother's warm invitation that Mother came to live there. It was a huge house, and old, which wasn't surprising since it had been build in 1803. It was also beautiful, descended from Palladio's magic and filled with antiques of various generations. Obviously there was plenty of room for Nannie's clothes, furniture, paintings, books, and other treasures. Further, she would be cordially welcomed in the community.

Unlike most of the women there, Mother did not play bridge, a major element in their lives, and instead of tea-table talk Mother was given to unexpectedness. At least she had many old friends, and countless cousins, in the neighborhood. Best of all for Mother, Rosalind, too, went to live at Long Branch, although she was married a short while later in a great big wedding there and went to live with her doctor husband in Baltimore. She came to Long Branch to greet me, so I was able to get my arms around her, and my mother and my grandmother in one swoop. Nancy and her family came there shortly afterwards, and brother Huidy came from Harvard to welcome me home and join the happy family throng.

***

Soon after our noisy, harmonious, reunion, Mother and we four children went to visit our dear lawyer friend and his wife, Jim and Mary Lewis Carey at their lovely, old, brick Georgian house Octarara, high on the banks of the Susquehanna River.

They had kept Daddy's ashes there, awaiting my return to the US We gathered in the small boat at the Careys' dock below their house, prepared to cast Daddy's ashes, as he had wanted, in the Susquehanna River. This was an occasion I had long awaited and looked forward to with apprehension and with the full awareness that it would my final goodbye.

This service took place in the last week in June, several weeks after France had given in supinely to the Nazis and had signed a peace treaty at Compeigne. At least, I thought, Daddy died before that so he never knew about the disgrace of a country he had loved so dearly.

It was a moving, sad-sweet rite on the Susquehanna which we preformed with deep reverence, but our ignorance of such procedures added an element of surprise. We laid the simple box with Daddy's ashes (I, for one, was amazed at what a small amount of ashes our bodies turn into) gently on the water. Then we realized that the box would float and that, of course, what we were supposed to do was to strew the ashes themselves on the water. So we retrieved the box and held it upside down.

The ashes spilled out and a glint of sunshine fell on them. We watched, dry-eyed and breathless, as the ashes floated briefly on the surface of the river and then melded into the current.

Afterwards, back at Octarara, the beautiful welcoming house, we consumed generous draughts of bourbon in our toasts to Daddy and his profound contributions to our lives, all telling about how much we loved him and missed him. The booze relaxed our inhibitions against maudlin emotionalism and we all, Jim and Mary Lewis, too, wept copiously into our booze.

I woke several times in the night, and was surprised each time to find myself crying. And I knew what people call "closure" was a category I had not reached. Nor did I think how I ever would.

***

Some days after that ceremony, I moved to New York, where I went to work for British War Relief. I wanted desperately to make that small obeisance to the England that I adored. I had only been there a few days when I got a cable from Joe Kennedy from London. He said that most of the time since I left he was sorry he had sent me home, "But the last two weeks have completely justified my judgment" and that all were glad I was "out of this."

"This" meant the ferocious Luftwaffe attacks on British airfields, docks and shipyards along the Thames, factories, the monuments of London, and the homes of civilians. We listened, in thrall, to Edward R. Murrow, broadcasting from London nightly about the devastation the German planes wreaked on England and at the same time about the doggedness and the resilience of the British people.

I pinned up on the wall next to my desk at my British War Relief impromptu office my most recent favorite Churchill quote, which I had copied in big bold letters on a piece of cardboard. It was in response to the comment a French general had made when France folded and thus left England alone fighting the Germans. The French general had predicted that the Germans would "take England like a chicken and wring its neck."

Churchill's answer looked great on my office wall. "Some chicken. Some neck," it roared gloriously.

I had known when I went to work for British War Relief that it would be a brief sojourn, since it was a volunteer job. I figured I would run out of money soon. I hadn't been able to save much on a salary of $1,200 a year. So after a few weeks in New York I headed for Washington to seek a real job.

Life on a Dizzy Newspaper

In Washington, dear old friends, Jane and Bob McIlvaine, opened their hearts, as well as their house to me. They insisted I stay with them and take over their large third floor as my abode. Jane was writing a novel and Bob was working at the Navy Department. He told me that since the dreadful bombing of England had started he had felt the US should be helping that brave country to defend itself and defeat Hitler, and the sooner the better, so he had joined Naval Intelligence. I said that I agreed with him wholeheartedly and congratulated him on having joined up already.

He and Jane and I were delighted that Roosevelt had now given fifty destroyers to England (aged ships, granted, but manna for the British Navy) in exchange for our use of British naval and air bases in Newfoundland, the West Indies, and several other spots.

I later got a note from a British Navy officer friend of mine, saying that, believe it or not, the American destroyer he had inspected had hand soap and toilet paper already in the head. I had not realized that such commodities could nearly move me to tears.

Further, as an indication of his increasing awareness of the encroaching war overseas, the President led Congress to enact the first peacetime selective service act. Now men between the ages of twenty and thirty-six had to register for action in the armed services.

Meanwhile I had settled haphazardly in my lofty new quarters and prepared to call Arthur Krock. Jane had already filled me in on some recent skinny about Arthur. His ailing wife had finally died and sometime afterward he and Martha amused their friends by announcing that after their "whirlwind courtship" (they had been shacked up together for some eight years) they were getting married.

Arthur seemed pleased to hear from me and invited me to lunch with him the next day. On my way to meet him, I happened by one of the few bookstores in DC in those days and picked up a paperback copy of a collection of Ogden Nash poems to give to Arthur as a present for Martha and him.

Arthur was delighted with it and said that Nash's poems were among his favorites. Mine, too, I assured him, and just to think of them makes me laugh. I told him that a niece of Nash's was one of my dearest childhood pals in Baltimore and that I had seen her Aunt Isabel and Uncle Ogden frequently and that he was wonderfully funny in real life, too.

Then Arthur and I automatically fell into conversation about the horrors of what was happening to London, how deep was our admiration for the courage of the British warriors and the resolution of the British civilians.

During lunch Arthur surprised me by informing me he had already set wheels in motion for a job for me. He said that an old friend, Frank Waldrop, managing editor of the *Washington Times Herald*, was anxious to meet me and had suggested I come in to see him as soon as possible. Arthur explained that he had gotten to know Waldrop when Martha had been writing a column in the style section of the *Times Herald*, but which she was no longer doing.

As I thanked Arthur for his help, he smiled and told me that in exchange for the pleasure that gave him, he was going to extract a promise from me. I crossed my heart to indicate that I would promise him whatever he wanted. He told me that Cissy Patterson, publisher of the *Times Herald*, was not to know that it was he, Arthur, who had recommended me for a job on her paper. I was mystified by this odd stricture but agreed anyway.

***

A few days later I met Frank Waldrop in his office in the graceful art deco building that housed the paper. He told me that what he was actually looking for was a slave but that in polite company he would refer to this person as a special assistant. The job would involve doing research for articles he would be writing for the paper, mostly for the special Sunday section, and finding appropriate pictures to go with such articles. If there were no appropriate pictures in the paper's "morgue," where clippings, photographs, and reference papers were filed, I'd have to scout all over the city to find them. He said he would be writing editorials for the paper.

Maybe, he said, he would welcome suggestions about articles he might write, but mainly, he said, the job would involve warding off people who would waste his time. "And other such heavy responsibilities," he added, with the shadow of a smile. Then he said the job might lead to regular reporting.

We talked for about an hour and I decided that I not only liked Frank Waldrop, but the noise and the sense of vitality that drifted in from the city room outside his door sounded like music to my ears. When he asked me if I would like to work with him as his assistant, I told him I would indeed.

I managed to get a little background on the publisher from the McIlvaines and some of their friends before I started work at the paper. I already knew that since the late thirties, the publisher had cobbled together two of publisher mogul William Randolph Hearst's papers and morphed them into the *Washington Times Herald*. It was now a round-the-clock publication with ten editions a day.

It also had the rare distinction of being the only paper in a large metropolitan district in the entire United States that was published by a woman. This woman was Eleanor Medill Patterson. She had abandoned her title, Countess Gizycki, which she had acquired as a young woman when she married a rake of a Polish Count. Now she was known, by friend and foe alike, simply as Cissy Patterson.

When I tried to learn more about her personally, there seemed to be a consensus that Cissy was too quixotic and complicated to characterize briefly.

However, I did learn that she herself had tried. "I am," Cissy had said, "just a plain old vindictive, shanty Irish bitch."

I figured the Irish was applicable because her forebears had been Irish but I guessed she had thrown in the word "shanty" with a satirical twist since I knew that wasn't a valid adjective for her. I had learned that she owned a white marble Italian Renaissance house in Dupont Circle in Washington with nearly a dozen servants there to tend to her needs; an apartment in New York City; a big spread in the Tetons in Wyoming; a house in Sarasota, Florida; a house in Sands Point, Long Island; a historic pre-revolutionary house (the Dower House) near Marlboro, Maryland; a 280-acre farm in another part of Maryland, with a bluff overlooking the Potomac River; some property in Nassau; and some in North Dakota. Further, Cissy tooled around the country in her private railroad car named Ranger, after a favorite cow-pony. "Shanty" hardly applied in her self-description, I thought.

As to the other words she had used in her portrayal of herself, "vindictive" and "bitch," I figured I would find out sooner or later whether Cissy had been accurate in suggesting them as applicable.

Early on, I was befriended by an old reporter who seemed to want to fill me in on the common folklore on the paper and I asked him to tell me about Martha Blair.

It seems that for several years Martha had been writing a column, ostensibly about social functions taking place in Washington. However her stories hinted at spicy goings-on among some of the best known characters in the city, so that it was basically a column about "political gossip with libidinous innuendo," my new friend explained. A column written by an attractive woman which concentrated on such a steamy combination was a great hit, he said. Indeed the publisher considered the column one of the shiniest jewels in her garland.

That is, Cissy doted on the column until Martha and Arthur got married. Now most of the cognoscenti knew that Martha's zesty political tidbits were a result of "pillow talk," this young man told me, which was OK when she wasn't married to the chief of the *New York Times* Washington bureau.

Subtle word came down from the *Time's* headquarters in New York that the source of Martha's political information was too obvious now, and therefore, Arthur Krock best not pass on so much "color" to his wife. After that dictum her column seemed to have lost its life's blood.

Late one evening, after the white-washing of Martha's column, Cissy, who might have indulged in a drink or two, the friendly reporter suggested, telephoned Martha to tell her that since her column nowadays seemed confined to descriptions of the delicious strawberries and clotted cream at the summer parties at the British embassy and other such fascinating tales, it was no longer necessary for her to write for the *Times Herald*.

When my friend finished his story, I realized that I had learned why Cissy should not be told that it was Arthur Krock who had recommended me to Frank Waldrop. And I, of course, never broke my promise to Arthur. Cissy never knew that it was he who had recommended me to Frank Waldrop.

Later, as I got to know more about my publisher, I figured that Martha Krock had gotten off lightly the night Cissy fired her considering that Cissy had a reputation for colorful syntax. She could have laid into Martha in any one of the several languages in which she cursed with special aplomb: English, of course, and Polish, for she had learned Polish during her marriage as a young woman to the no-account Polish count, or French because she had lived in Paris for a few years. Or she could have shouted in what was known as "Cal's special language," which she had learned from a cattle rustler named Cal, when he was living with her on her ranch in Wyoming, or visiting her in Washington.

Over my several years on the paper, I soaked up other more sub-stantive tales of the life of our idiosyncratic but talented publisher. From the beginning of her newspaper life Cissy had sought out bright, aggressive young reporters, Waldrop being among those she had hired early on. He was a southerner who had built a reputation as a brilliant reporter and as editor on the *New York Journal*. He was quoted as saying that all *Times Herald* reporters were "notoriously wild" and all thought they worked for Front Page, but he was actually one of the few that didn't fit into that category. He was calm and collected, I learned nearly immediately, and scarcely drank at all. He was extraor-dinarily bright and had a wry sense of humor. It was clear that he and Cissy admired each other inordinately.

History was his passion, especially military history. Every now and then I could feed him a small, unusual item about what was going on in England from letters I got. I remember, for instance, that he incorporated into a story about British pilots a line a friend in London had sent me. "Our pilots," my friend had written, "all fly as if they are eighteen years old and crossed in love."

I often shared with him news I got from my Richey family, just because he was curious about anything that had to with England at war. I had had a letter recently which told me that Paul, despite his terrible wounding and against the advice of his doctor, his parents, Teresa and her family, had been able to wangle his way back into the war. Not as a pilot at first, at least not during that ghastly sum-mer of 1940 with a seemingly invincible Luftwaffe beating down on a desperately fighting RAF. He had been confined to what was known as a "ground assignment" at a field headquarters, but he banked on the hope that he would soon be flying a Spitfire again. Frank used that little story as an example of British defiance and courage.

Cissy and FDR

Meanwhile in Frank's office we were readying for the coming election, with Roosevelt running for a third term, this time against a New York business tycoon named Wendell Willkie. I remembered, of course, that it had been four years since my remarkable visit to Hyde Park, where I was seated next to the President as we all celebrated his namesake son's birthday. That was the year that Roosevelt ran against Governor Alfred Landon of Kansas, and had, of course, defeated him soundly.

1940 was a significant year, of course, and Roosevelt desperately wanted to win his third term. He still had a lot on his plate that he wanted to accomplish. He was busy now juggling his role as the leader of the country which served as the arsenal for democracy during the desperate war in Europe.

For the *Times Herald* it was also a significant year. Only a couple of decades ago it had started off as an unimportant, piddling newspaper. And now because of the ingenuity and drive of its publisher, this year it had the biggest circulation and the biggest advertising income of any of the other papers in Washington, the *Washington Post*, the *Washington Star*, and the *Washington Daily News*.

The *Times Herald* was different from the other Washington papers in another significant way too. All the other Washington papers were run by men. Hell, Cissy was heard to say, not only was she the only damn woman in the whole damn country who was the publisher of a metropolitan newspaper, further, she, a woman, was the publisher in the capital of the United States whose paper was making the most money. She loved to point that out.

The *Times Herald* was also different from the other three papers in a fundamentally important way and the way that appealed to me the most: Of the four newspapers in the capital of the United States, the *Times Herald* was the only one to come out in support of Franklin Roosevelt in the election of 1940, especially crucial this year because the war was raging more furiously than ever.

I stood behind Frank Waldrop in his office and watched him as he typed the editorial in support of Roosevelt's fourth term, and marked it up for the composing room in the arcane newspaper language. I watched him closely even though he had told me it annoyed him to have anyone hovering over him. I asked him please not to be annoyed with me. I was so immensely excited to be working for a paper which had supported Roosevelt's ideals from the beginning and was continuing to do so.

I told Frank that I just had to be close as I watched him endorse this further commitment to FDR. He smiled at me, but I don't think he meant it because he considered I had hovered. I smiled back at him and he knew I meant it.

Cissy had supported Franklin Roosevelt since he first ran for president. She had been a fervent advocate of the New Deal because of her genuine concern for improvement in the life of America's poorest and she had stuck with Roosevelt through thick and thin. She had plumped for many of the social changes the New Deal advocated; she had once said she was a "big advocate of social justice." (When I heard that I became a big advocate of that Cissy).

Horrified by the poverty she had seen on a trip in Appalachia some years ago, Cissy and Frank Waldrop had written a series of articles for the paper called *Dixie's Dead End*, exposing the "hard scrabble" life of the people there. Her editorials urgently called for action to help improve their desperate situation. Now after all these years of hard work on her papers, Cissy was immensely proud to have earned the distinction of having supported Roosevelt all three times he had run for the presidency. She had celebrated each of his inaugurations joyously.

However, soon after Roosevelt's inauguration this time, Cissy's attitude toward the president went into an acute about-face. The admiration she had felt for him had now been replaced by a deep antipathy.

She saw him as a "turncoat" or even a "traitor." In her eyes, Roosevelt had totally abandoned his attitude of neutrality in the European war. Now he had signed the Lend-Lease Bill, which allowed the US to lend munitions and matériel to the countries fighting Hitler, which, of course, meant England.

Cissy read this as a betrayal of all that President Roosevelt had promised before the election about his commitment to non-belligerency during the war. This apparent change of heart on Roosevelt's part sent the isolationists, of which Cissy was an ardent proponent, into a frenzy of fear that the president was inching the country into an actual state of hostilities.

Now it was clear that at this point her vaunted liberalism had stopped at the ocean's edge. I was especially fascinated by that idea because it seemed the exact opposite to what would have been my Father's attitude. It would be his vaunted conservatism which would have stopped at the ocean's edge! He would have been gung-ho in support of Roosevelt's help for England.

Furthermore, Cissy's Chicago background, her inherent Midwest isolationism and its sustained fear of foreign involvement, had kicked in. And, after all, Bertie McCormick, publisher of the uber conservative and anti-British *Chicago Tribune* was a cousin, wasn't he? Indeed her father had been an editor of that right-wing paper, and her beloved brother, Joe Patterson, ran the *New York News* and shared Bertie's fierce anti-entanglement sentiments.

Both of the outspoken publishers of the *Chicago Tribune* and the *New York News* made it abundantly clear that they thought the US should stay the hell out of Europe's mess. And that became Cissy's mantra as well.

Now she threw the baby out with the bath water. Her sincere support of Roosevelt's liberal causes, were utterly cast aside for what she saw as his wicked desire to shimmy the country into the European war.

The *Times Herald* let loose Cissy's own dogs of war, not only against Roosevelt for his so-called betrayal, but against everyone around him. That included large numbers of men and women who had previously been warm friends of Cissy's. Many had broken bread and bent elbows with her on countless occasions in her white marble palace on Dupont Circle.

Cissy's infinite capacity to create enemies—which she had been honing much of her life—was now at its peak. As the storm swirled around the paper itself, Mason Peters, the engaging, driving, city editor told me that he thought William Congreve had Cissy in mind when he wrote that "Heaven hath no rage like love to hatred turned." No one remotely close to the President was exempt from Cissy's crusade against him, except surprisingly, Eleanor Roosevelt. Cissy never laid a finger on her, or allowed anyone on the paper to do so.

Evalyn McLean, a ditsy local social leader, whose family had once owned the *Washington Post*, wrote a column for the *Times Herald*, (even though her range of language was limited and Evalyn herself would never have recognized a dangling gerund if she bumped into one). The column was called "My Say" which was, of course, a play on the name of Eleanor Roosevelt's column "My Day," but Evalyn was forbidden personally by Cissy to ever write a fractious word about E.R.

Cissy herself wrote an article about Eleanor Roosevelt that seemed to me a blazing and unutterably sad understanding of her own self and further what she been totally unable to accomplish in her own life. "Mrs. Roosevelt has solved the problem of living better than any woman I have known.," Cissy wrote. "There is none of this business of self-destruction going on in her heart and soul, no longer any anger, envy, un-charitableness, remorse...Eleanor Roosevelt is master of her own soul."

It is clear that Eleanor Roosevelt was one of the few people in Cissy's world that she loved permanently and without reservation. As one small, tangible evidence of this, she ordered that only flattering pictures of E.R. were ever to appear in the paper, and this was strictly enforced.

That solicitude did not apply to columnist Drew Pearson, Cissy's former dear friend, and also former son-in-law, father of her only grandchild and further her protégé. Nearly a decade ago she had given him the prize that political writers dream of: regular national publication of his column. And now, Drew Pearson's *Washington Merry-Go-Round* was one of the most broadly syndicated political columns in the country.

As the war heated up in Europe, Drew's column increasingly endorsed the arguments of the interventionists and criticized those of the isolationists. He paid paeans of praise to President Roosevelt and became an ardent advocate for all possible military support for England. The sooner, the better, he insisted.

Now Cissy reacted as if she had been nursing a viper at her breast. She sought out the worst pictures of Drew that she could find. She ran his column in the ad section of the paper, then on the page with the comics. She referred to him so often in the paper as "S.O.B" that Drew claimed that envelopes mailed with only those initials were delivered to him. He was a Quaker and he told his daughter Ellen that her grandmother evidently thought that he was a "Son of Brotherhood."

Drew, not surprisingly, fought back and said nasty things about Cissy to all who would listen. On his radio show he once referred to her as the "craziest woman in Washington." These two reminded me of children throwing spitballs at each other, except that these spitballs had rusty nails embedded in them.

And, of course, the fallout from the venom landed on Drew's pretty little Ellen. Now a fight ensued with Ellen the victim. Drew (or his wife, Luvie) wanted the glorious farm on the Potomac that Cissy had given Ellen on her tenth birthday. Drew offered Ellen $100,000 for it. Cissy was horrified that Drew would offer what she considered such a paltry amount for such valuable property. She told Ellen she would buy it back from her for much more.

And now the "round the clock" fights between her father and her grandmother forced Ellen to take sides. She decided to sell the farm to her father.

***

When Cissy had first ventured into the newspaper world some ten years ago, she announced she would rather raise hell than raise vegetables. And one of her favorite ways of raising hell was to fire people.

Now to get back at Drew for his apostasy, she fired his wife, Luvie, who was writing a movie column for the paper, and then she fired Luvie's former husband, who was also writing a column of some sort.

Now to everyone's surprise, one morning Drew's column, the Washington Merry-Go-Round, disappeared from the *Times Herald* and turned up in the *Washington Post*. It had always been in the *Times Herald* and apparently there had been no agreement for it to be transferred to the *Post*. In any event Cissy and the *Washington Post* had had a curious relationship for a long time. Indeed as far back as 1929, in pursuit of her dream of becoming a newspaper person, Cissy flirted with the idea of buying the *Post* when its owner hinted it was for sale. At the same time New York banker Eugene Meyer offered five million dollars for the *Post*, but it turned out that the owner had decided not to sell it after all.

Undaunted by that hurdle to her ambition, Cissy persuaded her friend, newspaper mogul William Randolph Hearst, to let her run his Washington morning paper.

And she went into her new role "with all her tremendous energy, put all her wit and emotion into it," *Current Biography* wrote.

In 1931 when the *Washington Post* really was for sale, Cissy persuaded Hearst to buy it, but a mystery buyer outbid Hearst's representatives. It turned out that Eugene Meyer was the unnamed buyer and had now succeeded in getting the *Post*. Cissy knew that Meyer had deep pockets and that he would surely turn the "run-down" *Post* into a formidable rival to her *Herald*.

While the legal ramifications of the sale of the paper were being worked out, Cissy bought the rights to the comic strips which the *Post* had been running. By the time Meyer took over the paper, Cissy's contract with the funnies' syndicate had expired, but she continued to print the comics. It took two years and a Supreme Court decision to convince Cissy that the comics belonged to the *Post*.

That wasn't the end of the brawls between Cissy and the *Post*. In 1937 Cissy learned that Eugene Meyer was now trying to buy the *Washington Herald* from Randolph Hearst. Horrified, Cissy called her boss and old friend at three o'clock in the morning and pleaded with him not to sell the *Herald* to Meyer. Hearst succumbed to her tears and entreaties and agreed to her suggestion that she lease the *Herald* and also his evening paper, the *Washington Times*, with an option to buy them both. She also loaned Hearst some money at this time.

In 1939 Cissy bought both papers, and she did the logical thing. She combined the two papers. The new-born *Washington Times Herald* was published around the clock, with ten editions a day.

***

It was a broad-shouldered, bright, and racy paper when I went to work there in 1940, with the loud jazz of the constantly-running Mergenthaler printing presses singing of the paper's success. And Cissy was riding her hobby-horse with obvious pleasure. Not too long after I started there I had occasion to find out whether the two other words in Cissy's evaluation of herself—vindictive bitch—were valid or not.

She called me into her office one day and handed me a typed article; she said she would like my opinion of it. I started out the door to go to my desk to read the article. She indicated a chair in her office and suggested I sit there and read it. I had not been in her office before, although I had heard it had once been a grungy storeroom, and that it had undergone a magic conversion. I cased the room without being too obvious. I was beguiled by its charm—the oriental rugs, the elegant antiques, and the tulips in an old Chinese ginger jar on Cissy's desk. I sat down and started to read the article.

In a short while Cissy's hairdresser came in. I sincerely tried to concentrate on the article on my lap, but occasionally I had to look up to see what was going on. The hairdresser, Pierre or Andre or some such French name, put a towel around Cissy's neck; she leaned back in her chair and he loosened her hair. He started to brush the long chestnut hair with vigor. I saw that she shut her eyes while he brushed.

I continued to read the article but subconsciously every now and then I heard Cissy talking to her secretary in the corner of the room. My attention was diverted from reading when a reporter came in. The hairdresser went on brushing Cissy's hair and I noted that her eyes were still shut.

George, the reporter, moved over closer to her chair. "You wanted to see me, Mrs. P.?" he asked.

The hairdresser continued his brushing. "No, George," Cissy responded, speaking slowly. "I didn't say I wanted to see you."

George looked surprised. "Oh?" he said in a questioning voice.

"No, George," she said. "I didn't say I wanted to see you," she repeated. "I asked for you to come to my office." Cissy was always precise in her language. Now she articulated her words slowly.

"Yes," George said in a puzzled voice.

The hairdresser didn't miss a stroke. Cissy's eyes were still closed. "I asked you to come in, George," she paused slightly. "I wanted to tell you that you're fired."

In order to avoid seeing George's face, I looked down so fast at the paper I was supposed to evaluate that I knocked it off my lap. I picked it up, all five or so pages of it, and went slowly out of the room. As I closed the door I looked back. Pierre or Andre whatever his name, was still brushing Cissy's hair and presumably her eyes were still closed.

She never asked me what I thought of the paper she had given me to read and I never returned it to her. But I had learned that those other two words Cissy had used to describe herself were absolutely 1,000 percent accurate. They suited her to a T.

***

A few days after that dreadful episode in Mrs. P's office, I got home from work late one afternoon to find a letter from England in my mailbox, which I knew immediately was from Noel. It had gone to my address at Millwood, Virginia, and been forwarded from there. When I had left England, naturally I had no idea what my new address in the US would be, but I told Noel that a letter addressed to me at that little post office, the same address as my Grandmother's farm, would always be sent on to me. He had been amused when I described the post office in Millwood. First, it was in a small old frame building and I had told Noel that the man who currently was postmaster (a cousin of mine, of course, as nearly everyone in the county seemed to be) thought he had the best job in the world. He loved playing chess and frequently a good friend of his would drop by and the two could spend hours playing chess. Further, the postman was a passionate fisherman and when he thought the trout in the nearby Shenandoah were awaiting him, on a couple of occasions the postmaster had let a reliable friend man the post office for a while when the postman went fishing. Noel had liked those simple stories and I imagined he had thought of them when he wrote me this letter.

I fixed my self a long vodka and tonic, got out some cheese and crackers, and sat down at a little table where I could look out at the trees on Twentieth Street. I wanted to create a small rite for myself as I read his letter.

He wrote that he still loved me "foreverly" and told me of an odd episode which had proved that to him. He said that there was a new beautiful young woman recently recruited to work on the same kind of missions that he worked on and that they were nearly immediately attracted to each other. He said he had really not planned it but they fell into bed together one night. The next morning, he was awoken by her caressing his forehead and then her hand moved down to his closed eyelids. "And, of course," he wrote, "you know what happened!"

And, as if I didn't know, he went on to say that he screamed at her and yelled to never do that again. "And, indeed, she never was given an opportunity to do so again," he wrote. He said that he apologized profusely to her, explained his peculiar problem, and that now they were reasonably good friends. He ended his letter by telling me that he was now embarked on a sincere commitment to get over me.

I reread his letter and I took an especially big guzzle of my drink. Of course, I knew what he was referring to. It was the bizarre experience with him once when I had run my fingers gently over his closed eyes. He sat up with an amazed expression. "You are the only person in the whole damned world that I would allow to touch my eyes." He went on to explain that even when he had had his eyes tested for glasses, he always made certain that the doctor never got to touch around his eyes. He was terrified that the doctor might touch his eyelids. It was then he told me of his phobia: as a child after a nanny had put iodine in his eyes instead of the drug which had been prescribed for a mild case of pink eye. He said it felt as if his eyes had been set on fire; that it was so painful for such a long period that, from that time in his life on, he had never let anyone come close to touching his eyelids. Except, it turned out, me! Totally unaware of his paranoia, I had run my fingers once over his sleeping eyes. He looked at me in utter amazement, and kept murmuring something to himself, then smiled as if he couldn't believe what was happening and then told me the story about the iodine in his eyes. Now he used to plead with me to caress his closed eyes, and also to flick my fingers over his eyelashes. "More, more," he would say, and smile in delight.

I wrote him a long, warm letter some days afterwards, told him how much I loved that he had loved me so much and now I was trying to create a perspective on us and compel myself to think of him as someone I had loved in a long ago past. In time, our letters to each other began to look like letters from old friends, except for a lapse or two every now and then.

After a while, we sent postcards to each other, and then it was only notes at each other's birthdays and then we just forgot to communicate.

Jack Kennedy's Book: *Why England Slept*

In the summer of 1940 Jack Kennedy pulled off a literary coup: he turned his Harvard senior thesis on British foreign policy in the 1930s—which had earned a magna cum laude—into a highly successful book.

He called it *Why England Slept,* as if it could be an adjunct to Churchill's book, *While England Slept,* of three years earlier. Kennedy's book was a profound analysis of the cascading events that led to war and of England's total unpreparedness for such a catastrope.

Henry Luce, publisher of *Life* magazine, added a little fillip to the book by writing the introduction, in which he praised it to the skies. Arthur Krock, who had done some editing of the book, wanted to write the introduction, but in any case, Poppa Joe felt that Luce was a more appealing selection.

I could easily tell from Jack's penetrating insights how valuable his father's extracurricular assignments had been for him. All of those trouble spots in Europe that Joe had sent Jack and Joe Jr. to, or had arranged newpaper assignments for, had taught them a lot. They had learned to hone their observations and to write sharply about their conclusions. I felt that in Jack's writing I could see that Poppa's tutelage had paid off handsomely.

However, I didn't go as far as one admirer of Jack's book had. He said that Jack's father had "prepared him for destiny."

In any event, I thought Jack had a fine sense of values when I heard that he had given the British royalties from his book to an English town, Norwalk, which had recently been brutally bombed by the Luftwaffe. With his US royalties, he had blown himself to a super, jazzy car.

The Wild Goose Chase

Listening to Ed Murrow and Larry Laseur broadcasting from London for CBS, I felt I could hear the thud of the bombs as they fell, especially in the East End, the part of London that seemed to be a special target. I sensed the impact of the diabolic explosion which immediately followed. I could visualize the radiating blazes set off by the bombs, but I could never hear the cries of the wounded or the dying. At least, thank God, I never conjured them up.

It was obvious that the Germans were trying to crush the morale of the British in order to pave the way for the planned invasion. If successful, this would be the first time that England had been defeated since the Roman legions in the first century BC invaded the island. However, the Nazis had not reckoned on the amazing resilience of the people nor on the raw courage and determination of the British fighter pilots to fend off the Luftwaffe bombers.

I told Frank, who was writing yet another article about the Battle of Britain, that I had heard that my old friend Paul Richey was still not considered fit enough to fly a fighter plane again. However he was among those now dispatching the fighters out to greet the bombers. Frank said that must be a tough job because from all accounts the Germans had now set up scores of bomber bases in occupied France. This made their flight to England that much shorter than it had been.

I started to say that it looks as if the English Channel is getting narrower all the time, so when the Germans try to invade England... I didn't dare finish that thought. Instead I commented to Frank how extraordinary it was that the Nazis had already established military bases in France. "Well, look how fast they got there," Frank said. "Rommel and his tanks rolled through the Low Countries and into France in a matter of weeks."

I asked Frank, remembering always what a Civil War buff he was, if he had ever heard that Rommel had come to the US once to study General Philip Sheridan's brilliant cavalry tactics to see if those tactics could be adapted to other kinds of warfare, for instance tanks.

He scoffed at my question and wondered where I had ever gotten such a notion. I told him that I really didn't have the foggiest idea where I had ever heard it but I did remember hearing someone mention it years ago.

Now, what with one thing and another, I found myself with an assignment to go to Winchester, Virginia, and other places near where General Sheridan had fought. My object was to see if I could find anyone who remembered anyone who might have seen a German officer named Erwin Rommel visiting any of those places.

So I set off for my grandmother's beautiful old house, Long Branch, some fifteen miles from Winchester. I figured I would stage out of there on my odd quest. I was greeted warmly by my grandmother, known by all her grandchildren as Danny, and by her dear old friend, Cousin Lolly Bunch, who had come for a week's visit one summer twenty-six years ago and hadn't left yet.

After I had hugged them I sought out "Poppy" Bannister, whose parents had been slaves at Long Branch. After the Civil War they had continued to live at Long Branch and later "Poppy" had moved to a little house nearby. He had never worked anywhere except at Long Branch, so I had seen him over the years and was especially fond of him. I had taken a sugar lump with me and asked "Poppy" to go with me to the stable to see Trim, an old Percheron work horse, whose ancestors had come from a section of France called Perce. I had liked big old Trim since my childhood summers spent at Long Branch. He had been called a roan then, but his color now looked like that of a too-ripe old strawberry. He took the sugar lump gently out of my flat hand and I gave him a pat on his muzzle when I left him.

I had heard that Trim's breed had carried the Crusaders on their feckless missions to wrest the Holy lands from the Muslims. Despite his distinguished genealogy, Trim never appeared haughty about his background. I often wished I could say the same about some of my Virginia family. Every one of them had a non-subtle way of letting non-family friends know that our great-great-grandfather had signed the Declaration of Independence (he was simply called "A signer") and that he had been in Yorktown to receive the defeat of the British soldiers. Heck, my great-great-grandfather had not only a signer, but another one of my ancestors had been the first French envoy to the nascent United States.

After my little visit with "Poppy" and Trim, I joined Danny and Cousin Lolly for supper. Later, I noted, as we sat on the porch and had the house drink, bourbon on the rocks, with a morsel of water, that neither of the women had the gaucherie to suggest to me that my Rommel mission was like looking for the proverbial needle in a hay stack. Instead, right away they tried to think of ways they could help me.

"Tell her about the stories your mother used to tell you about the Confederate soldiers and the Union soldiers seesawing through Clip when she was living there," Cousin Lolly suggested to Danny.

I thought Danny responded a little sharply. "I don't know what that's got to do with the price of peanut butter in Australia." I always had to suppress a laugh at that odd but common expression of those days.

Lolly pointed out that maybe someone in Clip might remember Rommel coming there since it had been Sheridan territory from time to time. I smiled at my grandmother, as if to say please tell us the stories your mother told her about the soldiers.

As a child her mother, Molly Nelson, Grandmother started, was visiting a family cousin, named Mann Page, who lived in a little town called Clip in western Virginia when the war broke out. Since the soldiers from both the Union and the Confederate armies were ranging all over the countryside it was considered safer for Molly, who was thirteen, to stay there rather than risk traveling home through the countryside, awash with troops from both contending armies.

Mann Page was a joke in family lore because of his totally inappropriate first name. He was considered to be more a mouse than a man. For example, he had used some excuse about eyes being so bad that he could scarcely see in order to avoid joining up with any Confederate troop, yet he could see perfectly. Grandmother remembered her mother telling tales about that period when she was visiting Cousin Mann, saying that whenever the Yankees came marching down the main street of Clip (and it was Yankees one day and Confederates another), he fled upstairs and hid under his bed. If he heard fierce banging on the kitchen door, he crawled a little further under the bed. Now safely hidden, he would yell to Molly to go downstairs and see what the soldiers wanted.

Molly said that several times Yankees had knocked on the door, asking for a drink of water, which she had given them. They had thanked her, politely enough, she said, and one had even patted her terrier, Gyp.

She got used to having soldiers from one army come by, and then a few days later soldiers from the other army came by. Occasionally she and her well-trained little dog, whose real name was Gypsy, would sit on the bench on the porch and watch the soldiers, all of whom looked dirty and weary, march by. Gyp would never bark at either contingent; he would just sit there and look at them all with soulful eyes, she said, as if he felt sorry for them.

Grandmother told this tale in a soft, unmodulated voice until she got to this part and then her voice rose to an emotional pitch: "But one of those days, a soldier stepped out of line, leaped up the steps to the porch and, quick as greased lightning, grabbed Gypsy. Molly yelled at the top of her voice but the thief had slipped back into the line of marching soldiers so swiftly that Molly could not even see her dog any more. She still yelled her little heart out for Gyp."

Now I had heard my grandmother tell tales passed on to her or old family adventures, and had heard many of them so often that I could nearly repeat them verbatim myself, but still I drew my breath and sighed along with poor Molly as Danny spun out her tale.

Molly still spent a lot of time on the porch, and whenever a cluster of Yankee soldiers—yes, without any bias, Grandmother interjected, we can say it was a Yankee who had stolen Gyp—came into view she was watching them, but she had no idea who it was she was looking for. He had moved so fast that Molly didn't think she would recognize the man who had stolen her dog.

One warm dusty summer day she looked carefully at the soldiers as they trudged past. She stood up as she stared at one. Sitting on his shoulder was her little dog. Molly ran from the porch calling. "Gyp, Gyp," she yelled at the top of her little lungs. "Gyp, come here. Jump, Gyp, jump." She waved her arms frantically.

She started to cry as she realized that the man was holding Gyp so tight that though the little dog was struggling wildly, there was no chance he could get away. The whole line of soldiers was moving, and she tried to keep up with it. The soldiers seemed to be walking so fast that she lost sight of Gyp, but she kept calling wildly for him anyway.

Suddenly, it seemed as if out of nowhere, came a clear commanding voice. "Give the little girl her dog. Immediately," the voice said, and then it repeated, very loud, "Immediately!" Gyp leapt out from the throng of marching soldiers, ran like a hare, and jumped up into Molly's outstretched arms. "And the well-trained dog couldn't stop barking for joy," Danny added.

After she finished the story, I suggested I might go to Clip and see if anyone there ever remembered seeing a man who looked anything like the man in my newspaper clipping. I had tried to find a picture of Rommel as he must have looked say, twenty years before, but the best I could muster was a fuzzy picture from the *New York Times* of him in uniform taken in Berlin, I believe in the early thirties.

However Danny told me that Clip had been one of the hamlets incorporated into West Virginia when that state was formed at the end of the Civil War. Unfortunately, she said, she had no idea what is was called now.

Just before Danny blew out the kerosene lamp to close out our evening—there was no electricity at Long Branch then—she said she had to tell us a little story about General Sheridan, or at least some of the soldiers from one of his battalions. Any family in the countryside that owned anything valuable set about hiding it as the Yankees came into the Shenandoah Valley, she said. And their troops came in droves. So all the silver and any other valuable objects at Long Branch, the big pieces in the silver tea set, trays and flat silver, and the copper sauce-pan which LaFayette had given to my great-great-grandfather, John Holker, at the end of the American Revolution, were buried in a big hole dug in a field known as the Sod Field. It was far from the house and it had been covered over with the thick turf in such a way that there was no evidence that it had ever seen a shovel.

Shortly after the secret burial rite, it happened that a group of Sheridan's soldiers set fire to the wheat fields at Long Branch. For-tunately those fields burned themselves out quickly and no buildings caught on fire. Anyway, the valuables had been hidden and there they stayed until after the war.

There was one woman in a nearby house, Grandmother told us that night, who didn't try to hide her valuables, especially her jewelry. She was just going to put it all at the bottom of the stairs, she told her friends, so that when the Yankees came they could take it without waking her up.

After the war was over and the Long Branch men came back—that is, those of them that did come back—retrieved the silver and other treasures. All of it was there, filthy but intact, except for the lid to the LaFayette copper saucepan. The main part, engraved with the initials LF, in which he cooked while encamped during the Revo-lution, was there, encrusted with dirt. But its matching copper top, engraved also with LaFayette's initials, could not be found. The men on the treasure hunt dug around the area for a long time, but there was no sign of the missing lid.

Some fifty years after the Civil War, Danny was a young bride at Long Branch. One day talking to Susan the cook, she noticed that Susan was holding a dirt-covered oddly shaped object in her hand. Grandmother asked her what it was and Susan said she didn't know, but that someone had found it in the Sod Field where it had been routed up by the hogs.

As Susan talked, she scratched the object with a straight pin she had plucked off her dress, over her ample bosom. It seems to me that the cooks I knew always had a straight pin or two tucked on them. As she scratched the object in her hand, Grandmother said she thought she saw a glint of copper. Sure enough, after they cleaned it, they dis-covered that it was the lid to the LaFayette saucepan.

The next morning before I left to go to Winchester to start my search for clues of my German general, I paid a visit to the LaFayette saucepan. It was sitting, shining and content on the bricks in front of the black marble mantelpiece in the living room.

***

In Winchester, I went to the largest of the few hotels in the town and after a little discussion with the pleasant man at the desk, discovered that there was a porter who had worked there for nearly thirty years, who had a phenomenal memory for everyone who had ever been in the hotel. He fit well within the age group I had wanted to talk to. I had figured that if Rommel had really come to Virginia to chase General Sheridan's ghost, it would most likely have been between 1920, sometime after Rommel's experience in the German army during the First World War and, say, the early thirties, probably the time when Hitler was beginning to build up the huge army he was preparing for his assault on the Jews of Europe.

It was true, I discovered: the porter not only remembered everyone he had ever seen in the hotel, but wanted to tell me all about each one of them. I suffered through a lot of descriptions, but none seemed to fit my limited concept or the newspaper picture of Rommel. Next I went to the local chamber of commerce and got nowhere there either.

Then I wandered on some of the roads that Rommel might have travelled and dipped into several gas stations which looked like they had been around a while. Luckily, in two of them there were men who had worked there for fifteen years so that fit in my arbitrary time frame. I would describe Rommel as best I could, show them the fading newspaper picture, and point out that he had a German accent, but got no satisfaction.

Once one of my interviewees thought he might have hit the jackpot, but on further discussion the person he identified turned out not to be a German soldier speaking broken English but a colporteur from Texas. A colporteur, I learned, is a bible salesman, who was speaking Texan English.

***

I spent that night in an old fashioned bed-and-breakfast in Berryville, Virginia, a town famous for the scene of great Civil War battles between the enemy armies. Some of these battles had surely involved General Sheridan and his troops, the man that ran my abode said. He was a crisp ninety-year-old and an amateur historian; he reminded me that Berryville had once been known as Battletown for its position during the war. He told me that there were stories after the war about the damage done by the large number of Yankee horses stabled all over Berryville and in neighboring towns. He also told me tales of the damage Sheridan had done to the rolling stock railroads, to barns with wheat or other grains stored in them, and his general ravaging of the countryside. But he had never heard any tale about a German visitor.

Nowhere did I find a scintilla of a story about someone who might have been a German soldier named Erwin Rommel scouting the countryside looking for the secrets of one of the great tactical warriors of the American Civil War.

I called Frank Waldrop and told him that I had to confess that I seemed to be on a wild goose chase, that I was thoroughly discouraged and that I didn't see any sense in chasing this fantasy any longer. He said that if I had checked with him sooner, he would have told me the same thing earlier. I reminded him that he had assigned me the job.

Anyway, he told me that he needed me there badly. He was working on a long article on the unusual uniforms that some units of both armies wore in the Civil War. I seemed to be fated to stick with the Civil War a little longer. "I have heard that there were voluntary units fighting for the Union dressed as *Zouaves*," Frank said. "And I need you here to check out these stories and get pictures and drawings and so forth of these *Zouaves*."

"*Zouaves*," I fairly yelled into the telephone.

"There really were. Much more flesh and blood than your Rommel story."

All the way driving to Washington that evening, I kept repeating that exotic word, *Zouave*, to myself and trying to picture American soldiers in the Civil War dolled up like the dashing soldiers of Algeria.

Busy Nocturnal Life

Generally I was working hard on the newspaper checking on research for Frank, or finding appropriate art work for his stories, such as I had just done with drawings of the *Zouaves*. I liked doing research and learned a lot in the process. Occasionally he asked me for advice on an article he was writing, and sometimes I had ideas for articles he could write, and every now and then he gave me an assignment to write.

Meanwhile I was enjoying my evenings in Washington, too. Nearly all the people I saw were engaged in one way or another in support of the Allies. This included the Dollar-a-Year Men, or their families, or occasionally I saw a friend from somewhere outside of Washington who came to consult in a program for the Allies.

Rex Benson, as the British military attaché to the US, had an important role at this juncture of history. He and Leslie had rented a slightly overwrought house in Georgetown, where a steady stream of soldiers of lofty rank turned up. Most of them were English, also many Americans, and occasionally Poles or Dutch or Belgians, who had been able to escape from their occupied countries. In any case, all dripped galaxies of medals. Furthermore, distinguished British economists, journalists, and politicians drifted in and out of the house.

I was, of course, delighted to be a frequent guest at dinner parties in that esteemed house. And it was esteemed: I once overheard one guest ask another if he was staying at the embassy meaning, of course, the British embassy, or was he staying "chez Benson," as if the prestige of the two establishments was equal.

Rex had a reputation of being astute and cool-headed and he looked charming, too, I thought, except when he was engrossed in a serious conversation; then he frowned so much that he appeared forbidding. I knew he had already traveled a lot in the US and had good American friends in various levels of power even before he was assigned here. From all I had heard about him he was efficient and popular, and furthermore he was married to a delightful American woman.

***

On the ship coming to the US, Leslie and I had wondered and worried about what would happen to the French Navy if France fell. Since then, of course, we had seen the haunting photographs of Hitler goose-stepping through that most iconic example of French history, the Arc de Triumph. I had cringed at all the other pictures of the Nazis, smiling broadly in front of familiar French landmarks.

Later Leslie and I had learned what had happened to the French Navy once France had surrendered to the Germans. We discussed that tangled episode, to our vast sadness, one day at her house in Washington. Most of the French Navy had been tied up in Oran, a large French base on the Mediterranean coast of Algeria, when the French had given up the ghost. What we had discussed on our ship was the British fear that if France fell, the French fleet might be captured by the Germans, like sitting ducks, or it might even go over willfully to the Nazis.

What I learned from Leslie was that the British, try as they might after the collapse of France, could get no indication from the French navy as to its intentions. The officers of the British navy stationed in the Mediterranean were ordered to smoke out the French and find out what their Navy now planned to do. They got nowhere.

Finally, unable to get any hint from subtle approaches to the French Navy of its decision, so crucial to the course of the war, the British felt compelled to send an official ultimatum to the French Commander: either join the British Navy or destroy your own ships!

There was no word from the French Navy. The British let the time for a response to the ultimatum pass and still there was no response. There was another ultimatum, and again no response from the French.

There had to be some resolution to the status of the French Navy, the British felt, given the dreadful possibility that it could join up with the German Navy. The British waited several hours longer for an answer to the second ultimatum. Now since there was no answer from the French, word came down from London, that the British had no alternative: The British fleet was driven to the drastic measure of firing on the French ships.

The French battleships in the harbor were destroyed and over 1,000 French sailors were killed. Leslie told me that she had learned that Churchill was "unutterably sad" that he had been forced to deliver such an order to the British fleet, but he believed the French had left Britain no other course.

Over a drink Leslie and I discussed the agonies all around in this predicament. Churchill's, the British admiral that had to give the order to fire on the French fleet in Oran, and to say nothing of the French sailors killed or wounded.

***

Leslie ran her little Washington fiefdom with a deft touch, seemingly informal, but actually in her own gently contrived formal fashion. Her warmth and genuine interest in everybody created an atmosphere of conviviality that even blunted the sharp edge of the war, at least for a while. A simple motive underlay the many gatherings she gave: simply to do whatever she could to enhance British-American amity.

Dinners at Rex's and Leslie's house that I went to were mellow and light-hearted. It wasn't that evenings there were frivolous; it's just that the tragedies of the war and serious discussions that could lead to weighty decisions took place elsewhere.

One evening at a dinner party there I found myself seated next to a tall, intense-looking man in a rumpled suit. He had unkempt curly, dark hair and his necktie was wildly askew. Before we had even introduced ourselves to each other (although we had place cards so we could see each other's names; his was John but I couldn't read the last name) he turned to me and surprised me by asking, in a low voice, if he could say that he thought the dress I was wearing was "smashing."

I smiled and asked him what he would do if I said he couldn't say that? He didn't answer, but he didn't say it. Not then, anyway.

He immediately surprised me again when he told me a little later that Leslie had wanted us to meet because we both shared a predilection for the same odd book. I wondered briefly, looking at him, if she was referring to a childhood favorite of mine called *Slovenly Peter*, but instead I asked him politely which book she had in mind. "We are both *Tristram Shandy* nuts, she told me." He paused slightly and then added, "But I wouldn't have taken you for a *Tristram* fan."

I was about to ask him what he meant by that but just then the woman slated to sit on his other side turned up and engaged him in conversation.

Meanwhile, I wondered how in the world Leslie knew that I liked *Tristram Shandy*. Then I remembered the incident on the ship coming to the US.

Somehow John and I never got to around to discussing books any more the evening we met. The more we talked throughout dinner, the more I laughed at his off-beat sense of humor. I also realized that despite his disheveled look, he radiated charm. When he asked me if I was free for dinner the next evening, I accepted with alacrity.

When I got to know him better I learned that he had some special title in the embassy, something to do with legal advice, but in any case I felt that was not important. Somehow it became clear to me early on that his assignment, whatever it was called, was to get the US into the war alongside England as quickly as possible. Of course, I reckoned, nearly every official Brit in Washington had a part in that act, but I felt that my new friend John was assigned to play a major role in that critical scenario.

In our various discussions, either at his small house, at my apartment, at dinners with friends, or occasionally at a restaurant with him, I discovered that he had managed to get to know several important members of Congress, including some of the most isolationist. He had also made friends with a number of administration officials and some important political columnists in the city.

He knew that I had figured out his real assignment and one evening I told him that I marveled at what a great job he was doing but that he still had a long, long way to go since the large majority of the Americans were dead set against getting involved in what they called the European War. He thanked me for my congratulations. He smiled a wicked smile and said he had reported "home" that he was really lucky to have gotten to know one of the most influential newspaperwomen in Washington and that he was working on her. I asked him to please mind his language.

Once I remembered to ask him why, when we had met, he had thought I wasn't the type to be a *Tristram Shandy* fan. First he said he had to tell me how he and Leslie had happened on the subject that had brought us together. Leslie had told him a few days before the fateful night we met, he explained, that some general, who neither she nor Rex had met, was going to be visiting them for "consultation" and she wondered if perchance John knew him. "I said I did and that she and Rex would like him a lot. I found they already knew that he had an important background in German military tactics and they would also find him very good company."

John said he had also warned Leslie not to let the general get started on any tales of some battle he had fought in the Marne or somewhere else in France in the First World War. "'He will go on and on and on about it,' I cautioned her. 'He will remind you too much of Uncle Toby in his battle in Namur, so just don't let him get started on it.'"

I smiled when he told me that. He laughed and said that Leslie hadn't a clue as to what he was talking about and so John had to explain the parts in *Tristram Shandy* where Uncle Toby talks incessantly about his former battles, especially in Namur.

And that's when Leslie had told John she knew another Shandy nut. "I wouldn't have believed there were two of you here right under my nose," she had said "but sometime soon I am going to arrange for you to sit next to each other at dinner here."

I asked John again why it was that simply by looking at me that night, he was surprised that I was a *Tristram Shandy* buff.

He said he thought I looked "too fragile" and then he added, "maybe even too vulnerable."

I didn't say anything. I just wanted him to go on. He paused for a minute. "I didn't think you looked lusty enough. I had always thought, mistakenly, obviously," he went on, "that people who really liked Sterne, would look more..."

"More what, John?"

"Hell, just more robust."

I laughed and told him that I would now tell him what had really put him off in his judgment of me that night. "It was the dress I was wearing."

He interrupted me immediately. "I tried to tell you that night that I thought it was a smashing dress. And I've told you that since."

"The problem is that that print that looks like a pale sunset, with its soft oranges and dusty reds, put you off so much because it was so light and airy and you felt it made me look fragile."

"Yes, I thought you just looked like you might blow away and I was afraid I would never see you again."

***

Once that winter, John went back to England for an extended visit. Among the notes I got from him when he was away was one in which he said he wouldn't be surprised if I didn't recognize him when he got back to Washington. I wondered if he had been through some kind of a metamorphosis after which he would come back to the US looking "sheveled," as distinct from "disheveled." I often told him that it was incredible how he could be so sparkly clean all the time and also be in such total disarray. He would simply answer that he guessed he was just talented.

Anyway when I first saw him on his return I didn't have any problem recognizing him, but I was startled for there was John in a British general's uniform. "Not only that," I said as we embraced, "but you have two stars. My God, what hath the British empire wrought?"

"Well," he said, in response, "a guy has got to start somewhere, hasn't he?"

I noted with great pleasure that he appeared wonderfully unmilitary. His hair still looked as if it could stand a clipping, his elegant khaki uniform was well rumpled, and I think one of the stars on his shoulder was slightly off kilter.

Coventry

My paper, and all the papers in the country as well, and all of the radio broadcasters, erupted on November 20 with the monstrous story of the Nazi bombing of Coventry, one of the largest cities in England and an important manufacturing town. Five hundred and fifteen German planes had dropped incendiary bombs on the city, returned to their bases to re-arm, and flown back to Coventry again to drop more bombs. The Germans had plastered the town with explosives and with parachute mines.

The wreckage was so complete that Coventry got memorialized by a verb the Germans invented, to *Koventrieren*. The British simply added the term *Coventrate* to the English language. I saw it even used in American papers, including my own on one occasion.

***

The German bombers which attacked Coventry took special and deliberate aim to destroy the headquarters of the city Fire Department. This guaranteed that there would be few firefighters to cope with hundreds of fires which were now burning over the entire city after the bombing by the Luftwaffe. The huge numbers of factories and buildings, including especially houses, would burn endlessly. It must have seemed to the men and women and children of Conventry like unadulterated hell. There had been a rumor mentioned by a broadcaster from London, Frank told me one morning, that the terrible toll that the bombing inflicted on the civilian population of Coventry so shocked the British leadership of war strategy that a change was being considered by the British Air Command.

If this change took place, Frank said, it could affect the character of British bombing from now on, counteracting what had been a policy of aiming carefully for specific targets and thus avoiding, to a certain extent, non-combatant casualties. The British would no longer be constrained from attacks on areas which included also numbers of civilians. Some days later there were stories in my paper, especially and on the radio, of the British bombing of Mannheim in Germany, an important industrial center on the right bank of the Rhine. According to the accounts of that raid, there had been a huge number of civilians killed.

Frank mentioned to me that he thought that was a different kind of raid for the British. He wondered if it was aberrant or if the British were just getting careless or if they were really changing their tactics. I asked if there was a term for the bombing which paid little heed to civilian populations? He said it was called "carpet bombing."

Some few days later Frank said he would teach me the adjectives for certain kinds of bombing. He mentioned "strategic bombing" and then they got worse. He said there was also "saturation" bombing and even "obliteration" bombing. I looked at him, shocked. "My God," I said. "The British would never go into bombing so completely immoral as that, would they?"

He said it depended, "Depends on how much they would need to." If I had looked at Frank horror-struck a few minutes ago, I can't cough up the language to describe how I stared at him now. "Depends on how much they would need to," he had said.

I had a violent sinking feeling in the pit of my stomach: now civilized men are not to spare civilian women and children in their warfare, or worse, but I didn't allow myself to go down that road of despair.

Mint Juleps

Now Frank, the fiercely objective military expert, must have realized how much he had frightened me by citing the gradations of bombing. But without referring to our conversation, one morning a few days later, he said that he thought maybe this was the right time for the paper to have an article "of no social value whatsoever." And one where the word "war" would be banned and so would any thought of it, he added. He reminded me that I had once suggested that I would like sometime to write a "fluffy" article on how mint juleps were made at various Washington bars. Bars and nightclubs had flourished in London during the war despite the blackout, I remembered, and they were hugely popular now in Washington too. Frank assigned me to haunt them and write about how they made mint juleps.

A staff photographer, Dmitri with an unpronounceable Russian last name, was assigned to accompany me on my research to take appropriate pictures. He and I looked forward to the evenings we would spend at the various watering holes around town. I really liked the idea of my assignment, not only for the juleps we had to drink in the line of duty—for which, of course, the paper paid—but also because it gave me an opportunity to tell every hoary mint julep joke ever devised.

I threw in a little history of mint in my article, including that it was an element in Greek mythology. Minte was a nymph who was Pluto's lover; mint is mentioned in the Bible, in the Book of Matthew. I even managed to tell that my Shetland pony had wallowed in a mint bed by a stream at our old family place in Virginia and that for days I had a pony that smelled deliciously of mint.

After my article was published, Cissy told me she had hugely enjoyed it, and had found it amusing and original. Also she had liked Dmitri's photos. I was pleased but also disappointed that I couldn't write about the best part of my exploratory evenings: Dmitri. He was delightful company throughout our basic research. Further he was quite dashing looking in his black turtleneck sweater and the black patch over his left eye which gave him what I had learned to call a little *je ne sais quoi* look, which expression was one I used only when talking to myself since it is so pretentious.

The first night out when we were sipping away—the juleps at that bar were too sweet—he asked me if he'd ever told me how he lost his eye, about why he had to wear that patch. I told him no he had not, but that frankly I had often wondered.

We settled comfortably in our chairs, our long frosty glasses in front of us. Dmitri spun out a tale of an affair he had with a woman in Sweden, unfortunately married. He told me all about his first meeting with this glamorous woman. He talked about the various places they had visited in Sweden where they carried on their illicit romance. We sipped on our juleps while he went into details of all they had done to elude the husband.

"One evening," he said, now talking faster, "my dear woman's husband found us together on a sofa in his den when we thought he was away on a distant trip. Right then and there that man ran a sword right through my eye." I looked appropriately aghast and kept saying what a terrible story that was.

The next night, while concentrating on our research—I didn't like the bourbon in our drinks at that place—my friend said, "Say Page, have I ever told you how come I am wearing this patch over my eye?" Looking him straight in the eye (his right one), I told him "No, but I'd sure like to know."

Well, it seems he had fallen in love with a woman in Holland. She, too, was married and it turned out her husband, too, was a jealous type, but Dmitri explained that she was so irresistibly enchanting that he could not leave her. They found one safe place after another but unfortunately, caught by the husband behind a barn in the countryside around Friesland *in flagrante delicto*, he came at Dmitri with a huge knife aimed at Dmitri's eye. I clucked something such as, "My God! How awful. Dmitri, you poor guy."

And the next night, when I nodded no to his usual question—the juleps here happened to be the best—he told me he had met a beautiful Australian woman, married of course, on a boat going to India. The weather on the trip was beautiful; she had long amber hair, the ship had wonderful private spots. Everything conspired to making love, Dmitri told me. They continued their romance after they arrived in Delhi. One night her husband, a subaltern in the British army, happened on us alone together in a park near a restaurant in Delhi, he said, now speaking in a breathless voice. "He came at me with a dagger and pointed it right at my eye." Dmitri quickly put his hand over his patch and contorted his face as if in agony.

Unfortunately he and I only spent three evenings together on our julep research. I have wondered many times since how Dmitri really lost his eye.

Mackerel Sky

"Mackerel sky, mackerel sky, starts with a smile, ends with a cry," Mother chanted as we walked out to my car to head back to Washington on a cold day in early December 1941. We had spent the night at Long Branch and exchanged early Christmas presents with Danny and Cousin Lolly. It was nearly three weeks until Christmas but we knew we wouldn't get down to The County, as it was called proudly by the people that lived there, again before the holiday. We boasted that we didn't have to be bound by a date to have a merry time together, and besides we all promised not to open our presents before dawn on December 25.

In a spirit of religious congeniality, Mother and I had even accompanied the women to church the next morning. I had to hide a secret smile under my house-of-worship face at the little Episcopal church because I was always amused that most of the pews there had names, that is they had a brass plate with the name of the house owned by the people who sat in that pew. I was amused enough to be in a community where the houses had names, but the pews? We were sitting in a pew which sported a brass plate marked "Long Branch."

This Sunday we four gave up the ritual of cocktails at a friend's house following the service. Man thirsteth after religion, a local wag had said. We had foregone that pleasure because we were to have an early lunch since Mother and I wanted to get off early to stop off briefly to see a friend in Middleburg and still be back in Washington before dark.

This visit to Long Branch was only the third or fourth time that Mother had gone back there since she moved to Washington some months ago. It was my idea that she should move and together we had found the ideal, small house for her in Washington. I was annoyed with myself that I had been obtuse so long about Mother's plight at Long Branch. Everyone said how lucky Nannie was to be living there with her mother in that great, big, beautiful house, blah, blah, blah. It took me a while to realize that what she longed for instead was her own little house where she could cook—she had not been allowed in the kitchen at Long Branch except on occasion to have a cordial half hour or so with Cora, the incredible cook—gather up her own friends and be her hospitable, natural, irreverent, witty self.

Now she was living in her own little pink house in Georgetown where she had been joined by a beloved aunt, Mary Decker, who was actually some years younger than Mother. They were wonderfully congenial and deeply devoted to each other. The two of them held a kind of court one evening a week with a lively clutch of people of varying types, ages, and sexes. She was known affectionately by all of them as Nannie, which we children also called her most of the time.

The two delightful women had carved out a pleasant life for themselves which was not just lightness and fun. Mother worked twice a week for an organization that taught young women, whose soldier husbands were overseas, how to cook for just themselves now, or for their children if they had them. All involved seemed to be enjoying it. Mother geared her lessons to include especially inexpensive ingredients which, I must say, was a stretch for her. Mary devoted a day a week reading to the blind at a home for the blind nearby.

Happy as Nannie was to be in Washington, she was also delighted to spend a day or so at Long Branch to be with her mother and in the old house of her childhood. As usual, when Mother and I were there, we all had a good time exchanging news of what was going on in each other's lives and kicking around the gossip of the county, which I particularly found diverting.

And we talked about the war. Always about the war. Now especially we talked about Operation Barbarossa, the name the Germans had given to their assault on Russia. We praised to the skies the raw courage of the Soviet defenders of Stalingrad and were delighted that the Germans were being routed in some parts of the city. The death and destruction was so appalling that we knew it was a major one for the history books. And we bemoaned the tragic loss of life in yet another theater of that bitter cruel war.

***

On the lighter side of life, Grandmother and Cousin Lolly always liked me to pass on whatever idle rumors I had picked up from old newspaper pals, or from indiscreet British friends who told me stories they should not have. I remembered that once, on a previous trip to Long Branch, I had told them a tale of Pamela Churchill, the wife of the Prime Minister's son, Randolph. She was engaged in what had been described to me as a hot and heavy affair with the distinguished American, Ambassador Averell Harriman, who was in charge of US war matériel in England.

The last night Mother and I were at Long Branch that early winter weekend, I mentioned that I had a tidbit to pass on. It was about an "off the record" conversation between Roosevelt and Churchill when they had met this past summer in Argentina Bay off Newfoundland. Churchill had sailed to this rendezvous in HMS *Prince of Wales*, Roosevelt in the USS *Arkansas*. There in that extraordinary background off of Canada, the great leaders had outlined their war aims in a document which came to be called "The Atlantic Charter." This meeting had been secret at first but later was well covered in the news. The women nodded when I mentioned the Atlantic Charter. We were all committed internationalists and pleased with the Roosevelt-Churchill declaration.

I said I had a little sidebar to add to that story. I guessed it was apocryphal, I said, but I'd tell it anyway and they could judge for themselves as to its authenticity. The famous meeting between the two great allied leaders had ended, I said, and Churchill was being piped off the President's ship. He had started down the improvised steps that would lead him to the launch in which he would return to the *Prince of Wales*.

The President called out "goodbye" to Churchill once again and then added, speaking loudly, "Can you think of anything else the

President of the United States can do for the Prime Minister of Great Britain?"

Churchill popped his head up above the gunwales of the American ship so he could see Roosevelt. "Yes, Mr. President," he responded. He paused and looked directly at his faithful friend. "Yes," Mr. Churchill repeated. "You can get your special agent in Great Britain, the distinguished Ambssador Averell Harriman, to stop screwing my daughter-in-law."

The next day as I told Grandmother and Cousin Lolly goodbye, I said that I hoped my story last night had not offended them. They smiled their shock-proof smiles for me.

***

As Nannie and I got in the car to set off, I looked up at the sky and noted that the small fleecy clouds did resemble a mackerel or some kind of fish. I told Mother I had never heard that jingle before but I could see a school of fish up there and I'd settle for mackerel.

I smiled as I thought that no matter how much I saw of my mother, she always had a new angle of vision on an old subject. She threw in lines from a poem, or a quote which could come from the Bible, or Dickens, or Jane Austen, or just something Rabelaisian, that perfectly fit a subject under discussion. Or simply come up with a funny old weather proverb, as she just had.

***

It was sharp and bright, a typical early December day, the perfect atmosphere for our drive, I thought. On this familiar journey I am acutely aware of my sense of anticipation of the glorious countryside through which we'll travel. I can see it with my eyes shut and I know the personal iconography by heart. It is etched in the landscape of my memory. First we will drive through the lush Shenandoah Valley. The hillsides will be sprinkled with beautiful horses, thoroughbreds mostly because this is fox hunting country and no respectable fox hunter would be caught dead on anything but a thoroughbred. Or the hillsides will be dotted with grazing beef cattle, mainly Black Angus, which to me are especially becoming to the bluegrass slopes of the Blue Ridge Mountains.

We will cross the Shenandoah, one of my favorite rivers, on a simple low bridge, follow a road that climbs steeply until we cut through a gap sliced by nature through the mountains, so that we are now on the other side of a part of the great chain called the Appalachians that arches its way from Eastern Canada to central Alabama. We look down to a broad valley so lovely that it defies imagination.

A slow drift down will take us into that valley and at the bottom there will be a white sign with black letters that says Paris. I ask Nannie to tell me the story of how the town got its name. I tell her I have forgotten it, but that is a lie.

Years ago, she starts off (I like her stories that start off like that. None of this, "some years ago," which could be reasonably recent). Years ago, she says, there was a brick tavern here built close to the road so it could accommodate people that came by in the coaches. It was on the main road from Winchester to Washington and a stop at the tavern at Pumpkinville, as the village was then called, had become a highlight for travelers on that route. (Mother took the time to say although the sign by the tavern indicated the town was Pumpkinville, in real life the town was actually called "Punkinville," since that is the way everyone there pronounced it.)

Sometime after the Revolutionary War was over, she went on, General Lafayette, who had been with my great-great-grandfather Thomas Nelson (the one who signed the Declaration) when the British surrendered, decided he wanted to see more of Virginia. One evening in these travels around Virginia, Lafayette came to Pumpkinville, and decided to dine at the tavern there.

When the famous French marquis had finished his dinner and was preparing to leave, he looked around the dining room at all the women waiting on tables there and was heard to comment to the innkeeper, "I hadn't known that there were so many beautiful women anywhere in the world except in Paris."

After Lafayette left the tavern, one of the waitresses who had overheard the remark and was naturally flattered, asked the innkeeper where was that place Paris that the General had talked about that had all those other beautiful women. The innkeeper explained that it was Paris, the capital of France, to which Lafayette had referred.

And some short time later, my mother said, the sign that had read "Pumpkinville" was removed, and instead there on the road right outside the tavern, there was an official sign that read "Paris France." If you had a friend who lived there then and you wanted to send her a letter, you had to put down her address as "Paris France, Virginia."

Sadly, a few years ago, Mother went on, a huge old tanker truck crashed into the tavern, wrecking it and at the same time the truck hit and destroyed the sign marking the name of the town. When a new sign was put up, the word "France" had been left off. And now as you see, the little town is simply called "Paris." She gestured with her hands, sort of opening them both outwards, which indicates that that's that and there is nothing you can do about it. It's just simply called Paris now.

Middleburg would be our next town and Mother knew that I had promised my dear friend Jane McIlvaine, who had moved back there from Washington, that we would stop in briefly to see her. She was living alone in the big house which she had inherited from her parents while her husband, Bob, was on a battleship somewhere at sea. She wrote to him every day, and kept the letters in a cardboard box on her kitchen table. As soon as she heard from him and got his APO, she would mail them to him.

Jane and I had been dear friends for a long time and I had lived for a while in her house in Washington. I had always admired Jane for her warmth, her devotion to liberal causes, and her odd little invented phrases. As we came to Middleburg, I told Mother that Jane had suggested that Middleburg "was a little town of seething rest." We were both smiling at that as we approached the turn to her place.

Once in the driveway, I was surprised to see that the big double doors to the entrance to the house were both flung wide open. And on a cold winter day, I thought! And then I saw Jane rushing out of the house. She had nearly reached the car when I stopped. As I came to a halt I realized that tears were streaming down her face.

I leapt out and threw my arms around her. She coughed out some words and I finally understood her to say something about the Japanese and something I understood to be Pearl Harbor. And then she kept repeating. "They have bombed, they have bombed," and then she added, "the guts out of our ships at Pearl Harbor." By now Mother was out of the car and hugging Jane, who grabbed her hand and said that the radio was still on and for us to hurry in.

I followed and had actually gotten through the open front doors when I realized I hadn't turned the engine off. I ran to the car, turned the engine off, and when I got back to the house and walked into the living room, both Mother and Jane were sitting utterly still as if the words coming out of the machine on the table had frozen them into immobility. Even their eyes were still. Now I had to interrupt the announcer. "And Bob?" I asked, trying not to sound too frantic. She actually smiled. "No, thank God, he is somewhere with the Atlantic fleet or in the Mediterranean."

I threw my arms around her and we all seemed to unfreeze a little. "I had planned tea for you," Jane said, "but I've got a more appropriate idea." She left the room hurriedly and returned nearly immediately with a tray on which there was a bottle of bourbon, three glasses, a bucket of ice, and a small pitcher of water. Mother indicated she would have hers neat, I poured a little water in mine— after all, I was the driver—and Jane poured herself a nice slug of whiskey over some ice.

Later Jane produced some fruit and cheese and crackers and I don't remember if any of us ate anything. We just sat there, listening to a voice which kept repeating the deadly story over and over. His voice now took on a sing-song quality as if the news he was telling had drained him of any emotion.

We sat in the dark for a few minutes before we realized that night had fallen. Jane turned on the lights in the room and then I noticed how pale we all looked. As Nannie and I prepared to leave, I tried to persuade Jane to come back to Washington and spend the night with me, but she declined. We said all the right things, I hoped, whatever they were, and it was probably nearly seven when Mother and I left. Anyway, by then it was pitch-dark.

In the car, we were speechless for quite a while and then I sensed that Mother was in a deep blue funk and I knew what she was thinking. "Oh, I wouldn't worry so much about that. With his asthma, the army wouldn't touch him with a ten foot pole. You know that, Mom."

I had figured correctly. She was concentrating on her beloved son, my brother Huidy, now at Harvard. She knew, as I did and as I am sure Rosalind and Nancy would agree, that Huidy would be signing up as soon as he could. He had talked about it before and now this Pearl Harbor tragedy surely means the US will go to war: Huidy will be hurrying to enlist.

I kept referring to his awful asthma but I don't think that helped her. A few miles further along the road, I thought I might get her mind off of the subject with a silly story. As we approached a hamlet called Lena—I couldn't see the sign but I knew the territory inti- mately—I asked her if she remembered what we used to call it when we were children and we drove past it.

Lena was significant because it had a huge wooden water tower next to an old barn right near the road. And once as we drove past, some child noted that the tower was off kilter, and that it actually looked like it was leaning.

"Yes, I remember," Mother said in a low voice

"OK. What did we call it then?"

She obviously wasn't being diverted from her main stream of thought but she tried to sound a little perkier. "You kids called it the Lena Tower of Pisa after that."

"I've got one better," I said. She didn't suggest that I go on. But I did.

"A couple of years ago," I said, "I was with an old pal, driving to Upperville to a wedding there, and when we passed Lena I looked for our friendly family symbol and I swear to God our old water tower was leaking badly. In fact, water was gushing out. So I told my friend all our old bad puns about the water tower but now, I said from now on, I am forever going to call it the Pissing Tower of Lena."

I looked to see if I could catch a scintilla of a smile on Nannie's face, but it was too dark to tell.

After a second or so she turned to me. "God," she said, "I'm not just thinking of Huidy but I'm thinking that this tragic attack is going to wreak havoc on so many American lives. Though the broadcaster never gave us any figures on the lives lost, they must have been appalling, don't you think?" she asked. "And now so many of our young men will be signing up to join the Navy." She paused and added, "Or the Army or the Air Force." Then she quietly went on, "So many people will be dying." I could not hear her sniffling, but I could hear her opening her pocketbook and even in the dark I could see her dabbing at her eyes with her handkerchief.

I didn't answer but I thought that the little doggerel about the mackerel sky had been right on the button. "Starts with a smile, Ends with a cry."

The Attack

The Japanese attack on Pearl Harbor had been devastating to our Navy. The ghastly details came out in the next few days; it seemed especially gruesome learning about the details of disaster on a newspaper, as I did, because it overwhelmed every single section of the publication. Obviously we didn't publish the funnies that day, nor the Advice to the Lovelorn, nor any ads. "Pearl Harbor," as it would simply be called from now on, saturated the news.

Nearly a quarter of our ships had been destroyed. The number of sailors who had perished was a sickening 2,400. Of those, nearly 1,600 had been drowned when the battleship *Oklahoma* had been torpedoed and capsized. On the other hand, the Japanese lost only twenty-eight planes at Pearl Harbor and three submarines. And midget subs at that, I learned, and could even snicker at that irony.

There was, however, one piece of luck for the US. Three of our Pacific Fleet aircraft carriers avoided the rain of destruction. Instead of being in port that fateful day, they were out in the wide Pacific Ocean on training maneuvers.

If my newspaper and the others were drenched with reporting about the attack, radio reporters talked of nothing, it seems, except Pearl Harbor and the other US areas which were also hit. The Japanese had laid waste to the Philippines (a protectorate of the US) with both our naval and our military installations spread around that little country. Every airplane at Hickam field in Manila had been lined up wingtip to wingtip, making them exquisite targets for Japanese bombers. I wondered at the time how General MacArthur, in charge of the Philippines, could have allowed those planes to remain there like sitting ducks when he must have already heard about the attack on Pearl Harbor, but no one else seemed to wonder about the same problem. I was not exactly in a position to publicly question General MacArthur, so I wondered alone. Scores of American troops and hundreds of local civilians were killed in the Philippines. Further, hundreds were captured and held in dreadful circumstances by the invading Japanese. Guam, also a protectorate of the US, suffered the wrath of the Japanese, with many of the US naval and land bases there destroyed.

The day following the Japanese attack, President Roosevelt, in his war message to Congress, said that December 7, 1941 was "a date which will live in infamy." Congress declared war on Japan, with only one dissenting vote, cast by Representative Jeanette Rankin of Montana as she had done in 1917. On December 11, Germany and Italy declared war on the United States.

Mason Peters remarked to me that he felt that there was an atmosphere in the air of unity he had only felt before in the earliest days of the Depression. There was no question, he suggested, but that Pearl Harbor had relieved us of any "half-assed" acceptance of war. Now the entire country was welded with a single-minded togetherness. There was now only one objective in mind.

***

Less than one month after Pearl Harbor, surveying a war that had spread over nearly the whole earth, President Roosevelt began to think about implementing a vague idea that had been kicking around among

some American foreign affairs experts: to create a more formal structure to bind together all the countries fighting against the Axis powers.
On January 1, 1942, joined by the Soviet and Chinese ambassadors,
Churchill and Roosevelt signed a pact in which they promised to fight
against the Axis with all their power and pledged that none would sign
a separate peace. The next day the representatives of the twenty-two
other nations fighting the Axis joined in this creative and sweeping declaration.

Naturally my paper, like every other one in Washington, was
totally concentrated on this extraordinary conglomeration of world
leaders. Every reporter was looking for "angles" or unusual stories. All
photographers were assigned to getting pictures of the distinguished
politicians gathered here for world-shaking news. Indeed, one day for
a brief period there seemed to be no one at the paper except a couple
of rewrite characters and Cissy Patterson and me.

So far there had been no decision on what to call this bold new
undertaking but the evening that twenty-six nations had agreed on
a common goal, Roosevelt decided that he had the perfect title. He
figured it should be called the United Nations.

He was so pleased with his idea that early the next morning he
had himself wheeled into quarters in the White House which had
been turned over to the visiting Prime Minister of England. The President opened the door to find Churchill just emerging from his bath.
Roosevelt started to retreat but Churchill beckoned him back. "Come
in," he called out. "The Prime Minister of Great Britain has nothing
to hide from the President of the United States."

Churchill is said to have later pointed out that that story was not
entirely true. First, he said, that he was wearing a towel when the President came to his rooms, and second, the Prime Minister of England
does have things to hide from the President of the United States.

* * *

Frank Waldrop and I used to have ranging conversations about whatever struck our fancies and we fell to talking about the profound
implications of Churchill's visit: these two extraordinary men were
now locked together as world leaders with much of the fate of the
war in their hands. We discussed what we knew of the first time they
had met. That had been nearly a quarter of a century ago, in London
in 1918. Franklin Delano Roosevelt, then Assistant Secretary of the
Navy, was in England to inspect American naval facilities there, and
Churchill was Secretary of War in the British Cabinet.

We had no clue as to what they had thought of each other, but Frank pointed out that as early as 1933 Churchill had expressed his admiration for FDR when the American president was inventing new initiatives to cope with the deepening depression. Churchill said that Roosevelt was leading the greatest crusade of modern times.

I had picked up another little historical tidbit. I one-upped Frank with it. I told him I had read that Churchill had gone on to pay Roosevelt what I considered the greatest accolade that Churchill, with his vaunted affection for alcoholic beverages, could dream up: he had said that the effect of FDR's leadership during the Depression was like the "uncorking of your first bottle of champagne."

Now, Frank said, what FDR had to uncork in 1941 was the total energy of this country to wage war. Whatever isolationist zeal there had been before Pearl Harbor had dissipated into thin air, thanks to the Japanese themselves. Instead the outrage over Pearl Harbor had morphed into some kind of a glue that made Americans stick together with one single objective: win the war.

One pundit wrote that the President had invited Churchill to visit, but such an invitation wasn't necessary. Immediately after he learned about the attack on Pearl Harbor, Winston Churchill had set out in a battleship in the wintry stormy seas to join his new brother-in-arms. On arrival in Washington, he was invited to stay at the White House and the two leaders of the free world and their advisers could make plans for the defeat of their formidable enemies in this widening world war.

Churchill was invited to address a special session of Congress. He would return to Washington two more times in the course of the war and each time he was invited to address the US Congress.

On his visit right after Pearl Harbor, he opened his speech to this special session of Congress with the quixotic suggestion that if the countries of his parents' births had been reversed—that is, he explained, if his father had been American and his mother had been British—he might have gotten there on his own! That was greeted with gentle laughter.

Then Churchill threw the book at the ruthless people that had made the sneak attack on Pearl Harbor and he spoke passionately of the absolute certainty that the United States and Great Britain, in their abiding close relationship, together would defeat the Japanese.

He closed by asking in a vehement voice, "What do those people think we are made of?" His audience seemed to answer his question. They clapped enthusiastically and cheered loudly.

***

Another one of the times Churchill was in the US, he surprised both President Roosevelt and Eleanor Roosevelt by his odd range of knowledge. The Roosevelts were taking him to the country place in the Catoctin Mountains in Maryland, about eighty-two miles north of Washington, which was an unspoiled recreation spot for the President.

The complex of small houses had been built in 1932 by the Works Progress Administration and it was now a Naval and Marine Support facility. Roosevelt decided to use it occasionally as a weekend retreat. A great admirer of the book by an English writer about an earthly paradise called *Shangri La* in the Himalayan Mountains, Roosevelt decided to call that lovely simple space in the Catoctin Mountains, Shangri La. President Eisenhower, less romantic than President Roosevelt, later changed the name to Camp David to honor his grandson of that name.

As the President and Mrs Roosevelt and their British guest were on their way to Shangri La, they passed near a town called Frederick, where Churchill noted a sign advertising Barbara Fritchie Candy.

"Barbara Fritchie!" he called out excitedly. The President explained to Churchill that she was the heroine of a poem about the Civil War that all American schoolchildren learned in the past. He remarked that he could only remember one stanza of the quaint old poem: "'Shoot if you must the old grey head,'" he quoted, "'but spare the country's flag,' she said." He went on to say that the long unsophisticated ballad had been written by a Lincoln admirer, John Greenlief Whittier, in the 1860s.

He had scarcely finished his comments when the Prime Minister of England started to recite the poem. He went on reciting *Barbara Frietchie* until nearly the end of their trip. He did so loud and clear, with great Churchill gusto, all the way, to the utter amazement of his host and hostess. Actually he had just finished his startling recitation when they reached the Shangri La complex.

I learned this tale about Churchill's recitation of the long, unsophisticated ballad from a friend in the Navy stationed at Shangri La, whom I had known sometime since the past fall when he was in Washington. He had heard the tale from one of the aides who had been in the car with the visiting group. My Navy friend pointed out that from what he had heard about that drive to Shangri La that the PM had quoted the whole thing and he felt that it was all accurate, but he didn't know for sure.

I wondered then and I am still wondering now how in the world Churchill ever learned that poem. I couldn't imagine it ever turning up in a British school. (I do not think it has even been taught in American schools in the last fifty years or so.) Is it possible, I still wonder, that Jenny Jerome Churchill had learned it as a child growing up in Brooklyn and found it so fascinating that she had taught it to her son? "Not half likely," I say to myself in my best British accent. I guess we will never know.

And then I remember one more amusing thing my Navy friend who had been stationed at Shangri La told me, although it had nothing to do with Churchill and Barbara Fritchie. He said he had once read an official description of Shangri La and where there was a line that asked "Architectual style," the answer had been "Other."

Gargantuan Preparations for War

Shortly after the attack on Pearl Harbor, so many young American soldiers and sailors and airmen seemed to be sent immediately all over the place—against the Japanese in the Southwest Pacific and in the Philippines and against the Germans in the Mediterranean and North Africa. Immediately a legion of older men descended on Washington to run the immense number of programs organized to fight the spreading war. These men were largely the top bananas of the US industrial and corporate world, and since they were now paid a pittance of their fat peace-time salaries they were known as the Dollar-a-Year Men. Some of them had been friends of my sister Nancy and her husband Cokie, I saw them from time to time and in the course of my various ventures around Washington, I got to know others.

Now these men, with their broad backgrounds, would be in charge of cobbling together the countless organizations to run the gargantuan machinery of war. This would include the rationing of strategic materials and other irreplaceable commodities, among them rubber, gasoline, metals, sugar, and coffee. When Japanese silk was embargoed, there was a great dash by women to get the last silk stockings they would wear for a long time. Someone on my paper had said it was the biggest run ever in silk stockings!

Naturally many of the young men on the *Times Herald* volunteered and some were drafted. Cissy was conscientious about looking after the families of what she called "my servicemen" throughout the war. A brilliant young reporter named Chalmers (Chal) Roberts was hired to help

Mason Peters on the city desk with the added work that would fall on the paper with the outbreak of war. Both of them told Frank that they wanted me to work there, a prospect which delighted me.

I had promised Frank that before I actually left him I would find some other benighted soul that he could cower into servitude. Oddly enough one day as I was wondering who I could suggest for the job, I got a call from Kick Kennedy, who was in the family compound in Cape Cod. She reminded me that she had been busy doing volunteer work, but that her father had said she had to get a job that paid her some dough. He said it was high time she learned how to earn her own living. "And," she said, "he suggested I call you and see if you had any ideas for me."

"Ideas for you," I fairly shouted. I told her I was leaving Frank Waldrop's bed and board for the city desk. "You could do research for him. So come on down here, and come pronto, because he needs someone immediately, or sooner."

***

She arrived in Washington a few days later. I had already told Frank about this young friend of mine and had chatted her up to him. I did say that she hadn't had much working experience (actually she had none), but that she was alert and eager. I did not say she was Joe Kennedy's daughter, although it did not take Frank long to learn that after he met her and talked to her.

Anyway, he liked her immediately and told her she was to start work the day I moved to the city desk. A short while later Frank collared me. "Christ, what hath Page wrought," he asked me. "She can scarcely spell 'cat.'" He also mentioned that she was "incredibly naïve." But I could tell that he already liked her hugely. She was a hard worker and she learned fast, but as Frank told me confidentially once, she never could fulfill the job she was hired for. He said he was working harder than ever now that I had deserted him. In any case, as it turned out, Frank and Kick became lifelong friends.

A short while after Kick was hired, another young woman came to work on the paper. She, like me, had been an Arthur Krock recommendation. After he had finished a speech to a group in New York, Arthur told me, a beautiful woman came up to him and introduced herself. She told him she was studying at the Columbia School of Journalism (where, among other things, she was improving her English) and was interested in finding a job on a newspaper in Washington. Her name was Inga Arvad and she was from Denmark. She had worked on a paper in Berlin before coming to the US, she explained, and she wondered if he could help her. He said he would try.

He told Frank about her, mentioning again that she was beautiful and seemed competent with an adequate background in reporting. Frank suggested she come to Washington and talk to him. Arthur asked me if I could put her up for a few days, which I was happy to do. Frank offered Inga what he called "a provisional job." She was to interview various Washington personalities for a column to be called "Did You Happen to See?" for a week or so and then he would make a decision.

Her sample columns were lively and sometimes sprinkled with Danish proverbs, translated freely, and since her English was not letter-perfect, her writing occasionally had an amusing twist to it. I told her once that her English sounded like Mark Twain's German translation of *The Jumping Frog of Calaveras County* and then his retranslation of it back into English. Inga laughed, but I'm not sure she understood my convoluted comparison.

Aside from being extraordinarily pretty (she had once been Miss Denmark, she told us), Inga was ambitious and had a nimble mind. She was soon asked to continue writing her column. She stayed with me for a week or so and then got an apartment for herself.

Lobster Heaven

Cissy turned up in the city room nearly every morning, wearing either jodhpurs because she had just come in from riding or a pantsuit so simple that it was clear it had cost a fortune. The first day I started in the city room, I remember she was wearing one of the elegant pant-suits and she was accompanied by one of her nippy Standard poodles.

They intimidated me but didn't seem to have that effect on anyone else. Anyway, I was never anxious to try to pat one.

She ambled around in that inimitable walk of hers, checking up on what was cooking. Someone had once asked her how she had learned to move like that and she had answered in her husky voice that she couldn't help it. Her mother used to make her walk around the house when she was a child with heavy books balanced on her head.

Anyway, she was the only slow-moving creature on the paper. Mason Peters, the Byronesque city editor, with his long hair swept back from his handsome face, could not sit still. He jiggled his legs and tapped his fingers on his desk, always poised as if to pounce on a breaking story. There was a copy girl who was incapable of walking. She didn't even run. She darted.

Cissy waved and smiled "good luck" to me across the city room my first day on the city desk and then disappeared into her command post, her office. From there, it was her wont to pronounce that she expected a scoop a day. She wrote or suggested editorials and looked over pictures, layouts, and galleys. She emerged from her sacrosanct office frequently to roam around the engraving department or the composing room. She often cased the "morgue," where clippings and reference papers were filed. She was indeed, as one article about her had said, "a hands-on publisher."

I was delighted to be in the city room and liked the buzz that characterized it and the sense of friendly bantering. "Oh, you lucky girl," Mason said warmly, but with a playful edge, even before I had settled down in front of my designated typewriter. Guys could call a female a "girl" in those days with impunity. "Look at you," he continued. "Your first day here and you already get to interview the Lobster Lady."

He pointed to a woman who had just gotten off the elevator; he motioned for me to go over to her. I heard subdued friendly laughter as I picked up a pencil and some canary paper, which I folded three ways, as I knew reporters did. Someone said, "Sic 'em, Page." Chal Roberts called out quietly, but with a smile in his voice, "Congratulations."

I went over to a gray-haired, worried-looking woman and suggested we move to a vacant corner down the hall where we would have some privacy. As soon as we got there the woman pulled out a fat roll of paper from a stiff cardboard tube she was carrying. I noted as she unrolled the paper that it was exactly the size of a page in the newspaper. She handed it to me and watched me anxiously as I looked at the paper.

A drawing in heavy, dark ink of a lobster filled the entire page. In the lobster's claws were wooden pegs so that the claws were immobilized. Great tears rolled down the sad crustacean face and fell to the bottom of the drawing.

What the woman wanted, she explained to me, was for the *Times Herald* to reproduce this drawing in full, on the page opposite the editorial page. In other words, to devote the op-ed page entirely to the lobster and the tragic plight that obviously lay ahead for him: being boiled in a large pot.

Furthermore, along with the drawing of the lobster, she wanted editorials (she used the plural) to urge a law against such cruelty to one of God's creatures.

I thought about how Americans were fighting their way onto the Solomon Islands and New Guinea as they tried to island-hop over the watery miles between Pearl Harbor and Tokyo. I thought about the British troops fighting desperately in North Africa, where American troops would probably join them soon. The news from the Pacific and the Mediterranean was filled with stories of the bravery, and the deaths, of so many of our soldiers and sailors and pilots.

I told her gently that I was deeply sympathetic to the plight of the lobsters, but that I did not think that this was a propitious moment for the *Times Herald* to mount a campaign on their behalf.

She rolled the paper up again and gently put it back in the thick cardboard tube. She thanked me quietly as she rang for the elevator. I told her goodbye, but I felt she wasn't gone for keeps. I felt certain she would come back sometime. She had obviously already been there before.

Clearly some people seated at their desks in the city room expected some sort of a reaction from me. I looked at Mason and gave him a sweet "that was a smartass assignment" smile, and I sat down at my desk and wrote a few lines.

I wrote that when there are no more wars anywhere in the world, when everyone has enough to eat, when there is no poverty at all and there is justice for everyone on the planet, I am going to be the aggressive champion of an organization to fight to outlaw cruelty to lobsters. And that I would expect the *Times Herald* to carry the story of the founding of such an organization on the front page.

I handed it to Mason, sitting at his desk. He read it, grabbed my hand, squeezed it warmly, and looked up at me with wide gentle eyes. He folded the piece of paper I had given him and tucked it in a pocket of his giddy striped shirt.

The Battle of the Coral Sea

Abroad the war was growing more ferocious and abroad seemed to be everywhere. Our troops were engaged in desperate battles in North Africa, where they met sixty-two-ton Nazi tanks. Our valiant troops seesawed day to day between defeat and victory in the deserts of Egypt. Once again I thought, this is a helluva way to learn geography.

In the Pacific, however, we had gained a victory over the Japanese in the Battle of the Coral Sea, an arm of the Southwest Pacific on the watery route between California and Japan. This was the first time we had defeated a large contingent of the Imperial Japanese Navy and it was seen as a turning point in the Pacific war. The planes involved in this battle had come from the carriers of the contending navies. This gave the Battle of the Coral Sea the distinction of being the first sea battle that had been fought entirely by airplanes.

I knew that Frank Waldrop was planning a comprehensive article on the battle, so I went to see him in his office to tell him that I would like to help Irving Belt, in charge of the composing room, select the florets for his article. Florets are the little pieces of type which are used in articles especially by people who are nuts about type. They are set between paragraphs or sections of an article to indicate a slight change of subject or pace. I saw them as sort of a metaphor in type, and I found them fascinating.

Irving and I had become close friends. I think he liked me because he knew that I cared about typefaces and because I shared his admiration for Ernest Dowson's poetry. He was also a Swinburne freak.

Irving welcomed me enthusiastically on this occasion when I turned up to talk about florets. He produced a whole tray-full of the abstract little lead objects.

We plucked out one floret after the other and examined them. I seemed to admire several but finally I fell in love with one, which I thought seemed to embody the essence of the article Frank had in mind. Irving smiled and told me he knew why I'd selected that one and he agreed with me that this was the ideal one. It looked something like a small wave, or an airplane, or a sailboat, or even a bird in flight, perfect for all the elements of the Battle of the Coral Sea.

They looked wonderful in the article about the first sea battle which was fought entirely by airplanes that had come from aircraft carriers.

***

The US victory in the Battle of the Coral Sea was welcome especially after the heartbreaking news of the Death March in the Philippines. The American and Philippine troops captured in Manila on, and immediately after, the Pearl Harbor attack had been forced to march eighty-five miles in six days with only one meal a day (of rice) the whole time. The details of such atrocities, especially the information that an appalling number of troops had died in that march, were trickling into Washington.

Many young men I had known well were wounded or killed on one side of the world or the other. For a while I actually turned the plastic globe I had on a table by my desk to try to find a spot near where I had heard some friend had been killed, but I learned that using the globe didn't ease the sadness. Looking at the maps that appeared in the newspapers all the time, especially in my own paper was bad enough, but I settled on that rather than consulting my globe.

Personalities on the Paper

Women were now agitating for more roles in the war. Large numbers took the places of the men in the armed forces who had been factory workers. Rosie the Riveter became the wartime heroine in posters throughout the country. I was happy that the government was responding to the pressures coming from women and wrote a long article about the establishment of women's roles in the fighting forces. Eighteen thousand women were now attached to the Marine Corps. WAVES (Women Appointed for Volunteers Emergency Service) was organized as a reserve unit of the naval reserve and WACS (Women's Army Corps) was made a branch of the regular army.

Kick commented to me that she liked my articles and said that she, too, was getting anxious to join something related to the war. I knew she wasn't fixing on joining any entity as unglamorous as any of the new women's units. I asked her what she had in mind. She told me she was thinking of joining the Red Cross. "Maybe I can get back to England that way," she smiled. "Maybe even to London."

She had hinted to me sometime previously that there was a man in England in whom she was very interested named Billy Hartington. He would someday be the Duke of Devonshire, whose family had been major supporters of all things Protestant in England. Indeed, for generations the family had been fiercely anti-Catholic.

Kick had laughed when she told me that an English friend had written her and said she better get back to London because Billy was seeing a great deal of someone else. She asked if I would help her if she ever decided she wanted to try to join the Red Cross. I didn't have any idea of what she thought I could do to help but I told her that, of course, I'd be happy to do whatever she suggested. Then we drifted off to a discussion of the dreadful cost of the battles taking place seemingly everywhere.

***

The inmates of the small world of the city room at the *Times Herald*, as befits people aspiring to be reporters, had a healthy curiosity about the lives of all the other inmates on the paper. Of course, the most robust curiosity was in their love lives.

When it was obvious that something was going on between Kick Kennedy and a reporter named John White, tongues began wagging but what was going on did not appear to follow the hallowed fashion of such rapport. Kick and John seemed to argue endlessly, on company time, and from the gossip around and about the paper, the arguing went on their own time, too.

Mainly John seemed to be trying to get Kick to see less of what he considered her superficial friends and to persuade her to be more liberal in her interpretation of everything she had learned at her hidebound convent. Among the problems that the latter presented to John, was her rejection of his warm advances. In public, she resisted his kisses, even a kiss on the cheek, and rumor had it that she had told him she was determined to remain a virgin until her marriage, as the good nuns had taught her.

John White was proud of his sense of humor, and the story that was prattled around the coffee machine was that he had asked Kick to get a special dispensation from the Pope for him.

John was amusing, but more importantly, he was a keen observer and he wrote well. On the few occasions that he and I did a story together, we wrote creditable pieces and we enjoyed being together. At the same time, I was put off by his selectively odd clothes, his chopped-off hair, and his sandals. His general appearance seemed to me to be forced and I found it plainly silly, but I kept my opinion to myself.

He and Kick came to slapped-up suppers in my apartment a couple of times and despite their hassles, it was clear that they were deeply devoted. I just figured that they would go on, at least for a certain length of time, liking or loving each other, and that John had just reluctantly accepted that Kick would go on wearing her psychological chastity belt. I wondered if her affection for Billy Hartington interfered with any warmth she might otherwise have felt for John. Or if she was concerned about the dreadful Protestant-Catholic schism any relationship she and Billy would have, and therefore had decided she just wasn't going to grapple with that problem. In any event she seemed to have forgotten or given up on Billy, for the moment anyway.

Now there was another affair of a very different color which fascinated the inmates of the city desk, and that color was torrid. Indeed Inga Arvad's romance with Jack Kennedy, son of former ambassador Joseph Kennedy and sister of the *Times Herald*'s own Kick Kennedy, was very high on the Beaufort scale in the city room.

Indeed, Kick had predicted this infatuation. She was at my apartment a few days after she learned that Jack was to be stationed in Washington working for naval intelligence. There she announced that she knew the moment he and Inga met they would fall for each other "like a ton of bricks."

I ran across Jack and Inga from time to time, and when I saw them together I thought Kick had way underestimated the specific gravity of their mutual tumble. Jack always greeted me warmly as a casual old friend. I had never gotten to know him well, either in London or in Washington, although in Washington we had drifted sort of inadvertently out together for dinner once or twice, mostly from some cocktail party (probably at Eunice Kennedy's. She was now working in Washington too and had a house there). What I found most interesting about Jack was his off-beat, mocking humor and that he was a very nice person and indeed quite sweet, but somehow he seemed to be a "work in progress." In any case, we were casual friends. Besides, early in my days in Washington, I had met an especially engaging man working in the British embassy, and we were having a glorious time together.

At that time, although Jack looked healthy enough, he was quite thin and there was always buzz that it was some sort of illness that kept him just this side of scrawny. His broad smile looked too large for his thin face and indeed I once noted that his Navy uniform looked too big for his slender frame. When Inga stood beside Jack, with his angular lines and her obvious curves, I thought they looked like a figure eight next to an exclamation mark.

In any event, they always seemed happy together. Everything seemed to go along smoothly and smarmily with them until there were rumors that an adventurer named Wenner Gren, with whom Inga's present husband Paul Frejos (she had been married before, too, and was divorced from an Egyptian diplomat) was traveling somewhere in South America and was pro-Nazi. Then there were stories around the paper of Inga's anti-semitic remarks. (I never heard her say some of the things that some others on the paper attributed to her.) She had talked to Arthur Krock, according to what he told me, about her days in Berlin when she worked on a newspaper there and about the high-ranking Nazis she thought she should to get to know for her profession. I didn't get the impression that she was hiding any history of her life as a reporter in Germany.

Our paper had once published a copy of a newspaper clipping from some years ago, of Inga Arvad, looking her pretty self, with a caption underneath which said that Hermann Goering, the power behind the buildup of the Nazi air force, had appointed her to be the representative of Nazi interests in Denmark. This had seemed so ludicrous that no one paid it much attention. However, some months later I was in our clipping morgue, and one of the attendants there asked me if I wanted to see something interesting. When I said "natch," she produced a large newspaper clipping of Hitler, sitting in his private box overlooking the Olympics in Berlin in 1936, and among the people sitting in the box with him was our own Inga Arvad. As I filtered the amazing picture, a memory drifted into my head of Tyler Kent, the code clerk in our embassy in London who turned out to be a spy for the Nazis. I remembered what a shock this had been to me and indeed to all of us in the embassy.

I wandered upstairs and ran across Kick. I asked her in a quiet voice if it had ever occurred to her that Inga could possibly be a spy. I immediately realized I had made a stupid mistake. Kick looked at me aghast and suggested, in a breaking voice, that we go in and ask Frank what he thought. Frank asked us both to sit down and said that if Inga was free, he would ask her to come and join us. She came in shortly and Frank explained our conversation. She smiled wryly and said she heard the same question about herself all the time.

Frank said he wanted to take us to the FBI and see what that organization had to say about this. Inga surprised us when she said she would like that, because she hoped the FBI could give her sort of a stamp of approval. She had in mind the kind of approval some magazine gets from an organization in this country. That, she said, would stop this kind of talk. Frank immediately pointed out that the FBI doesn't do that. They just don't operate like that. We were all quiet for a while and I dared to hope then that that was the end of this stupid mistake of mine.

Instead Frank picked up the phone, dialed a number, and asked the person who answered the phone, whom he obviously knew, whether he could come over there and bring two young women with him. The answer Frank got was in the affirmative and he told Inga and me to get our purses and coats and come with him. He nabbed a taxi for us quickly.

Once at the FBI building we stopped at the main desk, where Frank dialed his friend and said we were on the way to his office. I do not now remember the name of the bland man to whom we were introduced, but Frank spelled our names out clearly as he introduced us. The man wrote the names down carefully, and passed them on to a young attendant at a small desk in the corner, who immediately left the room. Frank explained why we there, and he had scarcely finished when the attendant came back with two files. Neither Inga nor I were shown what, if anything, was in the files.

Frank left then and told Inga and me to take a taxi back to the office when we were finished, and said the paper would reimburse us for the fare. This seemed so irrelevant that I smiled, for the first time in hours.

Now the man, whose name I've happily managed to forget, asked each of us a barrage of questions, some of which seemed to me way afield from anything to do with espionage, or war, and little about our politics, and he kept putting notes in each of our files.

I guess we were there for around an hour when the man said we could go, and he politely escorted us to the front of the building. I had the dough for the taxi and when it deposited us at the paper, I tipped the driver very generously.

Inga and I straggled into Frank's office, where he offered to get us each a cup of coffee. I'd have far more preferred a drink, maybe with vodka in it, but Frank watched us drinking our coffee, and he said it made him happy to see us drinking together as if we were old friends.

At dinner that evening with John, I told him that I hoped this episode had taught me not to jump to conclusions on invalid evidence and, additionally, not to go around blurting out those inaccurate conclusions, especially if they implied disloyalty. John told me I should forgive myself, but he agreed with me that I hoped I had learned my lesson.

***

Kick told me sometime later that Jack had learned he was to be given a new assignment. He was to be sent to the naval base in Charleston, South Carolina. Kick said that Inga and Jack had decided that once this happened, they would break up. This surprised me since I had seen them so warmly together such a short time ago. Maybe, I thought, the rumors were true that Poppa Joe had convinced Jack that he and Inga should call it a day. In any event, Kick told me that Jack sounded "low and lonely" in his letters from his base in Charleston.

Shortly afterwards, Jack was sent elsewhere for training in the handling of PT boats, and I figured he was delighted since he said he had wanted to get assigned to sea duty. PT boats (the initials stood for Patrol Torpedoes) were small, fast boats which were used for sneak torpedo attacks against large Japanese surface ships. I figured this probably appealed to Jack's desire for derring-do.

***

Inga seemed listless, I thought, and sometime after Jack had left Washington, she left, too. She moved to New York, got a divorce from her husband Frejos, and married an old Danish friend named Nils Block, who was living in New York. The marriage turned out to be only a glancing one, for she divorced Block within six months.

One day Frank and I got to talking about the odd turn Inga's life had taken and what a shame it was that she was no longer writing. Her columns had been getting better and Frank and I both felt that what we had seen of her and Jack revealed that they were deeply devoted to each other. We wondered if they would try to get together again. Anyway, she dropped out of our orbit like a shooting star and I heard much later that she had married a former cowboy movie star and that they had had a son.

Frank also told me at that time that he had not heard much gossip about me and my "carnal life." He congratulated me for being so discreet. "Of course, it was easier for you because you picked someone who was not on the paper and had no connection with it," he added. "But I know that you and that mysterious Brit have been an item for a long time. I wouldn't want you to think that I'm not keeping my eagle eye on you, my friend," he said.

"Thanks a bunch, Frank," I threw over my shoulder as I walked out of his office, back to my desk in the city room. I hadn't even bothered to tell him that my English friend and I had broken up quite a while ago. I was glad that we were still friends, but he no longer made my heart flutter.

My Left Wing Friends

A lot of people who drifted into Washington during the war had other things on their agenda besides the war. One such was an old friend of mine named Jim Ryan. Jim was appropriately neurotic for someone brought up by a mother who dragged a child along from one lush European hotel to another on the grounds that in moving frequently she can escape the ignominy of her husband's rotating love affairs at home in the US. However, since the philanderer had inherited one of America's great fortunes, his flings were grist for all the gossip mills and as soon as Mrs. Ryan heard that he had acquired yet another new mistress, she moved to a new hotel, dragging young Jim and his sister along.

Anyway, whatever Jim Ryan's psyche had suffered in his childhood, as an adult he didn't have many more quirks than lots of other people I knew. We had met some years ago at a party in Baltimore and we had grown fond of each other on a nice platonic basis. He was intelligent, warm-hearted, and good company. Among his special interests was politics, especially what were known as progressive politics, and the people who espoused them. He was, for instance, a great supporter of Walter White, the current president of the NAACP, an organization which I admired hugely. I liked Jim for his sense of social justice, a deep concern of mine, as well as for his good company.

One day he called me from the "gross gray stone palace," his own description of the huge place that his late father had built in the mountains near Charlottesville, and which Jim had inherited. He said he was coming to Washington to see me and an old Air Force friend who had recently returned to Washington from years overseas. I didn't get a chance to meet his old Air Force friend but Jim said he would like me to meet an artist friend of his who was going to be in Washington in a few days.

The artist Jim wanted me to meet was Rockwell Kent, of whose work I was ignorant, so before the artist turned up Jim told me a little about his paintings. Kent's work hung in the Met, in the Art Institute in Chicago, and in countless other important museums around the country and some abroad, I learned.

Jim had with him some reproductions of Kent's seascapes and landscapes, and now I was beginning to share with Jim his infatuation with this artist. I was moved by what seemed to be Kent's feeling of reverence for nature and what Jim called Kent's celebration of life. I learned that Kent had other creative talents, including being a graphic artist. Among the books he had illustrated were a collection of Shakespeare's plays, *Moby Dick*, *Candide*, and *Leaves of Grass*.

I was already beguiled by Rockwell Kent before I met him and then I was immediately struck by what an odd couple he and Jim made. Jim looked unromantically soft, with glasses so thick that they exaggerated his pale blue eyes. I never understood how anyone with sight as bad as Jim's was able to get his pilot's license, but he was an avid and legal pilot. The army had rejected him, he once told me, and the army doctor who examined him had laughed and suggested that

Jim's eyesight was so terrible that he was more likely to shoot a buddy than an enemy.

Kent, on the other hand, had radiant eyes and he looked as if he could wrestle any enemy to the ground single-handed. He was also aggressively attractive. He had earned his living, at various times, as an architectural draftsman, a lobster fisherman, and a ship's carpenter, and he told diverting tales about his various lives.

Early on when the three of us were together, I learned that a tie that bound Jim and Rockwell together was their shared left wing political affinity. Rockwell Kent was an admirer of the Communists; whether he was a card-carrying member of the US Party I had no idea. Personally, that was never my cup of tea. As I explained to them archly, in a conversation about Russia, the closest I came to Marxism was to be a passionate admirer of a man named Marx, by which I meant Harpo Marx.

Jim and Rockwell and I spent several lively evenings together. We talked about the war endlessly, all rapt with admiration for the Soviets for their courage against the Germans. In the course of our evenings together we covered a lot of territory, and I commented once that we shared in an ironic indulgence during the time of war to be able to bemoan together the cruelty and tragedy of the worst war the world had ever suffered and to eat and drink happily and simply to enjoy each other's company.

He and Jim once made me tell some background about a story I was working on. I had been assigned to write about a group of Norwegian men, women, and children who had sailed from Nazi-occupied Norway to freedom in the US.

They had left in winter, in the dead of night with only the small number of lifeboats they could muster and an inadequate number of life preservers. They had left the only home they had ever known and had undergone ocean storms in the terrifying North Atlantic and various illnesses and diseases and had been on the brink of running entirely out of food. As they awaited clearance at Ellis Island in the shadow of the Statue of Liberty, where I met them, one woman told me that she would happily go over the whole trip again and again rather than face "living under the fear and darkness" of the Nazis. All the others I interviewed said, in pretty much her same words, that they would make the same choice.

I hoped that my profound admiration for their courage and their values came through in my long article. Jim and Rockwell said they liked it a lot and Rockwell said he particularly admired my way of mainly using quotes I got out of various people and let the drama of their adventure come out that way. "You never got in the way of this heroic tale."

At dinner, the evening before my friends were to leave Washington, to my great surprise and vast joy, Rockwell gave me a set of copies of all the prints in his Shakespeare book. They are bold and beautiful and I have kept them together intact, in their big original box, except for the delightful print of Orlando carving Rosalind's name in a tree. I gave that to my sister Rosalind.

It was lucky that Jim had the exquisite taste and sufficient money to buy so many of Rockwell Kent's magnificent paintings, which he had hanging in his huge house in Virginia and which I have seen and admired several times, because a large majority of the American artist's work left the country forever. Kent's work had been wildly popular during exhibits all over the USSR in his lifetime, and he left his own collection to the Russian people. He admired them extravagantly, not just for their courage during the Nazi siege of Leningrad, but for their politics as well. I surely shared his admiration for their courage, even if I never shared that last sentiment with him. Indeed, today there are more Rockwell Kent's paintings in the great museums of Russia than there are of any other American artist.

A Modern Art Gallery

I met another, far better known artist, some weeks after my last evening with Rockwell and Jim. He was an artist of a diametrically different type, and if Rockwell Kent had given me a collection of the prints of his Shakespeare book, all this other artist gave me was the willies. At least that was my first reaction on meeting Salvador Dalí one morning as I was headed off to work.

I couldn't stop staring at the great, long, up-curled, waxed mustache and the dark eyebrows which were curving in the exact reverse of his mustaches, on a smaller scale. These two outstanding features seemed to be in some kind of a yin-yang relationship.

I knew immediately that he was the famous Spanish painter Salvador Dalí because Caresse Crosby, the woman who had just opened a modern art gallery on the ground floor of my lovely old apartment building, had told me sometime before that he would be visiting. Indeed, no one could pretend not to recognize him. After all, that face had been on the cover of *TIME* magazine, famous as the painter of the super surrealist *Persistence of Memory*. So I said something bright like, "Hello, Mr. Dalí, welcome to Washington." I introduced myself and was wondering where I would go from there.

Fortunately Caresse came in at that moment. She apologized to Dalí for having kept him waiting and said she was glad that he and I had met as she unlocked the door to the gallery. I was already late on my way to my paper, so I bid them a hurried goodbye as I darted out of the building. I really was a little scared of the configurations on the great artist's face now that I had seen them in the flesh.

Caresse, I had learned some weeks before, was an American who had been living in Paris for years and had come back to the United States a while ago and lived in a house in Virginia near a little town called Bowling Green. She and I were introduced by the super in our building when she turned the first floor into an art gallery. In 1939, with the outbreak of war in Europe, Dalí and his wife Gala decided to leave France and were now staying at their friend Caresse's house in Virginia.

Caresse also had a tiny apartment near DuPont Circle, and she and I got together in the evenings every now and then for dinner. Caresse and I both liked to laugh and we enjoyed our rambling conversations. We also shared long sad stories about the war; especially terrible tales she heard about occupied Paris from friends who were able to send her postcards from her beloved sad old city.

She had a brilliant, disorderly mind and she lived in a dream world, I discovered, which she was hoping to translate into a real one. I gleaned a lot about her and her life just from being with her, and I learned more from a woman on the *Times Herald* who had once worked for a magazine in France.

For instance, I learned that in the 1920s Caresse, originally from Boston, and her second husband, Harry Crosby, had been among that enterprising cluster of American ex-pats living in Paris who were running hand-printing presses. Both of the Crosbys were also writers. Harry wrote avant-garde poetry and Caresse wrote about art. Their Black Swan Press printed some of their writing and dozens of books by other writers, among them those of their friends, including E.E. Cummings, James Joyce, and Kay Boyle.

The Crosbys also found plenty of time to devote to the madcap escapades that seemed obligatory to Americans living in Paris in those days, the people who Gertrude Stein had christened "The Lost Generation." But the Crosbys did it up browner than anybody else. Harry, always restless, now grew brazen, and then reckless. He also began to wildly fritter away the huge fortune he had inherited.

He went on a spree of *ad seriatim* mistresses. In 1929, his life and that of his current lover ended in a violent tragedy. Both were found shot to death in what was considered to be a double suicide, according to my friend on the paper who had lived in France.

Caresse soldiered on, trying to run the Black Swan Press by herself, but could not make a go of it. She published an art magazine for a while, but that, too, fell by the wayside. Bloody, but unbowed, she decided to come back to the United States and try her luck there. I met her just as she started what she would call the first modern art gallery in Washington. I gathered from her that she had married again after the tragic death of her husband, but this marriage did not last long. The house she had now in Bowling Green was part of her recent divorce settlement.

For a time, she flashed briefly across my life. Every now and then she would come by my apartment two floors above her gallery and we would drift out to dinner together, or I dropped by the gallery often after work if it was still open. I noted the paintings of young American artists there but I don't remember them at all or even recall the names of the painters. There were several Dalí paintings there, which seemed to out-Bosch Bosch, that are glued in my memory.

I saw Dalí once or twice more at the gallery. We greeted reasonably affably and his face had begun to grow on me, so to speak, and I was no longer alarmed by it. Anyway, he and Gala moved away from Caresse's to California and other parts of the US.

It was sometime after their departure that Caresse decided to close the little gallery at 1606 20th St. NW, Washington, DC. Ever in pursuit of her dream, she and a distinguished Washington lawyer left his wife and set out for Europe to establish an international peace organization that would seek a permanent end to war. She hoped to rent a castle (it had to be a castle, I figured) to house the new enterprise. It was to be somewhere in Europe not occupied by the Nazis, which offered some difficulty, I thought.

As I bid Caresse goodbye and wished her all luck possible and offered her my ecumenical blessing, she told me that her daughter, Polly—which had originally been Caresse's real name—would come to Washington someday and would bring Caresse's love to me with her. Unfortunately I never heard from her daughter, but I got a couple of cards from Caresse when she and her friend were somewhere in Portugal working on their peace-forever dream.

The more horrifying the war got, the more I wished that Caresse and her lover's dream had turned out to be a reality.

No Dice on my Project

As Washington, and the rest of the country, focused completely on winning the war, some people worried about the lack of attention to the social advances that the New Deal had accomplished in the US and the need for their continued support. Eleanor Roosevelt was among those troubled by this neglect, and she expressed her concern several times in her syndicated column *My Day*.

I shared her distress and was hugely admiring of her for using her prodigious influence to persuade leaders to continue to fight for the liberal issues that the New Deal had espoused. I discussed my anxiety about this with Mason Peters in one of our occasional chats together. He said that the war was totally engrossing the time of even the most committed liberals and that unfortunately not many people had the time to work on these pressing social problems now.

It was sometime in 1942 when I had finished reading one of Mrs. Roosevelt's columns that I began to think that Joe Kennedy might be persuaded that he could play an important role in solving some of the domestic problems that had fallen by the wayside in our concentration on the war. It was patently clear he wasn't going to be offered any job to help in the war effort. Indeed I had gotten a letter from him sometime during the summer, in which he had expressed his bitter disappointment at not having had a word from the President after he (Joe) had written offering to serve in whatever capacity the President might suggest. Joe had ended his note to me by saying that it would be nice to have a chance to talk with me.

On the strength of that, I telephoned him and told him I was calling with a great idea for him. He said he'd be listening eagerly. He should gather together some of the brightest people he knew, I told him, ones that weren't working directly in war jobs, and set up an organization to do something positive about the squalor in the inner cities in the US. His organization could start with slum clearance in Boston, I proposed.

Begin by improving the appalling housing there and make that an example of what could be accomplished in other inner cities around the country, I suggested. And since I had boned up on the problem in preparation for this talk with him, I quoted a line from the famous reformer Jacob Riis, who said "the slum is a measure of civilization."

I thought that would impress Joe, and I added that I was sure he felt the same way. I stressed that, aside from the crying need for such a project, it would certainly burnish his reputation to work for a noble undertaking like this. With his drive and ingenuity, there's nothing we couldn't accomplish.

He had listened attentively that far and then I heard him laugh gently. He said he was certainly flattered to think that I believed that he could accomplish such a goal as that, or even make a dent in those devastating problems. And whatever else he said, I realized, I had definitely not sold him on my slum clearance idea.

We talked a little more about one thing and another. He wanted to know how everything was going for me. When I hung up the phone I remember thinking that I had been silly to think he'd go for such an idea as I had suggested. And besides, at this juncture, I guessed he was probably concentrating exclusively on doing whatever he could to advance young Joe's career so he would be poised for a glowing political career as soon as the war was over.

Indeed, Poppa Joe had already tried hard in London to peddle Joe Jr.'s political future. He had talked to various people about Joe's brilliant writing and his evaluations of numerous events taking place in various parts of Europe, especially young Joe's report from Madrid as Franco was winning the war in the spring of 1939.

Since then, Joe Jr. had already officially dipped his toes into the big river of national politics in the US. While at Harvard Law School he had been elected a delegate to the Democratic Convention in 1940, where he had acquitted himself well. Many of Big Joe's friends reported favorably on young's Joe's performance there. And furthermore, unbiased people, too, had been impressed that young Joe stuck to his guns even when his position was not entirely popular.

After leaving Harvard, Joe enlisted in the US Navy. Now he was back in England flying US bombers across the Channel. In that happy day when the war was over, young Joe would have a brilliant political future ahead of him, and the sky was the limit as far as his father was concerned.

My instinct told me that Joe Sr., acutely aware that he had wrecked any chances he might ever have had to be the first Catholic president of the United States, felt that, by God, Joe Jr. could make it.

Part Four

A Rose is a Rose is a Rose

"A Rose is a Rose is a Rose."

-GERTRUDE STEIN

Picnic at Lovers' Leap

One late summer weekend, my grandmother, whom I was visiting at her lovely old house in the Shenandoah Valley, reminded me that I had been invited to a picnic at Lovers' Leap Sunday afternoon. It was overcast that morning so I decided to renege on the picnic, but then I changed my mind. Thank God, I thought afterward, that I hadn't let a little wisp of fog keep me from that particular picnic.

Danny would see that I had a fine lunch in a paper bag to take with me and I told her I would drive back to Washington directly from the picnic. I was very prudent about using my gas ration so that I could afford to get off on a jaunt like this every now and then.

The picnic site was a huge slab of rock that juts out high over a narrow strip of land alongside the Shenandoah River. It was named for an old legend: many years ago a young Indian brave from one tribe fell in love with a beautiful Indian maiden from another tribe. Now it happened that these two tribes were at war with each other and the honor of each tribe prohibited inter-tribal relationships. Montague and Capulet all over again, I thought when I had first heard the story.

Faced with the cruel destiny that they could never see each other again, the young lovers made a heretical decision to defy their tribal taboos. One evening they met at this huge slab of outcropping rock, that had no name at that time. They locked themselves tight in each other's arms, ran down to the rock's edge and leaped to their deaths. I hope there was a big bright moon for the young lovers that night. Maybe there were young bats flying around that hapless night; I hoped so, since some Indians believe bats are a harbinger of eternal love.

On previous evening visits there at dusk I had often seen little bats around that area, but little bats don't tell tales, so we will never know if there was moonlight for the young Indian lovers.

***

By the time I got to Lover's Leap that morning, the fog had dispersed and the sun was beginning to come through as I drove up to our picnic site. I was happy that I had decided to come and I had nearly forgotten the sad origin of the name of our meeting place. There were ten or twelve people gathered by the rock when I arrived. There were more women than men, as at most gatherings now, since the men were away in one war zone or another. That was not true in Washington, since it was awash with the Dollar-a-Year Men and the others working in the mostly-improvised buildings that housed the vastly growing army of civilians organizing the war machine.

At the picnic site, I knew everyone except one young man, a lieutenant in a summer Air Force uniform. The stranger looked vaguely familiar to me. He came over immediately and said something about how wonderful it was to see me again and how sorry he was that we hadn't seen each other for such a long time. I finally figured out he was the younger brother of two women I knew and that I had seen him last with them four or five years ago.

I remembered that I had thought then that when he grew up he was going to be extraordinarily attractive. And now I was thinking to myself how prescient I had been. It wasn't just that he was smashingly good-looking. Beneath that mop of curly hair, he had a remarkably sweet expression, especially appealing, I thought, on a strong face.

He smiled a warm smile and asked if he could sit with me at lunchtime. I told him I would be delighted and that I would go and reserve a table. He held out his hand to take my bag of picnic fare and said he would bring it. He had to give a message to someone and would join me in a couple of minutes. I set off to find a place for our luncheon party.

There is a glorious view from the rock although it is not possible to actually see the river from there. You just know that somewhere below the overhang of the huge rock, the Shenandoah flows past.

I chose a spot that seemed to be especially glinting in mica schist, that silvery-looking grain from certain rocks. I sat down at what I considered a sparkly table for two and surveyed the peaceful scene. In the near view, across the river, was a soft looking meadow where a dozen or so Holstein cows were grazing. I figured some people were going to have delicious milk this evening. Over to the left a large field of ripe wheat, golden-brown in the still-bright autumn light, swayed in a gentle breeze. It was probably going to be cut soon, but I figured the voles and mice would have plenty of cover in the stubble after the blades had gone through, and there would plenty of grain left for them to eat.

As a backdrop to all of this rose the Blue Ridge Mountains, reddish blue in the distance. I was moved by the sense of harmony that the landscape evoked and was surprised that it had struck such a tender cord in me. Indeed I was so absorbed that I hadn't realized that my new friend, Frazer Dougherty, had sat down beside me.

He placed our two picnic bags in front of us and carefully tore each bag down its sides and splayed them out flat as if they were plates, with all our food thereon. He put our paper napkins by each plate. He put my napkin by his plate and his by my plate, I noted with amusement.

We fell into easy conversation. We already knew some salient facts about each other so we didn't have to start from scratch. For instance, our families knew each other. My family on my mother's side had been in the county forever and though we lived in Maryland now and visited only seldom nowadays, it was still "home" to all of us.

The Doughertys (pronounced Dockerty) had moved to Clarke County some thirty years ago. The rumor was that Maria Dougherty, doyenne of the family, had moved the family from the Philadelphia countryside to Virginia because she thought there would be fewer fetching women there to beguile her husband Graham. There weren't.

Anyway they were a nice, proper family with all the credentials to fit into conventional county life. All in all the family was a welcome addition to the community. Maria was engaged in all the constructive works of the area, including especially the Red Cross. Graham became Master of the Blue Ridge Foxhounds, an estimable role in a fox-hunting community that patterned itself in many ways on the same kind of life that country conservatives in England practiced. He was a committed farmer, that is a committed "gentleman farmer" and a pillar of the local National Guard. If books were not a major interest in their lives, that lacuna was not a social problem. There were also four delightful children in the family, two pretty girls and two handsome boys, one of them, this charming young man sitting beside me.

After Pearl Harbor, I learned from my companion, he had signed up to join the army and thus forego the scholarship he had been offered to Cornell College. He had been stationed at an air base in Texas learning how to fly small military planes and would soon be transferred to a base in Columbia, South Carolina, where he would be trained to fly B-25s, which is what he really wanted to do all along. He suggested that when he was stationed there, he would be able to come to see me in Washington frequently. I assured him that I would look forward to that.

It seemed to me that he talked about flying generally in an impressionistic fashion and that he had been thinking about it for a long time. I was amazed that he knew that my father had bought an airplane for his company so many years ago; he said that he admired my father's early sense of innovation. I told him about my excitement at flying in that plane when I was five or six years old. He was amused by my tale of guiding "Wrong Way Corrigan" around London after the fey pilot had flown the Atlantic in a Curtis Robin like my father had had.

He was curious about my life in London and about stories I was writing for the paper. From our general conversation and the range of questions he asked, it was clear that he had broken out of the conventional family traces. I don't remember what he asked that elicited from me the information that there was no special man in my life at that time.

Our chat rambled on until I suddenly realized that I should have to leave immediately in order to be home in time for a supper date. He asked for my telephone number and I gave him my number at home and my number at the office. He smiled and said he would call soon. I chided him that he hadn't even written them down. "I'll call you," he said.

He picked up our picnic trash and I took one last look at the countryside before we left Lovers' Leap. I turned to Frazer and asked him if he knew that years ago buffalo had roamed there. He smiled at me as if he was pleased to learn that, and especially, to learn it from me. And I thought about "flower fed buffalos."

I wondered what had made me think of that. It's the only line I know of a poem of Vachel Lindsay's and it struck me as an odd thing to suddenly spring to mind. Odd, largely, because it sounds so romantic. Frazer walked with me to my car.

My Favorite Washington Visitor

A few days later I got a call from Frazer, saying how much it had meant to him to see me and that he was trying to finagle a way to get to Washington. I told him I thought that sounded like a fine idea.

Sometime the next week he called to say he had the next weekend off and he would be getting to Washington early Saturday morning. I told him I would be delighted to see him, but as it turned out, one of those *SNAFU*s (Situation Normal All Fouled Up, though the fourth word is far more dramatic) the military seems to love to create. It had forced him to cancel his leave. He sounded even sadder than angry and I was surprised at how disappointed I was.

One day, a week or so later, he managed to spend a day in Washington. After a long leisurely lunch, I went with him to the bus station to see him off on his trip to his base. He held me very tight when he kissed me goodbye.

Within a day or two after that, I got a letter postmarked Columbia, South Carolina. Actually what I got was not a letter. The paper enclosed seemed to consist of various letters, all in upper case, penciled in square blocks that covered the page. I couldn't make any sense of the letters and then I figured that maybe Frazer was filling in letters in response to a test of some sort. Perhaps a Morse code test, I guessed. With that in mind, I looked more closely and saw that he had written the letters I LOVE YOU, not only once, but several times. I figured that whoever was giving the test would see that the student was writing away and that no one would notice what he was writing. The instructor probably just vaguely looked at the test. I hoped that Frazer got a good mark for it but I bet the instructor wasn't half as amused as I was.

Before I had answered that correspondence, I got a call from him. He said he had an odd proposition to make to me. He was going to be given a day of leave for some special family celebration. It was a special birthday of a grandmother or some such occasion. Anyway, he was going to be in Virginia the following Saturday, for the day only. He would not be able to stop off in Washington. Could I possibly meet him in Virginia? It was an awful lot to ask of me, but it would mean so much to him just to be able to see me and for us to be together, "even if surrounded by dozens of people?"

"Cripes," I said, "I'd have to take the bus down and back just for the day." I had used up my ration of gasoline. Then I asked him how he was getting there but before he even answered me, I said, "And of course you will have to take a bus, or buses, all the way back and forth and probably travel at night each way!" And I added that I was sorry I had even hesitated for a second.

We managed to be alone for a few minutes and we made the most of it. After we had said our miserable goodbyes, some kind friend attending the celebration drove me to the little town where I'd get my bus home. On the way to Washington that night I figured that Frazer and I together would have paid some twenty hours of bus time for our ten minutes alone there. Of course, I wrote him later that he had had to suffer the slings and arrows of outrageous Greyhound much longer than I had, but that I hoped he felt our brief time together was cheap at that price.

I guess he did think so because many telephone calls later, one Friday midday, he said he suddenly had a whole weekend of leave and was taking off immediately to be in Washington in time for late dinner. "I trust I find you free," he said as if he was in a Noel Coward play.

"As a bird," I responded joyously and immediately canceled a dinner date I had with a couple I knew.

Later I thought that my idea that I was free as a bird was not very appropriate. We were more like birds in a cage (gilded) because we never once left my apartment the entire weekend except for a few minutes Sunday morning to get milk for our coffee. And we had decided to get married, as early in the New Year as he could get leave.

The Price of All-Out War

1943 found the US forces still on the defensive: in the Pacific we were fighting a war horribly costly to us in lives, trying to dig the persistent Japanese out of the islands they seemed to have burrowed into for keeps. And were on the defensive also in North Africa where we seesawed back and forth between us and the German with their monstrous tanks.

But soon the remarkable power of our country, the vaunted energy of our citizens, our overwhelming equipment, and the rugged courage of our soldiers and pilots and sailors came into play, and a welcome change was taking place in the scales of the war: we were now on the offensive.

In the Pacific we were proving we could fight an amphibious war, a quality we had to master in order to advance on the route to Tokyo. The tables were turning, too, for our troops and those of the British in North Africa. Rommel and other defeated German generals were captured or else they fled to Germany.

My paper was among those which wrote glowingly that after three years of warfare in Africa, the Germans had lost more than half a million troops. We also added that they were among the best the Germans had.

But we also knew that we had lost many troops in the fierce battles. I was among the vast number of Americans who cringed when we realized the huge price we were paying for all-out war.

The Elastic Truth

At some point in my life I had invented a character called Lillian White. If someone invited me out and I didn't want to go, I certainly couldn't just bluntly tell my kind inviter that I did not want to go. So I invented my Little White lie and said that I was sorry I couldn't do whatever I had been invited to do because I had previously promised my friend Lillian White that I would have dinner, or whatever fit the bill, with her that night.

However, when I went to the Red Cross with Kick my answer to questions about her attitude to her Red Cross job was much bigger than a Lillian White lie.

I had figured Kick had forgotten about her Red Cross idea because months had gone by and she had not talked about it since our first conversation. So I was surprised when she reminded me that I had previously said I would go with her for her Red Cross interview and vouch for her. She explained that she had heard again from a friend in London who said that Billy Hartington (the future Duke of Devonshire and the young man to whom Kick had been so close) was seeing too much of a young woman in London. "He still misses you terribly," her friend told her, and the friend felt it was urgent that Kick get to London as soon as possible. I had no idea how much Kick had thought about the Protestant-Catholic brouhaha that might lie ahead. His family had been vocally and violently anti-Catholic for generations and still were. How would Billy and Kick resolve this ancient insane antagonism?

Now, Kick asked me, would I go with her for her first interview at the Red Cross? I told her I would do as I had promised. She looked at me directly and said that the person who would be questioning her had to be convinced that her sole motivation in wanting to go to England was that it was the country in which she had lived and learned to love.

In other words, there was no romantic reason for her to select England as the country in which she wanted to serve. I looked at Kick directly now and told her I knew that she wanted to go to England because she loved the country so much.

Without even crossing my fingers when asked *the question* at the Red Cross with Kick, I said there was no romantic interest behind Kick's desire to go to England to serve in the Red Cross.

Soon, to her joy, it was all set for her to go to work in a Red Cross canteen in England. Furthermore it was arranged that the canteen she would go to would be in London. It had been Joe Kennedy's idea originally for the Red Cross to set up canteens for American soldiers in England and now he gotten a pal of his to see that Kick was not plunked down in some canteen in the hinterlands. London was where she would be. She would be going through extensive training before setting off and she promised that she would come by to tell Mrs P. and Frank and me and others on the paper "goodbye" before she left for England.

She thanked me profusely for my help. She was highly excited and I was happy for her, and it was also true that she absolutely loved England. That was no Lillian White lie when I said that.

Who's the Lucky Bastard?

"Hey, Kick. Who's the lucky bastard? Do you know?" Frank Waldrop yelled to Kick Kennedy, as he saw her near the door to his office. She turned and started slowly in, but discovering me sitting there, she raced in.

She gave me a hug and said, "I've been looking for you all over to tell you that I'll be off in a week or so and I've wanted to give you a goodbye hug and to thank you again for your support. Are you free for me to take you to a farewell lunch?"

I told her that that would be great. Kick turned now and looked at Frank. "What's up, my friend? What's your problem?" she asked.

"I'll tell you what happened. Page came in to see me a few minutes ago and I simply asked her his name, and she looked at me as if she didn't know what I was talking about. So I told her that she had that tell-tale look, that glow all over. Thus I knew she was in love and all I wanted to know was, who was he? What's his name? It's not that English guy, is it? I don't think he's right for a permanent partner for her. What does this guy who's hooked her look like? How old is he? Does he have a wife or any other such impediment?"

Frank suggested other pertinent questions he had wanted me to answer and I simply let him go on for a bit longer before I opened up.

"Kick," I said, "I came in here a few minutes ago to tell Frank a deep, dark secret but before I could start to divulge it he attacked me like that."

Frank was looking amused. I went on, "I wanted to tell him and to tell you, too, that I am going to get married and I was just about to tell him the name of the man, when..."

"Kick, that's why I called you in. Do you know who this lucky bastard is?"

She turned to me, wide-eyed with excitement. "Oh, God. You and Frazer are going to get married!" And she threw her arms around me.

I told them that as soon as Frazer could wangle a few days of leave, I was going to make an honest man of him. I filled in more details about him, mainly for Frank's benefit since I knew that Kick had seen Frazer several times and therefore felt she knew him.

Frank expressed his approval but said he still didn't know much about this "Frazer Dougherty creature." He said that since Kick might be a little more objective than I was, perhaps she could supply some pertinent skinny. "I want more than the vital statistics," he said.

She looked at Frank and smiled broadly. "He is absolutely charming," she said. "I saw them dancing together in some joint here in town a couple of nights ago and it was clear they are wild about each other," She paused briefly. "He really is delightful, Frank, and you will like him a lot; further you will find he is one of the best-looking characters you've ever seen."

Frank was looking amused at the little scene playing before him when his phone rang. A split second after he had picked it up he said he would be there "immediately." Kick and I both knew who had called. It was Mrs. P. and Frank always responded with the same words to her. He gave me a running kind of hug as he dashed out. "Can't wait to hear more," he called as he fled the room.

Kick and I sat there quietly for a few seconds. Then she asked me what I figured was the earliest that Frazer could possibly get some leave. Probably toward the end of the month, I guessed. That meant she would have to miss the happy event because she probably would have already left, she said, looking sad.

***

When we met for lunch she hugged me again, warmly, saying that she really thought Frazer was "wonderful, so bright and real!" After we sat down she smiled and said, "You are both so very lucky to have found each other."

Then she looked at me with a puzzled expression. "But, you know," she said, talking slowly, "I had always thought that you were ambitious."

I decided to let that slide, and, in fact, didn't know how to respond to her comment. Anyway she had certainly spoken like a true Kennedy, I thought to myself.

Getting my Ducks in a Row

Mother rarely called me at the paper but she did one day in early March to say she had to talk to me and asked me to please come to see her right after I left work. She sounded worried, so I checked with my city desk bosses and they told me to finish whatever I was working on and to go see what my mother wanted.

She had gotten a letter from Huidy. He was "in the damned military hospital in Montgomery recovering from an asthma attack," he had reported. He made it plain that he was doing remarkably well and would probably be out of there in a few weeks. I suspected he was putting up a brave front, not only about his illness, but I knew that his real problem was that he was deeply worried that now his army career might be suddenly truncated. Frankly, I had been totally surprised that he had been able to get in the army when the vets saw his asthma record.

So Nannie and I went to Montgomery to visit him. After two days there we were assured that he was OK and that he would be headed home soon. Indeed we left at his insistence. His health was improving rapidly, but he already knew that he was being invited out of the army. He was even cooking up ideas of something else constructive he could do now, some kind of a job he could get that would help with the war effort.

There was a joyous letter from Frazer awaiting me when I got home. He was practically certain he could get time off toward the middle or end of March for us to get married. He called me before I had even had time to answer his letter to see how those dates sounded and said he could make it March 23 if I could, and that with luck, we might have nearly a week off together before we set up shop in Columbia, South Carolina. He was living on the base then but he'd find some kind of a place for us nearby.

I was overjoyed and told him I would start getting my ducks in a row since what we were talking about was only a few weeks away. And I had a lot of ducks, such as seeing if that date suited Danny because we wanted to get married at Long Branch. Any date would suit Mother; I'd check with other members of the family. Huidy would be well enough to join us by then, I figured.

And naturally I'd have to let my paper in on the definite date as soon as possible. Of course, they knew I was leaving and all purported to be heartbroken. It was going to be hard to leave my paper. I was feeling entirely at home on the city desk and further, there was the ironic fact that shortly before I met Frazer I had signed a contract with a publisher, which wanted me to write a book for them tentatively entitled "Washington Valkyrie." It was to be a series of essays on the general role of women in the US in wartime, with vignettes on special women in Washington who had important wartime jobs.

The editor there who had sought me out for this book figured I could do my regular work on the paper and write the book, too, and I had agreed to that. Not only that, I had gotten a small advance from the publisher. Now, I had to let the editor there know immediately that I was not going to do the book after all, and I figured I had to return the advance, too.

Frazer knew all this. I was just telling him in one of our extended telephone conversations all I had to do to get organized for a forthcoming wedding. Anyway, I had to telephone the editor one afternoon and tell him I was reneging on my idea of the book. As it turned out, the editor called me the next day and said they were sorry I wasn't going to be able to write the book, since I wasn't going to be in Washington to do my research, but the publisher wanted me to keep the advance. I was surprised and delighted with that outcome and wrote the most gracious letter that I could in thanks.

Now I had to call the publisher of the slick New York magazine and tell him about my marriage plans, which meant that I would no longer be writing my Washington column for him. I had been moonlighting for about a year, writing a column about Washington in wartime and about personalities involved in various agencies that I had found colorful and interesting. The publisher, Harry Bull, had really liked my column and said a fair number of people had told him they thought it was unusual and that they found the people I wrote about, and the jobs they were doing, original and creative. One had said he had found my writing "vivid." I thought that was the veriest accolade.

Frazer was sorry that I had to give up that column, although I assured him that it had kept me jumping and working a lot of odd hours so not to worry about that. Then I told him I was having lunch with his mother the day after the next and I wondered if he would be in touch with her before that to tell her our news. "You go ahead and tell her, please," he said. "I think she would be especially happy to hear it from you. And I'm sure any date will be fine for her."

Since Maria Dougherty had been working several days a week at the National Red Cross Headquarters in Washington, she and I had lunch together occasionally. We always met in the dining room of the Mayflower Hotel.

As usual, after we had greeted each other cordially and sat down, Maria reminded the waiter that she would have her "usual tea," at which he nodded knowingly. I ordered a vodka martini on the rocks. Now I knew that instead of tea in Maria's teacup there would be a martini. While she was in her Red Cross uniform, a handsome enough suit of slate blue with some red trimmings and Red Cross insignia, she was not supposed to drink any booze in public. I had been startled by this ceremony the first time I met it and now I accepted it without even smiling.

While we sipped I told her that Frazer and I had set the date! She was genuinely delighted. She and I really liked each other, which made me happy. We had a cordial lunch and discussed plans for the wedding, sketchy as they were. She would invite everyone from her team, as I put it, and Nannie would invite everyone from ours. Then she and I drank a toast to the adventures that lay ahead for Frazer and me and to a victorious end to the war soon. I said that we would all be sorry that Big Graham, who was now stationed in London, wouldn't be here. We toasted him. As we tapped our vessels together, I thought that my martini glass and her teacup made a happy zing.

Stalingrad

And if I was thinking I'd dance barefoot on my wedding day, to play with Shakespeare's line, I was aware and deeply grieved at what was happening a world away, in Stalingrad.

There one of the bloodiest battles in all of the ghastly bloody history of warfare was taking place. For five months, one week and three days the gallant soldiers of Russia had fought off the Nazi forces, who were determined to take this stronghold of Stalingrad on the orders of Hitler. The fighting was now taking place building to building, with losses on both sides reaching astronomical figures. Finally the defenders of Stalingrad had the upper hand: the Axis forces had run out of ammunition and food. Now the Germans, and their cohorts, so rock-ribbed only a short while ago, were either starving or freezing to death.

When the German Sixth Army surrendered, it was the final turning point of the war in Russia: Hitler was compelled to admit defeat.

These estimated figures tell the heart-wringing tale: there were 850,000 Germans killed, wounded, or missing and 107,000 captured. There were 1,150,000 Russians, dead, missing, or wounded. Furthermore, 40,000 civilians had died, but Stalingrad was free.

Wedding at Long Branch

Frazer and I were married a month later, and half a world away. And as full of excitement as I was, the war and its agonies insinuated itself in little streaks off and on.

We wanted our wedding to be informal, as befits a wedding in wartime. For instance, my family had telephoned those we wanted to invite and Frazer's family did the same. But I would follow tradition and wear the dress my mother had worn when she and my father got married in 1914, four years before the US was in the war. Apparently the dozens of old Harvard friends of Daddy's at that wedding had whooped it up more than was absolutely necessary, according to tales passed down to the next generation. My wedding, perforce, would be quieter. No dozens of young men at a wartime wedding. And those there probably would not be drinking to the gills.

Following tradition, I would sashay down the magic three-floor circular staircase as Mother had done at her wedding and so had lots of ancestors and both Rosalind and Nancy had done at their weddings. Benjamin Latrobe, who had designed the graceful circular staircase, must have had brides in mind at the time. If you listened carefully enough, I thought, you could hear the rustle of dozens of taffeta trains of two centuries drifting down that lovely corkscrew of steps.

Furthermore, in another sop to tradition, I would wear the veil, although it had lost some of its original pristine whiteness, which Mother and other generations of family brides had worn. I figured that I too had lost some of my metaphorical pristine whiteness, so...

Another rite I would follow was to have an older man give the bride away. Since my beloved father was dead, I selected a dear friend of his and of Mother's, Vassar Pierce, for that role. "Uncle Vas." He and his lovely Danish wife, Aunt Dagmar, seemed to be close-woven into all of our lives and had visited us countless times when we lived in Maryland. He was the president of S.S. Pierce, a company started in Boston by his great grandfather in 1886, which sold elegant food to discerning people all over the world. I remember that the fancy canned foods were decorated with the store's own coat-of-arms in bright red. He himself was as simple as the veritable old shoe and indeed he had once said—granted it was after a couple of drinks—that he was nothing except "a little old green grocer."

So here we were, Uncle Vas and I at the very top of the circular staircase. I, all dolled up in my bridal finery, and him in an elegant dark blue suit. There we found relaxing things to giggle about as we awaited the arrival of the minister who was to marry Frazer and me.

This minister, who lived about twenty miles away, was a cousin. Nearly everyone I knew in the community was a cousin and indeed his last name was Nelson, like scores of other cousins. I had already explained to Uncle Vas that the minister, Cousin Bob Nelson, was famous for being late for most events at which he was to officiate, including funerals and weddings and baptisms. On the other hand, he apparently always got to the local baseball games on time.

We entertained ourselves by looking down at the arriving guests, all of whom seemed slightly foreshortened because of our distance above them. I noted the paucity of young men among the arrivals. Indeed a dear friend had told me the day before that she was having a problem bringing up her little boy because his father and all the other males in the family were away. She couldn't get him to stand up to pee since he had never had a model to copy. Once when the mailman had to deliver a package, she suggested to him that he must want to use the bathroom and invited him to take her little boy in with him.

From where I was standing I could see that Rosalind, at the bottom of the steps, was having a problem restraining Seabiscuit, her Springer spaniel (named after the famous race horse) who was trying to charge up the stairs to jump all over me. I couldn't find Nancy but I saw both of her little boys wandering happily around, poking each other warmly in the ribs now and then.

At the same time, I saw a small group of Washington friends arrive and saw some special friends from the *Times Herald*, including Cissy, whose luxuriant mop of red hair identified her immediately.

Brother Huidy had been delegated to wave to Uncle Vas and me, at the top of the stairs, the minute the minister was sighted. I suggested that because of all the fox-hunting folk that would be there, he could just yell "tally ho" up to us and that would be the signal for us to start down the stairs. We saw Huidy wave, and he smiled as we responded by waving back to him.

Uncle Vas looked at me and said, "Let's hit the trail." He gently placed my hand on his arm, bent at the elbow and we set off. As we rounded the first curve in the staircase, I could see that Aunt Charlotte was headed for the living room, where the piano had been cached for this occasion. It was generally kept in the library, still known as the "New Room," although that room had been transformed from a pergola into an additional room to house books some eighty years ago.

Aunt Charlotte was one of my great aunts, that is, one of Grandmother's sisters who had come on hard times and who lived permanently now at Long Branch. She played the piano with both gusto and skill. She and my friend, the glamorous New York harpist, Daphne Hellman, comprised the orchestra for this occasion. Daphne came to Long Branch a day early not only to tune, but further to string, the gilded harp that decorated the hallway at Long Branch. She was aided in this enterprise by a young Marine friend of mine, who said he had never laid eyes on a harp until pressed into this service. I guessed Daphne was the first person to play that harp in probably a half a century.

I could see her there at the bottom of the stairs, with her tawny hair nearly hiding that strong, beautiful face. She plucked some strings with a graceful sweep of her hand and out came the first notes of "Here Comes the Bride." I could hear the piano meld into the tune and now we had a duet. I was touched that these two people, both dear in my life, but so totally different from each other, were playing so joyously for me. I turned to Uncle Vas with a proud smile.

Now Uncle Vas and I took our last step from the staircase and we were on the floor of the great hallway. Frazer mesmerized beside us, looking wonderful in an elegant, tight-fitting jacket which his father had had made of some exotic material, strictly non-GI, and had worn during the First World War. The three of us started over to where Cousin Bob Nelson was standing, with the white scarf of Episcopal priesthood hanging lopsided around his shoulders.

For a few brief seconds, there was a third contribution to the music of the harp and the piano. Seabiscuit let out several howls. As Frazer and Uncle Vas and I came to the spot where the minister stood, open Bible in hand, the piano and the harp playing "Here Comes the Bride" ceased and Seabiscuit, too, out of some mysterious canine respect, stopped his singing.

The ceremony itself proceeded without mishap, although several people told me afterward that when Frazer was supposed to say, "With this ring I thee wed," it had sounded as if he said, "With this wing I thee wed." He didn't lisp so I don't know what he actually said.

Some of the language of the ceremony is imaginative and lovely but I didn't hold with the high-flown theological demands that were an essential part of the Christian charge. However, there are occasions, I feel, when one must just suspend disbelief. I don't think there was anything in the ritual where I promised to "obey" my husband. If so, I hope I had at least my fingers crossed.

I had an odd sensation the minute the ritual was over. It was as if all of us, the bride and groom, the families and friends, and even the dog, had all been bound "round" by a strong thread of ceremonial tension that kept everyone still and absolutely quiet except for the traditional words. And when they were over, the thread was broken and everyone was greeting everyone loudly and laughing loudly and gesticulating, yes, loudly.

Then we all had champagne and other drinks and gathered around the big dining room table, said "ooh" and "ahh" at the beauty and the size of the wedding cake, which Frazer cut with the Civil War sword I had discovered in the attic the day before, the blade of which I had cleaned vigorously lest it still have stains of blood thereon.

Everyone seemed to have a jolly time. Certainly Frazer and I did. Once, however, after talking to Nannie, I wondered to myself if my marrying a man who was going off to war had brought back to her memories of her husband, my father, going off to war. Of course, the circumstances were entirely different. When Daddy sailed to France in 1918, Mother was left to look after their three little girls all by herself and the youngest—that was me—was only a few days old.

I remember so much of my wedding day yet I have only one vague recollection of the flowers I carried. I have such a clear memory of all the flowers around the house and the great simple arrangements of flowers in the various niches than lined the curved walls of the staircase. I must have been carrying flowers, since brides always do. But the only time I recall my having flowers is when I threw a bouquet, as is the bridal custom, in the direction of a female guest.

I was standing on the staircase, I had walked up a few steps so I could see everyone better—and, frankly, so I could be better seen—the party was nearly over. There were several women with arms outstretched for the bouquet and I threw it deliberately to those of a cousin of whom I am very fond. She was thrilled to catch it, she told me afterwards. Some months later she and the young marine, of harp-stringing fame, were married. I have to conclude that the bouquet I tossed was my own.

After a couple of hours, I had changed into more commonplace clothes, though Frazer was still in his spiffy jacket, and we set off for a journey which would end up at the Air Force Base in Columbia, South Carolina in about a week.

When we escaped from the festivities at Long Branch we headed for Middleburg in our slightly beat up Ford, which I called Cousin Zukie for no good reason. We spent the night there and early the next morning set off to dawdle our way down the eastern coast ending up in Columbia. Our plot was to stop at whatever looked appealing to us en route.

Dawdling Our Way to Columbia

We stopped when we found pleasant places to stay and whenever we were at a beach someone had a radio gurgling away and we were forever hearing songs from *Oklahoma*, a sort of folk opera by Richard Rogers and Oscar Hammerstein. We especially enjoyed the song "People Will Say We Are in Love" and like thousands of other Americans we were enthusiastic about the story of the *Oklahoma* girl who fell in love with a cowboy. It was a charming and ideal story, set in the early part of the century, to beguile a country generally awash with stories about the war.

Americans were also going to more movies and reading more. Although I'm not certain that the books were a diversion from the horrors of war because there was now a spate of books about the war, written mainly by well-known war correspondents, which were selling very well.

But Frazer and I were now were nearly able to tune out any news that had to do with the war, so we could revel in the music from *Oklahoma*. Fortunately, the last big story about the war we had heard was a happy one for the US. A short while before our wedding, the papers and radios had been full of wildly welcome news: a huge convoy of Japanese ships had been sunk by American bombers somewhere off of New Guinea.

This was a welcome victory for the US, but for my part I figured that many of the American planes involved had been B-25s, the very kind that Frazer would be flying, and none of the reports I had heard or read had given the number of American planes lost. I tried to stuff cotton in my brain so I could stop it from thinking of such contingencies.

Two day before we were to leave Florida and head for the house near Frazer's base in Columbia, which he had rented by phone from Washington, I remembered that when I had last seen Kick Kennedy she had asked if we would get away for a trip before we went to the Columbia Air Base. I told her we would probably futz around in Florida, and she made me promise that if we were anywhere near Palm Beach we would go see her mother and father. She said that I always cheered her father up.

I knew we'd never get closer than we were now and suggested to Frazer that we should call them. Joe was delighted to hear from me and he asked if we could come to Palm Beach the next night and have dinner with them. We could gather at a hotel that had a restaurant he thought we would enjoy and that was north of Palm Beach, so we'd have a shorter drive than if we came all the way to their house.

It was a big intimidating hotel but the minute we walked in the door we saw Joe waiting for us and the hotel seemed cozier. He gave me a big hug and put his arm around me, telling Frazer how glad he was to meet him as he guided us to the dining room. Rose was already seated at our table. She was pleased, she said, to finally meet Frazer although she felt she knew him already because Kick had written them extolling him. I was amused at that comment because I knew Kick wrote to her mother and father constantly, telling him all kinds of news and gossip, as well as quite personal things about herself and her friends.

We had a delectable dinner. I was the only one who had a cocktail and wine, too, but I deserved it. I told Rose how great she looked, which indeed was true. I smiled at Joe and told him the same thing, but it wasn't quite as true. Despite his tan, he didn't look well, I thought, or was it was just that he couldn't hide his concern over his children? I knew he was worried that three of them were either in, or headed, toward a war zone. Kick was waiting for the cargo ship which would take her and the other Red Cross workers to England. Its departure had been postponed because there had been a flurry of German submarines around the south Atlantic, which had now been more of less dispersed. Joe Jr. was stationed in England, where he was flying bombers. Jack was somewhere in the Pacific commanding a PT boat. No wonder Joe had an anxious look, I thought.

I had noticed signs pointing to what looked like a large gambling casino as we came into the hotel. After we had finished dinner, and had a too-rich dessert and coffee, I asked Joe if Frazer and I could go in and play a few rounds of twenty-one. Joe said no one in military uniform was allowed to gamble in the hotel (or maybe in was a rule all over Florida) but, he went on, if I would like it, he and I could go in for a while Frazer and Rose could entertain each other. So off he and I went.

Joe was exceedingly patient as I played my cards and it seemed to take his mind off his worries to watch me try to win at twenty-one. He told me how pleased he was to see me happily married. He added that Frazer really was as delightful as Kick had said he was. Joe promised he would send my special love to Kick next time he wrote or talked to her. He said he would also report that I had lost about twenty-five dollars in the casino.

As Frazer and I left, thanking them for the delightful evening, they in turn thanked us for coming to see them. Rose said she had enjoyed hugely talking to Frazer, and Joe wished Frazer all good luck in the war. He added that he could see that even if I had lost in gambling, I certainly was lucky in love.

It was quite a trek to Columbia, but since we still had a couple of days before Frazer was due to report for training, we didn't rush along. We were happy as the proverbial larks on that last trip we would take together for a long, long time.

Cissy's View of the Wedding

On arriving at the funny little cottage in Columbia we had rented, we were pleased to find some mail awaiting us there: letters from our families, a couple of cards from friends, and a large envelope from Frank Waldrop.

He had written a note on an enclosure which said "read this first, before you look at the enclosed clippings." He wrote that Mrs. P. occasionally got carried away by romanticism and that had happened to her "big time" at our wedding. First, she thought we were a special couple, but further the atmosphere of the wedding had triggered some of the few cheery memories she had of her life in Poland. He said that it might have been the patina that age puts on everything, the Palladian style house, full of antiques from different periods obviously collected over generations, the exquisite staircase, the Corinthian columns in the hallway, or the ancestors looking down from the walls. "In your case painted by no one less than Gilbert Stuart," he said. "And the old relatives in their well-worn finery and unfashionable hats."

Frank went on to say that Mrs. P. herself had guided the *Times Herald* photographer as to which backgrounds and which people he should take. "And at her direction, the Sunday edition of the paper ran a two-page spread of your wedding," he wrote, "Now you can look."

***

And there really were two pages of pictures of the wedding. There was a not-very-good picture of the bride and groom standing near the wedding cake, a charming picture of my two little nephews guzzling the cake, an excellent photo of two old women sitting happily together, one of them my beloved grandmother, and both of them with warm, strong faces. There were lots of pictures of young people, mostly women sitting on the stairs, a picture of Daphne Hellman playing the harp, and others that filled a page.

But there was another page with a large photograph of Frazer and me, taken from behind us as we were leaning dreamily toward each other. I remembered it had been Frazer's suggestion that we escape outside to be alone together for a few seconds. The caption under the picture in the paper says we are taking a walk in the moonlight. Odd, I thought. I hadn't even noticed the moon that night.

Sure enough, there is a big silver moon overhead in that picture. Frank had another note attached to that page. "The moon," he wrote, "was invented by Mrs. P. and placed there in the photograph at her direction."

Perspective Gets Skewed in Wartime

After a brief period in Columbia, I realized that time takes on a totally new dimension when your country is at war, even to an innocent bystander, as I began to identify myself. There is a weird sense of time being foreshortened, an illusion of its compression. The journey seems to take on the perspective of Paolo Uccello's painting of horses in one of his battle scenes. A print of that painting hung in the hallway of our house in Maryland. Now, in Columbia, with Frazer getting ready to train for war, I felt I was looking at the world in a new way, as if someone had moved the vanishing point.

Maybe that's why relationships build so swiftly and surprisingly and remain so solid, too. In any case, Frazer and I made fast friends fast; indeed we became friends of the Bissells just a few days after we arrived in Columbia. Julia Bissell and I picked each other up in a ridiculously simple scenario. We were both reaching to a high shelf for a particular kind of marmalade in the local chain food store. It was the last jar left, it turned out. We laughed at each other, both insisting, Alphonse and Gaston style, that the other should have it. Then we decided that neither wanted it, and each picked another kind of marmalade.

Shortly after we walked away from the contended jar of sour orange marmalade, I asked her to come by our house that evening for a drink. She said if the invitation included her husband, they would be delighted to accept.

Our house in those days was originally a two-car garage. The owners of the main house had done a speedy job of converting it, aware of how easy it would be to rent with all the military bases so close by. There was not only the Columbia Air Base but Fort Jackson, and there were others nearby, whose names I have forgotten.

There was a mild problem in the bathroom of our little house. The tall, cylindrical water heater had been placed smack between the basin and the toilet, making it too close to each and since the heater had no insulation around it, we learned that in order to use either facility and not get seared in the process, you had to lean precariously away from the water heater.

There were, however, redeeming features to our abode. There was a wooden table in our yard. There were several chairs around it and it was under a great catalpa tree. Further the catalpa was now in full bloom.

Frazer, Julia Bissell, her husband Alfred, and I sat under the catalpa tree that evening. We had cheese and crackers and drinks. We chatted, laughed, and became friends. Alfred was a captain in charge of some paper work for the commanding officer of the Air Base. He had been a stockbroker or had some such cheerless job in Wilmington, Delaware where they lived. It didn't seem to have done him any permanent damage and he was now a lively and sometimes witty guy. His favorite writer was Saki and he was always game for a joke with a refreshing, positive view about life. Julie was extraordinarily pretty, with long brown-gold hair which she wore pinned back with a large tortoise shell hairpin and she had very green eyes.

She had an oblique kind of humor; she always told a story with an unusual slant. You were surprised when you smiled at it, and more surprised when you laughed.

They were fairly rich but not spoiled by it. In our conversations we heard about trips they had taken to various parts of the world and I put them fairly low on what I called my "Lazy Susan" measure of travelers. That was my idea of the kind of people who can travel all over the world as if they are traveling on a Lazy Susan. They stay at the same fancy hotels, eat at the chic restaurants, and see the same kinds of people they see at home and have the identical lackluster adventures. They just stay at the same level all the time. I figure that those types of people could have better stood in bed.

The saddest of these people on my Lazy Susan rating get a ten. Julia and Alfred were about a number three, if not lower on my scale.

***

They were good friends, but the people that I really doted on in my camp-follower days were two men training with Frazer to be B-25 pilots, Monk Adelman and Tom Finnegan.

Monk, who spent many evenings with us at our house, had been taking an engineering course at some New York City university and selling Venetian blinds in the evenings "in order to eat" before he joined the Air Force, he told us. He had a repertoire of tales about his odd customers. He insisted that the kind of people who order Venetian blinds at night are weirder than any other people. He said he could now walk down any street and see someone who looked like he would order Venetian blinds at night. Monk was swarthy, slightly husky with very dark eyes, with a vivid personality and an ebullient spirit.

Tom and his wife Bea and their red-headed son Rikki, who was six, lived on the Columbia Air Base. They were often at our house in the evenings. Tom, who had just gotten a master's degree in history when he joined the Air Force, was tall and wiry. He had a guileless, disarming demeanor and a sharp Irish sense of humor. He was warmhearted and it was easy to slip into sympathetic personal discussions with him.

Frazer once said of our life there that he kept banker's hours, which was not quite true. He did generally leave the house around seven in the morning and was most often home in time for dinner. A bus from the base picked him up and brought him home. I always marveled at how he, and Monk and Tom, could slough off the work, if one can call it that, they did all day long and then be relaxed and thaw out in the evenings.

I don't think I ever heard Frazer, or any of the other people in training with him that I knew, talk in any detail about what they did during the daytime. But I knew; it was not exactly a military secret. They spent their days learning how to kill by practicing with the lethal equipment on B-25s to attack Japanese ships or land bases or planes. They were learning how to fly hot airplanes at terrifyingly low-levels so that the four gunners with them could be closer to the enemy and strafe him more accurately and thus more violently. Strafe, I learned, was a German word meaning to punish.

There were a couple of lakes not far from their base which apparently were ideal on which to practice skip-bombing runs and low level, sea-skimming attacks. I heard from a young woman at my "beauty shop" in Columbia, that a while ago, a plane in this precarious exercise had dipped too low in a mock strafing run and had gone down into the lake, with all lives lost.

I never mentioned this story to Frazer and I never knew if he had heard it. Anyway it was a tale that turned my heart to mush.

He was training with the crew that he would eventually be flying with when all the practicing would become a reality. He brought them to our house several times and I was sorry that I never got to know any of the foursome well. One I remember particularly because he seemed to me like the blondest, pinkest-cheeked kid I had ever seen.

***

Frazer and I had one weekend of R&R (Rest and Recreation) while there. We went to visit my sister Nancy and her husband Cokie at a house they had in Georgia called Beneventum, not too far from Columbia. I had been there once, a few years before, when our whole family had spent Christmas there, and had found it lovely. It was a nice simple old house, surrounded with wild open fields where Nancy and Cokie hunted for quail and sometimes wild turkeys.

Cokie was now a captain in the Air Force and was the aide to the general, head of the base at Mitchell Field in Long Island, near where they lived. Frazer and I were delighted to join them for the one weekend Cokie could escape from duty.

Nancy and I were very close and I knew she particularly liked the simplicity of life at Beneventum. She flourished in the unpretentious life there, especially compared to her life in New York. She never talked about it much but I sensed that she wasn't drawn to the kind of lives some of the women in her Westbury, Long Island, world. She said that when she first moved there after marrying Cokie, she didn't know some of the arcane female lingo. For instance, she had never heard of "Belgians" (shoes that were handmade in Belgium to your special order). Nor was she familiar with that fiercely expensive and enchanting long, silk pleated skirt made by an Italian designer named Fortuny, that all of those women had. A Fortuny skirt came in its own little round box that looked like a hat box in which you kept your skirt rolled up and twisted like a snake so that the pleats would retain their shape. I knew that Nancy reveled in her simple life at Beneventum.

Frazer and I wove our way to the house through a grove of live oak trees with great beards of Spanish moss hanging from them, then on to an overgrown pathway through an unkempt yard. On both sides of us were wild open fields. The house was casual, too, with a well-worn atmosphere. There was a clutch of wagging-tailed hunting dogs inside that we either had to step over, or to dislodge if you wanted space on the sofa.

Nancy had brought me some pictures of her two boys and her little girl. She said it was too hectic for them to travel so far for just those few nights, so she had left them with their Grandmother (Cokie's mother) in Long Island. She told me that my nephews had loved the pictures of themselves taken at Frazer's and my wedding, when they were stuffing their faces with wedding cake.

Cokie had gone hunting early on the morning of our arrival and so we had quail for dinner. We also had some fish eggs before dinner. The last time Nancy was at Beneventum she had preserved eggs from female fish caught in a nearby river called the Pee Dee. They were known at her house as Pee Dee caviar. They were delicious with a more robust taste, I thought, than that of the extremely expensive caviar from Russia which I occasionally had.

After dinner Nancy invited the men to take over the clean-up chore and she and I went for a walk out among the live oak trees. I had thought that the Spanish moss might make them seem eerie in the dark but there was a big, orange moon shining through them which gave the effect of a night-time fairyland.

We reminisced at length about the happy Christmas all of our family had spent with her and Cokie at Beneventum four years before. I told her, near tears, that I held that Christmas very special since it was the last one when we had all been together with Daddy.

For a while we remained quiet. Nancy broke our silence. "Say, I've been wanting to ask you a question. Are you and Frazer planning to have children?"

"Of course," I answered, slightly annoyed, because I thought it was such a silly question.

"When?" Nancy asked.

"When it's convenient," I responded.

"For God's sake, don't wait till it's convenient. If you wait till then you'll never have kids," Nancy said in a firm voice.

We didn't talk about that anymore. Instead we went in and joined our guys for a nightcap. It turned out, although I had thought we had tacitly agreed to a vacation from war news for two days, that Cokie and Frazer had been listening to the radio. Then they told us, with great excitement, that at a conference in Tehran, FDR and Churchill and Stalin had agreed on plans for the invasion of Europe. Our little group spent much of the rest of the night guessing exactly where and when that would take place. All of us were aware that there must be an invasion of Hitler-controlled Europe and also we knew of the monstrous risks in such a huge undertaking.

Cokie had said that he desperately wanted to be sent to an airbase in England, that he hoped he would be there before the projected invasion took place. Nancy was torn, because she knew how much Cokie wanted to be there and yet she wanted him to work in the US where he would be safe. Frazer, who was pretty sure that when he was sent to a war zone it would be against the Japanese, was thinking of the poor devils who would have to fight someday to cover an invasion of Japan. And I was thinking, God in heaven, will Frazer one day have to be involved in a land invasion of Japan?

The next day, when we were hugging and kissing each other goodbye and Frazer and I were telling them what a fine time we had had, I whispered to Nancy that I'd been thinking about what she had said. I confessed to her that she was probably right about that "convenient" bit.

Telling Frazer Goodbye

About four months later, Frazer, Tom, and Monk got word that they and their crews would be shipping out within a week for undisclosed overseas duty which we knew was somewhere in the Pacific. At nearly the same time, I had gotten word from my doctor, that as I had hoped,

I was pregnant. Frazer and I were both thrilled with that news. I was three months on the way to having a baby!

It had always been planned between Frazer and me that when he left to go abroad, I would go to my ever-loving, ever-generous Nannie and live with her in Washington until Frazer returned. Now we decided that I'd have our baby there in Washington.

We had already agreed to sell our car, Cousin Zukie, to our land-lord when we would be decamping from Columbia. Mother lived near the streetcar line in Washington and I figured I didn't need a car in the city. Our landlord would pick up our car after we left our little house with the slanting hot water heater and the lovely catalpa tree.

I could talk casually about "after we leave," but as the time approached for Frazer to leave I tried to bluff myself into thinking it would never happen, with little success.

Instead, I saw him off one sunny morning as I had done for months now. He was picked up by the usual bus that took him to his base and I wondered if we could just pretend this was an ordinary morning, that he was just going off for the usual day there, for the routine rehearsal for war. I would pretend as long as I could that it was maybe the dress rehearsal, certainly not the actual theater of war. I felt I just couldn't bear too much reality. But, of course, I had to. When I came to my senses that morning, I was doggedly determined not to cry and make Frazer even sadder.

The bus arrived at the designated time. We held each other very tight. He told me to turn around and not to look as he headed for the vehicle that would take him for the first lap of his journey toward war.

I slowly turned around as he had bid me and didn't watch him leave. I was afraid to look lest I would be turned into a pillar of salt.

I waited for Julie to come by and pick me up and drive me to the airport where I'd take the plane to Washington. She was too sen-sible or too sensitive to try to commiserate with me, for which I was grateful. Seated in the plane for take-off, as I fastened my seatbelt, I wondered if that pressure could hurt my baby. And it wasn't until then that I started to cry.

***

Such was the compulsion in my family to be in constant touch with each other all the time that some friend had said there were three ways of communication: telephone, telegraph, and tell-a-Huidekoper. I guess it was true because by the time I got to Nannie's house in Washington there was a message from my sister Rosalind telling me that Hugh had already made an appointment for me to see an obstetrician in Baltimore. Translated, this message meant that Rosalind already knew I was pregnant and she did not believe that anyone could have a baby anywhere in the world except at Johns Hopkins Hospital. Now Rosalind's husband, Dr. Hugh J. Jewett, was considered one of the best urologists in the country. Not that a urologist is exactly the right person to deal with childbirth, but anyway, no sister of Rosalind's was going to have a baby delivered anywhere other than Johns Hopkins and by no doctor other than one selected by Hugh Judge Jewett.

After I had time to settle down a little bit at Mother's, and read and reread ten times the postcard I had gotten from Frazer, with an unfamiliar APO post mark, but with an exquisite photo of the San Francisco Golden Gate Bridge, I called Rosalind. I told her I would be over to see her and see the famous obstetrician, Dr. Alan Guttmacher, on the date she and Hugh had made for me, only a few days hence. I thanked her, wearing a wry smile for her kind solicitude. I mentioned that I thought it seemed very early for such an examination, or whatever, at this point, since the baby wasn't planning to arrive for six months.

I checked with Mother and my beloved Aunt Mary, who was giving up her room to me for my Washington sojourn while she stayed with a neighbor. They agreed that we three would take a train to Baltimore on the day of the appointment. Since it was in the afternoon I would invite Rosalind, Mother, and Aunt Mary to lunch at Marconi's, a restaurant I remembered fondly from my Baltimore days. Then I would go and introduce my embryonic baby to Dr. Guttmacher.

San Francisco Surprise

However, as it turned out, that had to be a pleasure deferred for Dr. Guttmacher. I had gotten a surprise call from Frazer. He was in California and he would be there at least five more days. "My God," I said, "I'm coming there. I'm going to follow you to the ocean's edge."

"My God," he repeated. "I hoped you'd say that."

"Or even further," I interjected.

"I can't wait to see you. I can't believe it. How are you, my darling? Are you and that baby OK?"

I convinced him we were absolutely peachy, and he asked, talking very loud, whether I was really coming. "And when, when?"

"I'll climb on the phone soon's we hang up and call every airline in the world and see which has a seat for me the soonest." For some reason, totally unlike me, I suddenly thought of a logical question. "Hey darling, what's the source of your skinny that you will really be there for five days more?"

"Totally reliable," he said and I knew he was smiling because that's an old army joke meaning "don't believe it." "No, of course, I got it from some one I trust. You know I wouldn't let you and the baby come all the way across the country unless I was sure to be here for you and that we would have a few days together, maybe four whole days, depending when you can get here."

Since it was nearly impossible for him to receive calls, he explained, he would call me in two hours to see if I had made any headway on a ticket. "I was ludicrously lucky," I told him when he called. "I have a flight in mid-morning tomorrow and will be able to leap into your arms in San Francisco tomorrow evening."

"Caramba," he shouted, his favorite word when he was especially excited.

I didn't have a single word that was equivalent to his to express my joy so I simply said something prosaic such as "Divine." I sat still for a few minutes after I hung up the phone, exulting in the prospect of what lay ahead. I could already visualize the flight. I could see us flying low enough when we were over the arid areas of the southwest so that I could suddenly view the round fields of green. They look to me like huge emeralds and tell me that a wheel of pipes is sprinkling water in a circle to irrigate an otherwise barren land.

On my few flights to the West Coast I had been entranced by the rounds of live green farmland that sit like jewels in an inhospitable brown tract. I had learned that this form of irrigation is accomplished by what is known as a center pivot which forms circular irrigation. That is what makes the patchwork of green circles; when I could begin to look down and see emeralds in the countryside like that, I would know that San Francisco was not too far away.

I even remembered to cancel my appointment with Dr. Guttmacher and make it for a later date. I called Rosalind and told her about my exciting change of plans and rushed upstairs to pack for my wildly exciting trip.

The Army Steals Time

When Frazer and I were shown to the table he had reserved for dinner at the Top of the Mark the second night I was in San Francisco, I asked to be seated with my back to the ocean, as if the ocean gave a damn that I was feeling hostile toward it because it would be taking Frazer far away.

We both laughed at my nonsense and his laugh was so beguiling that I seized this moment to tell him once more how sorry I was that I had gone sarcastic on him in the morning.

He had had to report to his base early in the morning and planned to come back to our hotel and pick me up for breakfast. I should have known immediately when he came back that morning that something had gone horribly awry. He looked as if he was on the verge of tears. Then he blurted out that there had been a dreadful SNAFU (I knew what that meant). I winced. "Our departure orders have been changed," he said in a woebegone voice. "We are shipping out at dawn tomorrow."

"Those fine five days have suddenly winnowed down from five to two," I said sharply. "Five days you promised me! You and your vaunted impeccable source of information!" I regretted the angry words before I had said them but they rushed out anyway, and my profuse apologies couldn't make them unsaid. Later I thought, it wouldn't do any good to say, "out damned words." That wouldn't wash them away. It hadn't helped Lady Macbeth.

It would be our last breakfast together for a long, long time. Each of us must have silently promised ourselves to rise above our disappointment and my bad temper. We smiled sadly, and agreed that we were so grateful to have been able to have even these special extra hours together.

He asked me, over again, all the questions he had been asking me ever since I arrived. How was I really feeling? Was I taking the right care of myself and the baby? He told me again how marvelous I looked. And he wondered again how I managed to be over three months pregnant and still not show any evidence of it. He asked me, "Where is our baby hiding?" I didn't believe any of his shameless flattery but I needed it and reveled in it.

Anyway, Frazer said that we should celebrate this extra gift of time, even if it had been truncated, at the most wonderful restaurant in the city, the Top of the Mark, with its famous view of the San Francisco harbor.

I don't remember which of us decided we should invite Tom and Monk to join us. "Tell them that dinner is on us," I suggested. "They can pay for the booze we will doubtless inhale in the course of the evening." I told him to remind them that I would hit their wallets lightly since I was allowing myself only one drink, a single glass of wine or at most two an evening on account of the baby.

Frazer was due back at his base by noon. He would call the restaurant to make the reservation and the four of us would meet there at seven-thirty. I had been able to tell him now, without flinching, that during the course of the day while he was at his headquarters or "wherever," I'd try to see if I could get an earlier flight back to Washington. Meanwhile I was going to wander around and enjoy the enchanting city.

Now seated for dinner at the Top of the Mark and awaiting our friends, I had just finishing telling Frazer once more how ashamed I was to have lost my cool that morning and that was the last time I would bring the subject up. Sitting there, we had managed to snake our ankles cozily together and we were holding hands when Monk turned up with Tom close behind him.

I unwound from Frazer and got up to give Monk a kiss. I had scarcely laid eyes on Tom before I noted that he looked unutterably sad. I put my hands up to his shoulder, quite a reach since he was so tall. He leaned down for a kiss, and now that I could see his melancholy eyes, I asked him what was going on.

Before he had a chance to answer, Monk suggested we all sit down. I patted the chair next to me and indicated to Tom that he sit there. Monk sat next to him on the other side and started to explain. "Things have been FUBBed horribly for Tom." This was a military acronym I wasn't familiar with and I must have looked puzzled. Monk translated, more or less, "Fouled Up Beyond Belief."

"Tom is despondent," he said, "because he had just called home and learned that Bea is on her way here, and..."

Tom interrupted him gently. "She will be landing here tomorrow morning several hours after I will have left." He mustered up a brief smile. Then he reverted to a look that made me think of some poor dog that had been punished for a sin he had not committed. We all sympathized with him in whatever way we could. He drew a deep breath and then suggested we order drinks. He was going to have a double, especially dry, martini. "And that's just to start with," he said.

I reached over to him, took his hand, and told him that I would be at the airport in the morning to meet Bea (I knew that he had promised her the same five days). Tom asked if I could also promise not to collapse when I had to tell her he had left. I made some inadequate answer and from then on we got on to other subjects, including ordering dinner.

The three of them drank quite a lot that evening and although we never hit a maudlin, fake merry high, we managed to have a good enough time. I noted that Tom was able to smile occasionally. Monk, always sensitive, told us stories that edged on being raucous but instead they were just low-level funny enough to make us smile amusedly instead of roar with laughter.

I had noticed two middle-aged women having dinner together at a table near us. Once when one was saying something to the other, while they were looking fixedly at us, the other smiled a kind of poignant smile. I felt certain the first one had commented on what a handsome group of young Air Force lieutenants ours was. And it was true. Frazer was dazzlingly good-looking—I could say that even objectively—and Tom and Monk were both handsome by anyone's standards.

***

A little later as we were talking about getting ready to leave, the way you always talk about leaving long before you get ready to leave, a tall Air Force captain came in with a small dark-haired woman close by his side. She was wearing a lovely black satin suit and together I thought they both looked younger than springtime. He stared at her as if he could eat her up. I figured he was probably in his late twenties but when he took off his Air Force cap, I saw that his head was covered with gray curls.

"Yikes," I said to my guys in a low voice, "I hope you make captain before you get that old."

"I just hope I get to be that old," Tom said.

Part Five

O Brave New World!

"O Brave new world that has such people in't!"
— WILLIAM SHAKESPEARE, THE TEMPEST

Mairzy Doats and Dozy Doats and Liddle Lamzy Divey

The first words I heard when I came to on February 22, 1944, after the delivery of my child, was that I had a fine baby. Music from the spheres, to me. A fine baby boy, someone said. More music from the spheres, I thought.

The next words that I remembered were a different kind of music: those of the hit song of 1944, "Mairzy Doats and Dozy Doats and Liddle Lamzy Divey." Those dippy words ringing together in my mind and my heart with the birth of baby Frazer Page Dougherty. The words actually are "Mares eat oats and does eat oats and little lambs eat ivy," but when they are glided together they come out in that funny language. It was played endlessly on the radio, slurred along like that. I heard nurses walking down the hospital halls, singing it together. I heard it sung, jazzily to himself, by a passing intern.

It must have gotten itself deeply imbedded in my consciousness early. Sometimes I even found myself singing "Mairzy Doats and Dozy Doats and Liddle Lamzy Divey" to my own little lamb, Fray, lying next to me in my hospital bed.

I couldn't figure out why I was so enchanted by this song unless it was the pleasure it gave to so many people by its sheer nonsense, and this seemed such an innocent, childlike antithesis to the cosmic news of death and destruction that overshadowed our lives.

Anyway, my baby seemed to like that dizzy song, too, when he was there with me learning how to suckle or learning how to make marvelous faces like a minute little clown, or just snuggling close. He especially seemed to like it when I lullabied it to him.

Dr. Alan Guttmacher, my obstetrician, whom I had gotten to know and admire hugely in my visits to him over the past months,

215

came by shortly to see us and although I was still groggy, he told me what a beautiful little boy I had. He patted Fray gently on the head. He looked at me and offered me his congratulations for having such a healthy baby. And he congratulated me for delivering the baby with such dispatch.

Later that morning when I had been deposited in my room and worked my way entirely out of my groggy state, a nurse, feeding me sips of juice of some sort, told me with obvious admiration, that I had had that baby in less than five hours.

***

When Mother and Rosalind came to meet the baby, they said that they had immediately written Frazer to tell him that Frazer Page Dougherty had arrived. They had reported that a bonny boy who had weighed in at just under eight pounds had been born in jig time and that both the mother and child were thriving. They told me they had spread the good word to all members of the family and other special people they thought should know about it. I figured they had probably also passed the news on to people who couldn't care less.

Between the visits of the intern and nurses and the more welcome visits from my baby, I managed to get a note off to Frazer. I wanted him to know how enchanting his baby was. He was already proving to be smart, anyway pretty smart about the nursing bit, and whatever hair he had seemed to be dark blonde. I suggested another note saying that since Frazer shared quarters with Tom and Monk to tell them that I said the baby is a real keeper.

I was pretty tired, I admitted, and couldn't believe this had all happened since last night, so I told Frazer that I'd be writing him a long letter and sending some pictures soon's I got back to Mother's house in Washington, two days from now.

Sometime after my supper, Fray was brought in from the nursery for one more feeding. That's when I told him I was sorry that he would have to wait a while to meet his father. He would have been here except that he had to keep a previous engagement, I said, and that he was some seven thousand miles away, flying B25s out of New Guinea, bombing and strafing Japanese ground forces and ships. These were the things I had pieced together, I told my baby, from his father's letters and what I read in the newspapers. "You will like him when you meet him," I assured him, praying that that time would not be too far away.

Pattern for Poppa

After a month back at Nannie's house I figured that all the good photographers must be away at war because not one that I tried could get a decent picture of the most enchanting baby in the world, not even the excellent photographer that I knew from my old newspaper. Frazer seemed enthusiastic enough about the pictures of his son that I sent him, but I decided I would take another way to represent Fray to him. I would make a mock-up, a sort of pattern, of the baby.

I got out a fat, black felt pen, the kind you use to address packages in great big letters so you are sure they'll reach their destinations. I put the pen on the right side of my bed. I placed a large sheet of tissue paper in the middle of the bed and laid a naked, pink baby, just learning to smile, on his back on the tissue paper. I put my left hand on Fray's belly to hold him in place, reached over for the felt tip pen, and pulled its top off with my teeth.

I started to outline the little body, which began to wriggle. I think Fray thought that I was tickling him with my left hand splayed out on his stomach. He was laughing—it was a new accomplishment for him—he seemed to enjoy the tracing game so much that he was not a happy camper when it was over and I put him back in his crib.

I could scarcely wait to see what we had wrought. I started to cut the black line, but even before I had finished and had held the pattern up, I knew we had a problem. It was not possible, I discovered, to trace the outline of anyone that is kicking, even if in delight. Surely I was not going to send a mock-up of a baby with several legs or a tail like a young merman to his father. I reluctantly tossed that piece of tissue paper away and decided I would try again, but this time with a sleeping baby.

A little later I put Fray, so suffused with milk from nursing that he was sound asleep, on another large piece of tissue paper. I went deliberately through the same procedure. Fray awakened only once, half-opened his eyes, yawned, and fell right back to sleep. He was still sleeping when I laid him back down in his crib.

I carefully cut along the bold big black lines, held the pattern up by its shoulders, and smiled with delight. I knew what it would mean to his father, how happy he would be when he took it out of its envelope and was able to get a look at his baby, in at least one delectable dimension.

Next morning, after displaying it proudly to Nannie, I folded the pattern up tenderly, put other tissue paper around it, and placed it in the envelope I had already addressed to Frazer at his APO. I left Fray in the charge of his grandmother, and I went to the post office to mail the envelope myself. It took a lot of stamps.

When I put it in the mail slot, I thought of how far it had to go. It would have to pass over those dramatic-sounding parallels of latitude: the Tropic of Cancer and the Tropic of Capricorn, to say nothing of the Equator itself. And it would have to stay out of the way of enemy submarines or enemy aircraft before it would get into the eager hands of a faraway father.

My Little Christian and his Hobby Horse

Although I had not yet found the god I was looking for, the one that tempers the wind to the shorn lamb, I agreed to have my baby christened as a Christian, as a Protestant.

I knew that would please various close members of my family, many of whom were profoundly true believers and committed to various Protestant rituals. I admired the Protestant faith, and was mesmerized by its stories and the swinging language in the King James Bible. And I believed that people not well versed in the rich stories in the Bible can never fully understand much of western culture, its literature, its art, or some of its folklore.

Those who would be especially pleased with Fray's christening included my dear Grandmother and also Frazer's mother, Maria Dougherty. Regardless of the depth of faith, or lack of faith in any denomination, of all the rest of the family and the friends that were coming to the event, I knew all would have a happy and a sentimental time.

It is a lovely sight to see a small baby, dressed to the nines, in Fray's case, a dazzlingly white embroidered dress, with a deep lace hem, and a long petticoat also garnished with lace, which many of his forebears had worn for their christenings. Indeed, I was told, I had worn it for my own. And it is touching to see a baby in the arms of a minister who has a loving look in his eyes, especially if it was the minister who had married the parents. He was the one who, I had been warned, was late for all occasions at which he would officiate but never late for a baseball game where he had no role. True to his habit, he had been late to play his role at our wedding, but not by much and he was nearly on time for the christening.

Mother, Aunt Mary, my sisters Rosalind and Nancy, my brother Huidy, the baby, and I all stayed at Long Branch, my Grandmother's house. The christening took place at the Doughertys' home, Woodley, a lovely old brick manor house some seven miles distant. I was still amused that all the houses of the rich, or once rich, in the county had names.

The baby disported himself pretty well throughout the ceremony, except that he did not like having cold water sprinkled on him. Is the water meant to wash away a baby's sins? I just smiled inwardly at such nonsense; as if a baby has sinned. Fray screwed up his face and let loose a howl.

I knew that he was hungry, as well as frightened, so as soon as the ceremony was over I took him upstairs and nursed him for a little while. Then he and I went downstairs, both in high spirits, and joined the party.

Maria Dougherty always had delicious food for any gathering at Woodley, she managed it with all the rationing at the time and there was plenty of booze. That had not been rationed. We drank a toast to the father of the baby, Frazer, who was somewhere in or near New Guinea, and then to Graham, the senior member of the family who was with the army in England. Once I felt as if we all looked like characters out of *Pride and Prejudice*.

At some point during the reception, Frazer's brother, Graham Jr., of whom I was very fond, told me quietly that he had completed his "assignment" and would like to show it to me. In the confusion of all I'd been concentrating on, I couldn't immediately figure out what he was referring to.

And then I remembered: On my last day in San Francisco before Frazer and I were to meet at the Top of the Mark for dinner, I had wandered in the part of town awash with antique stores, walking from one to the other, gazing through the windows. A pleasant way to spend time, without even spending a dollar, I had thought.

About then, I had seen a hobby horse in the window of an elegant antique store and decided that my baby, due in about six months, must have that hobby horse. I was no longer just "licking the windows" as the French say. I went in the store and gazed at the horse. He was smokey grey with round black spots about the size of a fifty-cent piece painted all over him. He had glass eyes, and wore a tiny leather saddle, cinched in over a red saddle blanket. His mane and tail looked as if they were made of real horse hair. His ears were made of black leather and his rockers were bright red.

As I was staring, entranced at the exquisite, delicate little animal, the owner of the store came over to me. She explained that the horse was very early American, probably made around the time of the Revolution. She thought that his paint and maybe some of his tack was original and that he was for sale for nine hundred dollars but that if I really wanted him I could have him for less and if I didn't live nearby she could arrange to have it sent safely to me.

I staggered out of there without even responding to the woman running the shop, I fear, but fully aware that I was in love with the little wooden beast with the astronomical selling price.

A few months later, in a junk shop in Washington, I spied a hobby horse that I thought looked exactly like my San Francisco steed, except this one was simply raw wood; and not only did it have no caparison, but didn't even have a single layer of paint. I cased the naked little horse, wondering—and then was told by the man in the store that he had bought it at a yard sale in this undressed state. He continued, saying that he felt sure it was an original, very old hobby horse, probably carved about the time of the Revolution, but since no one seemed interested in it, I could have it for fifty dollars.

Mother's housekeeper, Georgia Stith, told everyone later that she had never seen a weirder sight in all her livelong days. "There was Page, coming home in a taxi, toting a wooden horse naked as a jay bird."

When I had introduced it to Graham several months ago, he was more responsive to its charm. He told me that he would fix up the little rocking horse for me as a special present. At his request, I had described to him all the details of my horse's fancy San Francisco cousin. I had no idea what he had in mind but I thanked him profusely for the offer. And now he had told me he had completed his job.

Here at the christening, I pawned my baby off on one of his doting relatives and followed Graham into a small dark room, off the bright noisy dining room. He told me I was going to be surprised when he turned on the light.

There against the wall, was my little horse, looking as if she was ready to go galloping off to the green pasture outside the windows. I threw my arms around Graham and told him I could not believe my eyes. He had poured so much originality and energy and obvious affection into the little carved wooden animal, that for a moment I thought I was going to weep with gratitude.

Graham had made a bridle of thin black leather for her. A small black leather saddle lay on top of a red saddle pad. A mane of thick, red knitting-wool grew on her delicate neck. She had a substantial tail of the same red yarn which came down to her hocks. She had ears of black leather, pricked up like those of an alert little thoroughbred. Her eyes, made of mottled marbles, looked proudly ahead. She was dappled all over with round black spots, about the size of half-dollar pieces, and the rocker on which she was poised was bright red.

When it came time for some of us to go back to Washington that evening, Graham and brother Huidy put my horse, well protected by a blanket from Woodley, in the trunk of our car. Fray, now a very sleepy little full-fledged Christian, already in his flannel pajamas, slept in my arms, or on my lap, all of the way home.

Instead of being sleepy, I was all charged up. Mother, sitting in front of me, on the right of Huidy who was driving and I kept up a steady conversation. We chatted back and forth about the various people we had seen, how smoothly and delightfully everything had gone, whatever gossip we had managed to pick up, how good Fray had been, and what a magnificent job Graham Jr. had done of breathing life into my hobby horse.

When Mother asked me if I had any idea of what I would name her, I responded in full. Dew Drop, I told her, Macaroni, (that was the name of a pony Mother had as a child, she had often told me), Pandora (Mother knew that was the favorite horse of a beloved great uncle, Rush Shippen Huidekoper), Traveler, Pegasus, Trojan horse…

"Stop," she said, "that's a lot of names for such a small horse! And you've mixed up the names of some mares with those of stallions and maybe some geldings, and so forth."

I told her that there were lots more names for her: Rocinante, I went on, Buccephalus, Black Beauty, Horse of a Different Color, Merry Legs, and Incitatus. And I stopped there for the time being. I leaned back, clutching my baby more tightly. And just before I fell asleep I heard my mother, who thought she was whispering, lean over and say to my brother, "Page is much more interested in that horse than any child will ever be."

Tom Didn't Get to Be That Old

In Mother's house a few weeks after the christening I shifted the baby over to my left arm while I picked up the phone with my right hand. At first I thought it was someone who had dialed a wrong number because, although the person, a woman, was speaking English I could not understand a word she was saying.

Then I figured it was a crank call and was about to hang up when I suddenly realized it was Bea Finnegan. "Bea," I yelled into the phone. I was about to ask her what was the matter. But I knew already! Tom had been killed.

As it turned out, I finally understood from her hysterical voice, that Tom was missing. Then she said, in a barely controlled voice, that she would call me later when she was able to talk. "Bea, darling," I spoke loudly into the phone to make sure she could hear me above her sobs. "Darling," I repeated. "Call whenever you can. Oh, my God, Bea. I'll stay off the phone so you can get me. Oh, Bea." And I think I just kept repeating that several times until I finally realized that she had hung up.

I thought back to the last time I had seen Bea nearly a year ago. She was desolate then, too. She had just landed at the San Francisco airport expecting to see Tom and it had been my woeful burden to tell her that she had missed him because his orders had changed. His leave had been canceled and he and the others in his group, including Frazer, were now somewhere over the Pacific.

I sat there now by the telephone, numb. I think I would have remained there forever had not Mother come into the room to find out what all that noise was about. She said she couldn't tell who was crying louder: the mother or the baby. It wasn't till she roused me from my shock that I remembered that I had been on my way to nurse my hungry baby. I put him down for his afternoon nap when I had heard the phone ring.

He was sleeping soundly when I heard the phone ring again and made a dash for it. I had had to compose myself for Fray so that I wouldn't wake him up and I was all right when I answered. And it was Bea, as I had presumed. She spoke in a controlled voice now, but low, and I wondered if Rikki was close by and she didn't want him to hear. She told me what she had heard this morning. She had gotten a call from an Air Force colonel from a base nearby saying that Tom was missing in action. He had been missing for several hours and a fleet of search planes was out looking for him, hoping to find him and his crew safe and sound. "Somewhere in the South Pacific," was all she could tell me. Then she was quiet.

I desperately wanted to console her. So I poured out all my genuine words of sympathy and love and then some of the false ones. My first reaction of course was that Tom was dead. But I did not want to say that. At the same time I thought I could not bring myself to say I was sure Tom would be found alive. But I did say it.

I could hear her taking deep breaths, as if she was struggling to avoid tears. I tried a new tack. "Bea, darling, how is Rikki doing?" He and I had been close in the days at the Columbia air base.

She said that he couldn't take it in. "And neither can I," she added, with a terrible finality. She was utterly quiet for a moment. In fact so long was the moment that I thought she wasn't able to talk coherently now. I waited silently and patiently. Then she started to talk again. She now spoke quite easily, saying it meant so much just to hear my voice. "It helps me more than you realize."

I told her I wished there was some way I could be of real help and asked if there was anything on God's green earth that I could do for her.

She didn't answer immediately, and then she said, in a low, nearly timid voice, that she wanted to see me more than anyone in the world. She said she knew my baby was just a few months old and she knew it was a terrible thing to ask of me. She paused before saying, "If you could come, even for just a day..."

I realized now the depth of her need for me in her anguish. Otherwise I know she would never have asked this of me.

Then she told me that Rikki, who I figured must be seven or eight now, had told her that it would mean a lot to him to see me now. He remembered me especially from our happy times in Columbia, she added.

Her voice trailed off, but only briefly. She asked me to think it over and see if there was any way I could arrange to come to be with them. Just for a day, she repeated. Somewhat to my own surprise, I told her I would call her back.

I think it was her comment about Rikki that triggered my decision to go. The minute I finished talking to her, I called Fray's pediatrician to ask his advice. He wanted to know if Fray felt secure with his grandmother. I assured him that he loved his grandmother and seemed completely at home with her. "In that case," the doctor said, "since it would mean so much to your grieving friend and her son, I think you should plan to go." He told me the pharmacy would have the equipment for me to pump breast milk and put it into bottles. I made a reservation on a plane to Hartford for tomorrow morning and one returning to Washington the following morning. I called Bea and told her I was coming and gave her the time of my arrival at the airport the next day. She sounded overjoyed and said that both she and Rikki would be there to meet me. She made a fine stab at humor, adding, "with bells on."

I left my baby with Nannie, who was armed with a dozen full bottles of my milk. She told me not to worry about Fray, to save all my emotion for Bea.

Once at Bea's house she and I spent endless hours just talking. I realized that none of our discussions could be rational in these circumstances; I had to let her pour out her agonizing heart. Her emotions swung back and forth from hope to fear of the worst. Occasionally when I had a chance, I tried to engage Rikki by talking about his school or discussing books he was reading.

I knew that Fray was fine with his grandmother, but I called home twice when I was away just to reassure my self that they were both OK. Mother reported each time that he was doing all right on his new milk container.

Before I left Bea, I told her how profoundly I admired her for her strength and courage in facing this tragedy. At the airport when she and Rikki saw me off I felt that, although we were all suffused with sadness, we had made secret pacts with ourselves not to dissolve as I was leaving. There wasn't even a sprinkle of tears among us while we hugged each other and I headed to my plane. As I buckled myself into my seat on my way to go home to my baby, I waved from my window and made a "thumbs up" signal to them, even though I know they couldn't see it.

I guess we were about halfway to Washington when I began to think again how close Tom and Frazer had been and what a shock this must have been for him. I had a sudden uncanny idea that the letter Frazer would have written me about his despair would cross somewhere over the vast Pacific with the envelope in which I had sent him enclosing the tissue paper "pattern" I had made of our son.

I got a call from Bea several days later in which she told me, in a voice so desolate it would make stones weep, that she had gotten word from the Air Force saying that Tom was now presumed to be dead. I could think of nothing adequate to say. I could only think of the last time I had seen Tom, for dinner at the Top of the Mark, when he said he just "wanted to get to be that old."

The World and His Wife

Naturally I was fiercely apprehensive about anything I heard about what was happening in the Pacific, but then it suddenly struck me that the war was taking place in every ocean and on all six continents. So now the world and his wife and all his children, too, were a part of the

war. I realized that if the loss of life of the combatants was astronomical, the number of civilians caught in the crossfire everywhere was
enormous, too. I thought back to the day when Frank Waldrop had
told me that he thought indiscriminate bombing would start soon,
and he was right on the button. Now war killed women and children
nearly as ruthlessly as it killed combatants. Was there no morality left
in the pursuit of war, I wondered?

Sometime after I was tossing all of this around in my befuddled
mind, my old pal Mason Peters from the *Times Herald* dropped by.
I poured him a glass of beer. I figured it was too early in the day for
anything stronger. I got Fray up from his nap and brought him down.
Mason greeted him with a big smile and Fray smiled a small smile
back. I gave him some orange juice and plunked him on the rug with
a box of toys. With luck, I thought, this would buy a little time for
Mason and me to talk.

First Mason asked for news from Frazer. All I could tell him was
that he was somewhere in New Guinea, very busy flying his B-25. I
had told Mason when he had visited me before about Tom Finnegan's
death and he had been appropriately sympathetic. Mason followed by
saying that over the times he had seen me, he had discovered a noticeable change in me. I looked at him quizzically. He said that he simply
he felt that I had a "more seasoned understanding" of people and
"what makes them tick." He went on to say that he was proud that
I had remained "undazzled by all the bigwigs" I had met throughout my life. I shrugged my shoulders and smiled especially at that
comment.

He said that it had been a pleasure all these years to be able to
keep a special eye on me and to remember "my commitment to justice
for everyone," as I had called it my first day on the City Desk. "You
were still pretty young when you wrote that paragraph after you interviewed the Lobster Woman," he said, "but I knew that your passion
for justice was tangible and permanent."

I took his hand and held it for a moment as a way of thanking
him for his understanding just when Fray let out a yelp. I sped over
to him and found he was delighted with himself because he had
put a few blocks over each other and knocked them all down. So
it had been a joyous yelp, on realizing a newly discovered power.
I went to the kitchen and returned with a piece of zwieback, gave
it to my little boy, buying thereby a few more minutes in which I
could neglect him. I told Mason that he could see that I believed
in bribery.

I was determined to get Mason to tell me how he judged the situation now. I always thought that newspaper people were better informed than anyone else and wondered if he shared my sense of optimism about the direction of the war, that is the European war. He said he felt in his bones that there would be an invasion in Europe soon since Roosevelt and Churchill and Stalin had promised at the Tehran Conference that the huge aggregate power of the Allies would be concentrated on the defeat of Germany in the near future. He went on to say that the Germans could be defeated, not easily obviously, but defeated because the American troops were so powerful. Hitler's crazy, ill-advised attempt to conquer Russia had ended in vast destruction of the Russian army, Mason said. "To say nothing of the German army! Indeed that tragic war has won the accolade of being the largest theater of battle in the history of the world."

I told him that I had read somewhere that Hitler himself, giving defeat a religious twist, had moaned that the "God of War had gone over to the other side." Mason smiled teasingly at me. I had read that in the *Times Herald* he pointed out. I smiled at myself.

Now I noted that my little boy was getting restless and I figured that he was ready for his supper, so we moved into the kitchen. Mason stayed for a little longer, expounding in more detail his views on the war, then he bid us both a warm goodbye, congratulated me on how well I looked in "my old age," and gave Fray a kiss on the forehead.

***

We had actually talked mostly about the present and presumed future of the war in Europe, but after he left I couldn't stop thinking about the fighting erupting all over the Pacific. The valiant Americans, especially the marines, were beginning to capture more and more of the Japanese bases in New Guinea and many of the jewels of the great necklace of islands which stretched toward Japan. Most of these were islands which the Japanese had occupied and fortified immediately following their attack on Pearl Harbor.

I shuddered whenever I heard about the battles in the largest body of water on the planet. I thought that, in view of what was going on there, Magellan had certainly given that ocean a grossly illogical name.

My heart was in my mouth every time I wondered which battles Frazer had been in, and the letters I got from him shed no light. He never referred to where he and his crew had been, or what they had been doing. I presumed the military wouldn't allow specifics but I knew that they were strafing and low-level-bombing Japanese installations and ships somewhere in that maelstrom.

Hell, I thought, that's what he and his fellow pilots had been trained to do, wasn't it? Occasionally I tried cynicism such as that, simply tried to treat the Pacific war matter-of-factly to see if that attitude helped me to stave off my fears. Not much, I found out. For a while I went in for conjecture. I wondered if it would help me to cope better if I really knew what Frazer's life was like that out there.

***

Anyway, he didn't tell me. Instead his letters were mainly full of questions about his child. Was Fray talking yet, smiling, what color was his hair now, and so forth? He occasionally went to Australia on an R&R jaunt and he wrote about that enthusiastically. I figured that by avoiding the reality of war in his letters to me he could at least give himself some respite from its horrors and instead think loving happy thoughts about me and our baby.

I was always very cautious in my letters to him. I happened to have a box full of letters written by my great-grandmother, Molly Page Nelson, to her husband, Hugh, a captain in a Virginia regiment, who had been captured during one particularly bloody Civil War battle. The treatment in the Union camp in which he was imprisoned was especially dreadful, apparently in retaliation against a Confederate camp notorious for its brutal treatment of Yankee prisoners.

I don't know what happened to the letters of my great-grandfather, who was incidentally a minister, for I never saw them. Maybe they weren't saved. I never saved letters. In Molly's letters she seemed quite unconcerned about the war and about her husband's fate in prison. Her letters struck me as superficial. She wrote to him mainly about the merry picnics and parties she went to. I suppose she did it to lift his spirits and to encourage him to remember that there was still fun and joy in the part of the world that he hoped to come home to someday.

In any case, he did come home eventually to enjoy that life, years later and dozens of pounds lighter and not much given to smiling, I had been told.

Not that Frazer was in prison, but I tried not to write him only of the frivolities in my life. I sought to avoid glittering generalities.

I wrote him minute details about his son, including how smart he was. For instance, he was already learning to throw things on the floor. Even his pediatrician considered that advanced, I boasted. Many babies don't start that until they are nearly a year old, the doctor had told me.

I sent Frazer news about members of our families. I remember that in one letter I told him that I had given to his sister Gerty my wonderful rabbit fur coat with the wolf-fur hood that Jim Ryan had brought me from Alaska years ago. She was sky-watching at night on some mountain top in Virginia, looking for enemy planes through huge GI binoculars. I figured she needed the coat more than I did, I wrote magnanimously.

I passed on news about common friends, as long as it wasn't bad news. And I wrote him about dear friends in England; Paul Richey, among them, who was flying again, escorting the huge bombers headed for German airfields in France.

I remember I wrote him once that there were now droves of American troops in England, getting ready, I supposed, for the invasion of Europe which all of the editorials and so-called experts felt was bound to take place sometime in the course of the year. I thought he would be amused by a story I had heard: the Brits were annoyed by the huge influx of American soldiers. "They are overpaid, they are oversexed," some English men beefed, "and what's more, they are over here!" Mainly in my letters to him, I told him how desperately I missed him and how much I loved him.

If my life in Washington during those days was totally absorbed by taking care of Fray and writing to my husband, I managed to find other things to enjoy, too.

My favorite diversion was having my friends or Mother's friends come by to see my baby and me. Actually, in much of 1944, my mother was away visiting my brother Huidy and his family in Milton, Massachusetts, and I was on my own in her house but her friends were still solicitous of me. Visitors, such as Mason Peters, still head of the city desk at the *Times Herald*, came by off and on, as he had done a few days ago. Sometimes a visiting friend was bemoaning the loss of a relative in some theatre of our far flung war. I personally spent an inordinate amount of time writing sad letters to friends sympathizing at the wounding, or often death of a husband, father, son, or lover.

One special old friend who came by fairly often was General "Mike" Scanlon, who had been the US air attaché in London when

I had been in the embassy there. I remember one afternoon when we spent hours marveling at the massive amount of military equipment our factories were turning out: weapons, ammunitions, ships, war planes of all sorts, and special kinds of uniforms.

He told me that the president of one of these industries now converted to crucial wartime production was an old friend of his. He had seen him recently and told him how much he admired him and the others like him for their wartime genius at "pulling so many rabbits out of hats so fast."

His friend had responded, that it was easy and snapped his fingers "Nothing to it," he commented. "All we have to do is to be sure that we have planted enough rabbits in the hats beforehand."

***

Other than seeing friends, my other indulgence was reading. Of course, I read to Fray from time to time. With great drama, I either recited or read nursery rhymes to him and he seemed to like my antic theatrics. At one point, I considered reading out loud to him the books I was reading then and thus kill two birds with one stone, so to speak, but since I was perverse enough to be reading mainly books that had to do with war, I decided against that idea.

I remember that *The Fifth Column* and *A Farewell to Arms* were among the Hemingway books I read sometime in 1944. I read *Mrs. Miniver*, a wonderful book about heroism on the home front in England during the worst of the bombing. I read it with special interest because its author, Jan Struther, and I had become friends when she visited Washington for a while the year before. Indeed I had taken her to my Grandmother's for a night since she had told me she would love to see Virginia. In the afternoon of our visit, we had gone to a little gathering at the simple little country club to honor the retiring Master of the Blue Ridge Hunt Club. He was a dear, sweet man and the ceremony was so like a page out of an English book of years ago, that Jan and I hid, with some difficulty, our smiles at the quaintness of it. Her own book, *Mrs. Miniver*, was totally contemporary and was such a tribute to the courage of simple English people that Winston Churchill said that that it had done more for the Allies "than a flotilla of battleships."

I read many books by wartime reporters, especially the dispatches of Ernie Pyle. He had the capacity more than any other writer to empathize with the G.I. You could look into the eyes of any infantryman, he wrote, and tell what he had seen of war. I don't remember any contemporary novels that I read then, unless they had to do with the war.

I distinctly remember a contemporary book I did not read. It was the novel that my dear Grandmother and her friend, Cousin Lolly Bunch, were reading then. They used to read out loud to each other, taking turns in the evenings after supper. This particular book was called *Forever Amber* which had sold one million copies in its first year of publication. And no wonder! It was a wildly explicit Edwardian romp, which had been nearly banned for obscenity in Massachusetts. When I was talking to Grandmother or Cousin Lolly about their book, to their amusement, I always referred to it as "Forever Under."

Incidentally, the Boston judge who ruled against its being banned for obscenity later said the book should have been banned for being "too soporific." That's what I had suspected and was why I didn't bother to read it.

***

I didn't get to movies much in those days, although movies during the year of 1944 were more popular in the US than they had ever been. I did see, and like everyone else, was enchanted by *Casablanca* and found every occasion to use its illustrious line, "Shocked, absolutely shocked."

But it was contemporary news, awash with stories of the battles in which our brave men were engaged all over the world, that captured me. I read reports from any action in the Pacific over and over, but it was the radio reports about fighting in the Pacific that engaged me most intently, that seemed so close to the bone, and that kept me on tenterhooks.

Omaha Beach

On June 6, 1944, as usual I flicked on my little battery radio, my preferred form of addiction. Every morning I turned it on as soon as the baby woke up. He competed with the news, crying noisily to be fed, but this morning it was the news that won out over my maternal instinct: The invasion of Europe had started.

I turned up the radio as loud as it would go, finally cleaned up Fray and automatically set about nursing him. He was happy now and except for an occasional gurgle, he was quiet. Now I was able to turn down the volume of the radio. At first it was impossible to locate exactly where the broadcast was coming from. But what I learned soon that in the pre-dawn of that morning was that large numbers of Allied paratroopers had been dropped on the hills overlooking the beaches of France on the coast of Normandy.

The mission of the paratroopers, now behind enemy lines, was to attack the Nazis in their fortified defenses above the beaches to stop them from firing on the boats bringing in the Allied troops landing on the beachheads.

The invasion of France was taking place simultaneously on five Normandy beaches, with those advance troops being parachuted above each of the five beaches. It appeared from the news that the largest invasion, and the fiercest fighting, was taking place on a beach now being called Omaha. As the broadcaster went on with his recounting of the bloody news, I wondered briefly if Omaha was anywhere near Villerville—that little fishing village Rosalind and I had gone to when she came to visit me in France a few summers ago.

The broadcaster had no news of the fate of the paratroopers, but obviously they had not been wholly successful in their destruction of German troops above the beaches. Indeed, the men trying to land on the beaches, and the ships which were bringing them in, were subjected to a vast barrage of enemy fire. Some of this fire was undoubtedly coming from the German installations above the beaches. Also firing was coming from the fleet of tanks that Rommel was said to have brought there in response to the rumors of invasion.

The longer I listened the more terrified I became. I fully realized that the future of the war was being determined in the outcome of these battles happening right before my ears. Whoever was doing the broadcasting—and I never heard his name—used simple words, never adjectives nor colorful language in his reporting. I don't remember him ever raising his voice but the scene he drew sounded so chaotic and so like a slice of hell, that I felt chilled right down to my bones.

Aware that I felt chilled, it struck me as very odd that I was weeping hot tears, weeping them right down on my baby. I guess he found it odd, too, because he kept trying to swat hot tears away, as if they were flies. I turned off the radio.

Several friends called in the course of the morning. We skipped the perfunctory greetings and immediately fell into exchanging our ill-informed ideas about the invasion. All of us were obviously profoundly moved by the intensity of the fighting and aware of what hung in the balance of the outcome. We expressed in one way or the other, our anxiety over our troops which we now knew included not only Americans and Brits, Canadians and Aussies, but maybe some who had escaped darkened Europe and wanted to be engaged in her illumination.

One friend said that she had heard that the Allies had tried some deceptions, one of which had worked. The Allies had led the Germans to believe that logically the invaders would take the shortest route across the Channel to France and had thus planned to land on the coast of the *Pas de Calais*. That subterfuge had tied up a lot of German tanks planning to greet the invaders there, my friend gloated. And, she reported that we had sent in a lot of dummies along with the real paratroopers being dropped above Omaha beach. Whether her skinny was accurate or not, it was clear that there was ferocious fighting going on the Normandy beaches.

***

To give my mind a change of scenery for a bit, in the afternoon I took Fray out to the little porch on the front of Mother's house. The last few days had been cool for early June and it had been overcast, but today was sunny and warm and the dogwood tree on the corner was in full bloom.

There were blossoms on some of the little pink begonias that Mother had planted. I pinched off a deep pink begonia and sat down in the only chair out there, holding Fray in my lap. I showed him the begonia and told him that Nannie, my mother (his grandmother), was crazy for pink. I was always passing on arcane bits of information to him. He looked totally uninterested. Then he frowned as if he was worried and I assured him that he should not worry about his father. He is nowhere near those beaches in Normandy, I told him.

After a little while I found myself making promises to him which I hoped the world would keep. I said that when this war is over, I promise there will never, never be another world war. He fell asleep and I put him in his carriage, pushed it into a shady spot, and took out of the carriage the book I had placed there a while ago. I put the pink begonia on the cover over his feet.

I read the same paragraph over five times before I realized I couldn't concentrate on reading. I resisted the impulse to turn the radio on and decided that instead I would focus on 34th Street in front of Mother's house. There was little action there today. Several cars went by, one driving too fast for a city street. I shook my fist at the driver despite that he had already long gone past. A little girl came by, riding a new-looking three-wheeler on the sidewalk, pumping away hard with little fat legs. She was followed by a woman, presumably her mother, who looked pained. I wondered if she was agonizing over the news from Normandy, or maybe, I figured, it's just that her feet hurt.

A few minutes later, a dog that I recognized—he belonged to a family I knew up the street—came sauntering by followed soon by one of the sons of the family. The boy was wearing the dog's leash, tied around his waist in a jaunty fashion. He saw me looking his way, smiled, and waved. As I waved back to him, I figured he must be seventeen or so. And I went on to think that he was lucky not to be a few years older than that and be on a beach in Normandy.

***

I went over to Fray's carriage and moved it slightly so he was not in the sun and when I turned around, I heard someone call out my name. It was the friendly mailman coming up the street. "Got something special for you," he yelled in a happy voice. By the manner in which he was waving a letter I knew it came from Frazer. The kind mailman had obviously noted that the letter was sent from an APO address and he knew how anxious I would be to get that letter.

I started for the steps so I could get to him, but he said that he just had to see that baby. I was forced to wait till he had stepped onto the little porch for me to get my letter. He said in a quiet voice that the baby "sure is getting bigger." All the time I feared he was going to drag me into a conversation, ask me questions about Fray and so forth. Thus I could not politely open my precious letter at that point.

And then he asked me if I had heard the news. I was clutching my letter, aching with anticipation to open it but I felt obliged to talk with him for at least a few minutes about the war. "We just got to keep on prayin'. Prayin' louder," he said, finally. I agreed with him heartily, and he left.

I ripped open the envelope. The letter inside was appallingly brief. "Darling, I am unbelievably sad. Monk has been killed. More later. Love," And the brief note wasn't even signed.

After I recovered from my immediate shock and realized what a desolation this was for Frazer, my instinct was to call Monk's girl. Then it suddenly occurred to me that I had no address for her. Monk had gone to New York on a few days' leave especially to say goodbye to Patricia, the woman he had talked about so much and was clearly in love with. She lived in New York but had never been able to get to South Carolina and indeed I never knew her last name. I just knew that Monk loved her and that had been good enough for me. But now...? Now, when I wanted so much to pour out my feelings of sympathy to the woman he loved, I knew no way of getting in touch with her. Aside from the shock of Monk's death, I felt the additional lament of frustration at not being able to even offer my thin gruel of consolation to Patricia.

After a while of futile thinking, I turned my attention to Fray's needs: his bath, his time on his stomach where he looked like he was trying to swim, his supper, and his fun and nonsense time, at which I was not very sharp this day.

***

Luckily he was asleep when my sister Nancy called because I wanted a long, uninterrupted conversation with her. She was genuinely sad over my news about Monk Adelman and my additional concern that I couldn't figure out how to find the woman he loved. Nancy had known about Tom Finnegan's death, too, and knew that both of these men had been good friends of mine, and she also knew that this made me a million times more apprehensive about Frazer.

I was about to show her that I could think of something other than my worry over Frazer and I asked if she'd heard any late news of the world-shaking events in Normandy, when she suddenly interrupted my train of thought.

"My God, you know what?" Nancy asked and before I could answer a non-answerable question like that, she explained that Cokie was at last getting the assignment he had been seeking a long time: to be based in the Eighth Air Force in England. There he would be engaged in what he called "hotter action." This meant, Nancy explained, that his present boss, General Hunter, will be looking for a new aide to replace him, and this time he wants one who is also a pilot.

"Give me Frazer's APO address," she said. "General Hunter can find out all about him from his General pals in that area and maybe, maybe..."

"My God," I said. "Do you suppose possibly, possibly...?" I gave her Frazer's address and said that it would be heavenly if... Neither of us seemed to be able to finish a sentence.

Just before she hung up she asked me if I knew how many missions Frazer had flown. I told her I didn't know but that he had flown a big bunch. Somehow, I said, I thought the figure was over sixty.

We ended our conversation expressing our hopes and prayers that all would go well in Normandy. Just before we hung up, I remembered to ask her to congratulate Cokie at getting the assignment he wanted.

***

My dear friend Jane had once asked me if I had dreams about flying in a bombing plane. I told her that I had not and asked her if she had dreams about being on an aircraft carrier (her husband, Bob, was an officer on a carrier). She laughed and answered, "Only twice, and each time a week or so afterward, he came home on leave." I was naturally so turned on after that conversation I'd had with Nancy that I had a hard time getting to sleep. But as I felt myself drifting off, I determined to dream that I was in a bombing plane. It didn't work for me. I didn't dream a thing that night.

***

The newspapers the next day were saturated with news of the invasion. One story, which curdled my blood, told of some landing boats carrying troops which by mistake had opened their landing platforms short of the beaches. These wretched troops were thus disgorged into deeper water than they should have been. With all their heavy gear they were unable to swim even to the beaches in the near distance.

The following day the papers were also full of feints that the Allies had pulled off, making the Nazis expect landings in several other places so that they were poised for enemies that never materialized there. So my telephone pal had been right. Mainly the stories covered the savagery of the fighting on the beaches and the difficulty of Allied planes trying to protect our soldiers.

The general conclusion, as far as I could tell, was that the Allies had successfully taken the beaches they had aimed for. The cost had been high, but now there were large numbers of Allied troops on French soil. It would be a tough row to hoe to take Europe back from Hitler's soldiers, but the Allies had taken the fateful first step.

Much as my thoughts and hopes were concentrated on our soldiers on the Norman beaches, there was no way I could hide my personal excitement at the project Nancy had set for herself. I had heard the expression that gods have long arms. I wondered if generals do too. But I knew it was too early to call her to try to find out. The next day it was harder still for me not to call her, but the day after that I had to nearly slap my hand as I started to reach for the phone to ask if she had any news.

My Fabulous News

Three nights later I was awoken by a call from Cokie. He apologized for calling me so late (it was around eleven, I noted) but he thought I wouldn't mind if he suggested that my baby and I should come up to Long Island soon to look for a house because...

I yelled with delight and then I started to cry. It turned out that everything the General had heard about Frazer had been "most favorable, indeed excellent" and that he was being appointed as aide to and pilot for General Frank O'Driscoll Hunter. Cokie said that General Hunter had made the decision about Frazer a few days ago and had put the wheels in motion that would bring him to Mitchell Field. The General had called Cokie to ask him to relay that happy news to Captain Dougherty's wife. Cokie was to tell her that Frazer should be at Mitchell Field sometime within the next month.

I couldn't talk. "Are you crying?" Cokie asked me.

"Yes," I was able to say. Then I added, "Of course."

"Well, you better stop. You don't want Frazer to come home to a wife with great tear lines that will look like the black lines cheetahs have, do you?"

I think I laughed. I know that I thought to thank him sufficiently and to tell him how grateful I was. I even remembered to congratulate him on his assignment to the Eighth Air Force in England. He said he was "hugely excited," especially now with the invasion of France and all that implied for the huge Eighth Air Force. He said he may have already left by the time Frazer gets to New York and he added that even before I would get up there to look for a place to live. We both wished each other good luck and love and good night.

By the afternoon of the next day, I had conned a young man, Frank Everts, a senior at Georgetown University, who was the son of a friend of mine, to drive me and Fray to Westbury, Long Island, for a small fee. I would let him know a date for the drive as soon as I had a clue when Frazer would be arriving. Frank was a reliable twenty-two-year-old and seemed pleased to pick up an odd job like this. Fray and I would stay in Westbury with Nancy and the children and Cokie, if he had not yet left for England. I would reconnoiter from there for a place to rent for Frazer and Fray and me.

I got a call from Cokie saying that he was again to pass on word from General Hunter. This time the word was that Frazer would probably be going to New York in two weeks' time. Cokie suggested that I make plans for me and my little boy to come on up, but he feared he'd probably have gone by the time we got there. When I thanked Cokie again, he congratulated me on not crying with excitement this time.

My hired driver, Frank, my baby, and I were to leave Washington in five days. The night before we were to set off I got a call from Frank's mother. She said she had to tell me privately that her son was wondering what he should do if the baby cries on our way to New York and I have to nurse him. He had never encountered a situation like that, he told her, and there I would be sitting next to him, nursing the baby.

I said that if such a problem arose en route, we could simply stop at the next gas station and that the baby and I would disappear into the confines of the women's room for a brief period. My friend and I both laughed, and I asked her, "For God's sake, hasn't Frank seen breasts before?" She said she was sure he had but not in circumstances such as this.

The three of us set off at the appointed hour. Frank and I had a fine time on our trip to Westbury. We found plenty to talk about and even some things to laugh about. Fray had a fine time, too, sleeping most of the way. And in any event, I was able to spare my breast-feeding-fearing friend any frightening situations. We stopped at gas stations a couple of times en route. He spent that night at Nancy's and left the next morning to go home with a fat check in his jacket pocket and said, again, what a good time he had had.

***

The second day at Nancy's house in Westbury, I looked out of the window and saw her three-year-old daughter, also named Nancy, walking by the swimming pool carrying Fray. She was wearing nothing except a band-aid (high up on her arm) and he was wearing even less. She was holding him firmly and I noted that she walked gingerly as she went down the few steps into the shallow end of the pool. She dipped down every now and then, as if she was a dancer, always careful to keep my baby's head well out of the water.

He was waving his arms wildly and smiling broadly. The children's Scottish nanny, Nana, standing next to Nancy, occasionally flicked a little water on Fray's face and that sent him into shrill sounds of ecstasy.

I was sorry that Cokie had already left for England several days before I got there, but Nancy, her two young boys, and her little girl made us feel wonderfully at home. Fray was happy with his cousins, obviously delighted to be with people closer to his own size, and particularly happy to be the center of attention of so many eyes and hands.

During the day, Nancy and I scouted the small houses or apartments she had gotten a line on, looking for something suitable for Frazer and me and our son. By the fourth day I had found nothing that I could afford or that was satisfactory but we had heard of one small house that sounded good from its description and we were to see it the next day.

I'd had only one letter from Frazer since he had gotten the surprising word that he was being transferred to Mitchell Field. He wrote that as long as the three of us would be together, he'd be joyous even in a pig sty. The Rathborne children thought that was wildly funny and every now and then they would ask me if I had found my "pig sty" yet.

***

It was clear that Nancy missed Cokie terribly but she was happy for him that he was now at the Eighth Air Force, perhaps the most important Allied air base in the world at the moment. He had long wanted to be in a more active post. Now he was stationed at the base from which the huge Flying Fortress bombers took off to attack Luftwaffe installations on the Norman coast and according to reports in the papers, these were the bombers who had already been ferociously hitting targets in Germany itself.

I asked Nancy to brief me on General Hunter, Frazer's future boss. She told me that General Hunter was known to his friends as "Monk," a nickname that he had picked up when he was a fighter pilot in the First World War. She didn't know how he got the nickname but it had stuck.

He had carved out a heroic role for himself, earned a lot of medals, and had been posted to interesting spots around the world after the war was over such as military bases and embassies, according to an article she had clipped from *Time Magazine*. His last station before he came to Mitchell Field as Commanding General of the First Air Force, Nancy pointed out, had been the Commanding General of the Eighth Air Force, where Cokie was now.

At Mitchell Field it was General Hunter's responsibility to protect the East Coast of the United States from enemy attack. Cokie had immensely liked working for him and had found him an exacting and challenging boss, Nancy said. Furthermore, he and Cokie had become good friends, Nancy said, and that indeed she considered Monk Hunter a good friend of hers as well.

In the evenings, when Nancy and I weren't chatting about our family, or telling "tales out of school" about friends, we hovered over the radio. We hailed the accounts of successes of Operation Overlord, as the Norman invasion was called. It was a desperate uphill battle, but the Allies were making successful dents in the German defenses on the coast. Our troops already there were joined by huge numbers of others coming in to help them. The newspapers suggested that a million troops had been landed in Normandy, along with a staggering number of tons of supporting supplies, including vast numbers of vehicles.

I commented that all the figures bandied about anything to do with Operation Overlord seemed to be superlative. Anyway, sitting with my sister in her lovely house in Long Island, some thousands of miles away from the agony of war, we shuddered for what lay ahead. The Battle for France had started and no one but an idiot could be unaware of the pivotal importance of these battles.

***

The house we went to see the next day turned out to be perfect for what I had in mind for our little family. It was the small guesthouse on the property of a friend of a friend of Nancy's. The owner's niece had been living there and had recently moved, and it seemed to me that the little house had been sitting there with open arms waiting to welcome us. It was fully furnished and if there was a mild overload of chintz, I could live with that. It had all the amenities a small family could need, including a tiny bedroom off the larger one, which was fine for a baby. I thanked my lucky stars I had fallen into such a house.

The owner, a woman named Bea McClintock, introduced me to her gardener and his wife, Rose, who lived in an apartment over the garage next to our abode. Rose promptly told me she needed a little boy to look after. I took the hint and hugged her. Bea and I settled on an informal lease agreement which she would write out and I would sign. I would move in within a month, just before Frazer was due to arrive. My family and I would live there for a year, paying her the rent and the cost of the utilities by the month. The lease could be extended, depending how long Frazer would be at Mitchell Field.

Nancy and I agreed that Fray and I would stay with her for another week and then he and I would move into my rented house and await Frazer's arrival.

Anyway, we finally had some happy news to report to the children, news which was over joyous to me. Nancy got a message from General Hunter to say that Captain Dougherty will be arriving sooner than planned. He would be in California in the next day or so and is due to arrive at Mitchell Field on August 26. The message asked Nancy to pass the word on to the captain's wife. We scurried around and made plans for me to move to my little house the very next day.

That happened to be the day that those gallant troops who had landed in Normandy had fought their way to Paris and set that beleaguered city free. The vision of the Allies in Paris now nearly counteracted forever for me the heart-searing photos taken in June 1940 of Hitler goose-stepping through the Arc de Triomphe.

***

So it happened that on the day of the liberation of Paris, August the twenty-fifth in 1944, a clutch of Rathbornes took me from their house to my new house. They carried my suitcases and the baby paraphernalia into what the kids called my "pig sty" and put some of the things in the right places. After they all left, I fed a tired and cranky little boy and tossed him into his portable crib that was still in the hallway.

I set the bottle of wine that Nancy had brought me on the table in the kitchen. She and I had already christened it with emotional toasts to Paris. We toasted in jam jars; we couldn't find wine glasses. And she had left me sandwiches and fruit for my supper.

Just before she left I thanked her for all the warmth and hospitality that she and the kids has offered to me and Fray, and I gave her an extra large hug.

That evening I consumed all of the wine that was left. What with reveling over the pending arrival of Frazer and rejoicing again over the news of the Allies being in Paris and all that wine, I went to bed with most of my clothes still on.

The following day Rose came in to show me the pictures in the *Times* of the glorious American troops walking tall through the streets of Paris. We threw our arms around each other in celebration. Staring at the pictures, I harked back to the day in 1940 when I was in Ireland

ready to sail home, when a driver, with his radio to his ear, yelled that
Paris had surrendered to the Nazis.

***

What a helluva lot of blood has flowed under the bridge since then,
I thought. Switching gears to an upbeat mood, I found myself singing my personal version of the Oscar Hammerstein song about Paris,
and I cast it in a happy future. "The next time I see Paris, her heart'll
be warm and gay, I'll hear the laughter of her heart in every street
café," I sang to my little boy who was creeping on the rug in the living room. Fray didn't mind that I couldn't carry a tune. He smiled,
showing those nifty, tiny new teeth, especially, it seemed, when I
added a line and sang: "And your father'll soon be here and that will
be some sweet day."

I still had an hour before Nancy was to pick us up to go to meet
Frazer at Mitchell Field. Rose popped her head in to tell me that Nancy
had called to say she would pick me up at quarter to two instead of two.
(The phone in my house had not yet been connected.) That seemed like
a century away and I knew it was futile for me to try to be calm. Instead,
all morning long I kept turning in circles. I reminded myself of a dog,
the way it turns in circles, reverting back into its wolf memory, turning
to press down weeds so it has a soft spot in which to curl up and sleep. I
wasn't going to sleep, but I still seemed to be turning in circles.

The time to leave crept up painfully slowly. I had nursed Fray and
fed him those bland mushy carrots that he seemed to like so much.
I had bathed him, not once but twice. He had managed to blotch
through to the pants of his little bright blue suit, so I had dressed him
again in his second best suit and prayed to the god of diapers that my
baby would remain good to go.

Rose offered to take care of him while I "polished myself up."
After my shower I stood in front of the long mirror in my room and
looked at my body from the front and then I stared over my shoulder
and looked at the back of it. I decided it looked damn near exactly the
same as it had looked when I last saw Frazer or, more to the point,
when he had last seen me. I got dressed, threw on my jazzy bra, and
slithered into my good, beautiful beige pongee dress.

***

I was careful to have a pillow on my lap to protect that dress as I held
Fray on my lap on the way to Mitchell Field to welcome his father

home. Apparently General Hunter had called Nancy to tell her that Captain Dougherty had caught a ride on a military plane in San Francisco and would be getting in around three. He asked her to please get the word to Dougherty's wife.

On the way Nancy tried to cool me down. She asked questions such as what had I planned for dinner tonight. I told her that the day before I had filled up the fridge with food enough for a week, so I had no idea what we'd eat tonight. She finally gave up on practical questions and simply asked what I was wondering about the most at this point. I didn't have any problem with answering that.

"Oh, I wonder constantly about a man who has to spend all his time and energy concentrating on killing? Does tenderness just get abraded off? Is the capacity for sensitivity rasped out of him?"

She assured me that the human psyche is able to contend with two sets of emotions that have opposing qualities and still not be schizophrenic. "That's either my watered-down, or my souped-up, Freudian answer to your questions," she said. We were both laughing as she turned into a parking space with a sign that specified it was for guests of General Hunter. I looked at my watch, which told me that it was a little before two-thirty.

We were met there by a rather breathless young lieutenant who told us that the plane from San Francisco was landing right now and he would take us to it. I clutched my baby, who had slept all the way in the car and was still sleeping, and the four of us set off with the young lieutenant in his jeep.

The plane had taxied onto its designated spot on the tarmac by the time we arrived there. It was a small Air Force plane of some sort and the steps were just being let down. The first incoming passenger was an Air Force colonel, who walked down nonchalantly; and walked off, obviously knowing where he was going. Next came a woman in Air Force uniform who was immediately met by a man who took her suitcase. She, too, looked at home; as if she was greeting someone she saw all the time.

And then there he was. Frazer. Coming slowly down the steps, carrying a big duffel bag. He was sweeping his head around, looking anxiously, and even worriedly, I thought, at the groups at the bottom of the steps. And then he saw me. He smiled and I noted with wild, pounding joy that it was his same riveting smile. He ran down the stairs the rest of the way.

He threw the bag on the ground. In seconds our arms were around each other so tight that we squeezed Fray in the process. The baby woke up suddenly, wide-eyed and surprised. We piled into the jeep and thanked the young lieutenant graciously. There was a scrawled message addressed to Captain Dougherty under the windshield wiper of Nancy's car when we got back to it. Frazer held his child close to him, cradled in his right arm. Fray looked up at his father's face with an expression of vague curiosity.

With his left hand, Frazer picked the note from under the windshield wiper and read it to us. It said that he didn't have to report in until eight o'clock tomorrow. It was now four in the afternoon so that was only a little over a dozen or so hours away, I noted, annoyed. Not a great span of leave time. The writer said he was delighted that Captain Dougherty had arrived and that he looked forward to seeing him in the morning. Frazer smiled and told us the signature was scrawled unintelligibly, like that of a doctor's on a prescription form. "But," Frazer added, "I presume it is that of General Hunter."

Nancy knew that one of my first priorities was for Frazer and me to buy a car. We all agreed that General Hunter took precedence over General Motors (or any other car manufacturer). Nancy insisted that we use her car until we had time to look for one of our own. She would use Cokie's car, she said.

She drove us to her house. Frazer got out still holding Fray and hugged her warmly. They were very fond of each other and I had noted happily how they had embraced when we met him at the airplane. He climbed in the driver's seat and I sat down beside him. "I hate to give this little creature up," he said, as he handed Fray over to me. "We were just getting to know each other."

He stopped the car at the end of the driveway and paused. He took his hands off of the wheel, placed them on my cheeks, and gently turned my head toward him. "Caramba," he said, as he reached over to give me a lingering kiss. "You can't imagine how happy I am," he said as we set off again, headed for our joyous "pig sty."

General Hunter

Two friendly young men turned up the next afternoon and connected our telephone service about ten minutes after Rose had come over to say my husband had called her and asked her to take a message to me. He wanted her to please tell me that he loved me. "That's all he had to say," she said. I smiled as I thanked her and told her that would have to suffice for the moment.

He got home after his first day working for General Hunter in time for us to have drinks before dinner. He seemed disappointed that I had already put Fray to bed but I assured him he need not worry. He would have a chance to see Fray when he woke him up in the night, although, I boasted, he was getting close to sleeping through the night now all the time. He had slept through the night before.

Frazer reported that he liked his new boss. He was "crisp and cordial." But, Frazer went on, he personally had no idea yet of the scope of his job as the General's aide and pilot. Today he was given papers explaining what went on at the other bases in General Hunter's command. Mainly, he said, he spent the day trying to absorb all of that.

General Hunter had asked him to come in to his office before he left for the day. He told Frazer that he could imagine what a pleasure it was for him to be back with his wife and baby after all the grim time in New Guinea. General Hunter told him he hoped to meet his wife soon and had suggested that maybe Nancy would arrange that. Further General Hunter had added that he had grown very fond of both Cokie and Nancy.

Frazer and I had glorious times together and I discovered early that I needn't have worried that his warmth had been scoured away in the Pacific. He and his little boy had gotten to love each other quite early on and it was clear that Frazer was extra gentle with him. Somewhere in the back of my mind I carried the memory of Big Graham Dougherty and his relation with his children, or at least with his two sons. He had seemed to be afraid of demonstrating any tenderheartedness to them. I knew that a non-loving attitude was not genetic but I feared it could have been contagious. Anyway, I rejoiced to see my two guys being genial and sweet with each other.

As for the relationship between Frazer and me, it was clear, I felt, that our love for each other had withstood our extended separations and was indeed wider and deeper. And if I didn't think two people capture that first careless rapture again after a prolonged absence, it was because neither one was the person he or she had been before. When Frazer and I were together again, it was after he had been through all those hellish months of war. I didn't expect him to be precisely the same person again. I had been through the loneliness of missing him and worrying desperately about him, but most importantly, I had bore a child. And I felt that was a transforming event in a woman's life. So I wasn't the same person either. We had both evolved, I figured.

In any event, I was not given greatly to introspection. All I knew was that we were having a great time, and we were both overjoyed when I learned I was once again pregnant. We decided nearly immediately that we would see to it that Fray would be taught to welcome the new baby instead of treating it like a little monster that threatened his world.

And then we laughed at ourselves to suggest that we thought we could order our lives, or anyone else's so precisely. Anyway, we were having a fine time, on every level.

I was delighted with the present he had brought me from the war zone, my beautiful fleece-lined Australian boots. They fit perfectly and he said that I looked marvelous in them. Furthermore, they felt wonderful, even for bare feet, since the entire foot section, too, was lined with fleece. My naked toes wiggled happily in them.

Once, however, that winter I discovered that a family of mice was also delighted with the fleece-lined feet. I yelled at the top of my lungs when my bare foot discovered furry little rodents. Ever after that I shook my boots vigorously upside down before I put them on.

***

We had dinner at Nancy's house frequently. The first time we left Fray with Rose, but we got so much flack from the Rathborne children and Nana that we brought him the next time and left him with them. And at long last, there I met General Hunter, who nearly immediately told me to call him "Monk." I found him bewitching, and not just because the next thing he said to me was how much he liked Frazer and how much he was already depending on him.

I remembered that article Nancy had read to me about Brigadier General Frank O'Driscoll Hunter. "Tall, lean, fiercely mustached," it had said. I didn't buy the "fiercely" adjective and I would have added "handsome" to the description.

He was simple in that easy, worldly way that some secure people are. He had a distinctive style and just from our conversation over dinner, I felt that he was totally integrated as a person. I also felt that he had a sharply perceptive mind. I don't remember how that evening I learned that he had a special interest in history and the events that shaped it. Furthermore, I sensed that although he was obviously a self-sufficient character, he was also lonely. Nancy had told me that as far as she knew, he had never been married, and she did not think that he had a special friend here. When it became time for Frazer and me to retrieve our sleeping baby and head for home in our reasonably-new car, I told Monk that I hoped he would come around to our house and have dinner with us sometime. He smiled and said he'd be delighted.

We saw him another night at Nancy's. He chided me then for not having invited him to dinner. About a week after that, Frazer called from his office and said General Hunter had said to him that if he had any pull with the "aide's maid," he should see if she would like to invite someone to dinner that night.

"Tell him that I was just about to telephone and see, if by any chance, General Hunter would be free to join us for dinner tonight." I scurried around, asked Rose if she was free to give Fray his bath that night and by the time Frazer was home, I was nearly ready for our visitor.

Later I figured I had read Monk correctly: that he was lonely. Frazer agreed with me. We both noted that he seemed relaxed and at home at our little house. Anyway, he was there several times a month, it seems, and often at his own instigation. I was always glad to see him. He made a mean martini, which delighted me, and he said he thought Fray was one of the brightest little boys he had ever seen, which convinced me of his perspicacity.

However, those two did not start off on a good footing. The first time Monk picked him up and sort of cuddled him, Fray's cheek came into contact with a prickly mustache. Several howls later, Monk tried again, saying he would shave the goddamn thing off rather than have it make an enemy of his new best friend. Now Monk held Fray more gingerly and from then on they were pals. Fray soon got brave enough to feel the mustache and it turned out to be a source of huge delight to him.

It was apparent to me that Monk liked Frazer hugely. He was turning over more responsibilities to him and he mentioned several times to me how much he enjoyed his trips to other Air Force bases when he was flying with Frazer.

***

Conversations between the three of us those evenings covered a range of subjects, with the war always eventually dominating. The correspondents on both the radio and in the newspapers were so graphic about the fighting taking place in Europe that I, for one, winced at the brutality of the battles and shivered along with our soldiers in the bitter cold that had enveloped them that winter.

After a series of relentless battles, the Allies had liberated all of France and Belgium, as well as Luxembourg, and were now in Holland. There they were poised for the fearful struggle that they knew lay ahead in the thickly wooded Ardennes region as they scuffled their way toward Germany. They knew they had to defeat an iron-clad enemy, now fighting for its very survival.

Listening one night to a reporter in Amsterdam, where many of the canals were frozen in the coldest period to hit Europe in years, my mind flicked back to the time I had spent there with Dutch cousins. It was in the late spring of 1939 and I stayed with them in their glorious old family house on Herrengracht Street on a canal in one of the most elegant parts of the city. The rainbow colors of flowers, my swinging young Dutch cousins, and that mildly licentious but harmless older cousin, that whole sunny, carefree spring weekend now seemed an eon ago.

***

By contrast to the cruel winter in Europe, that winter in Long Island was milder than usual. There were days in December when Fray played around outside in summer clothes.

Indeed it was so warm one evening near Christmas when Frazer and I went to dinner at the house of an old friend of mine, that we had cocktails outside on the patio. Our host, Grover Loening, whom I had known in Washington, had been an airplane designer for many years and had built up a reputation for being so gifted and farsighted that he had been hired to design war planes for all the biggest and most advanced airplane companies in the country. When he heard I was living nearby, he invited Frazer and me to meet some of his friends.

There were about a dozen of us there for dinner and we indulged in the usual agreeable introductory conversations. Outside in the dusk, Frazer and I and a couple we had just met fell inevitably to talking about the war. We knew the Germans were making huge counterattacks against Allied troops in what got to be called the Battle of the Bulge for the shape of the area in which they were fighting. It grew into a general discussion and I mentioned that an editorial I had read said that the Allies were unprepared for the strength of the German counterattacks. The man standing next to me commented that he had heard that these battles, now taking place in the Ardennes, were the bloodiest the US had fought in the entire war.

Once again a superlative about another theater of war, I thought in horror, as we drifted into the house for dinner.

Inside Grover picked up his wine glass and quietly drank to me, sitting on his right. Then standing, he drank a toast to all his friends at the table, said a few pertinent words, and ended with a toast to that "thankful day when we will be in Berlin." After he sat down he turned to me again. "Speaking of the future," he said, "that man I seated near your husband represents the future. He is a genius, an inventor, and I am glad to see that he and Frazer are talking together." I looked down at the other end of the table and saw Frazer and a dark-haired man with the eager expression of a fox engaged in animated conversation.

I asked Grover to tell me more about him. His name was Bob Fulton (no kin to the other Robert Fulton) and he was amazingly gifted and adventurous. He had a totally creative mind and invented training machines he called "Gunairinstructors" for the Air Force, Grover went on. This machine simulated a cockpit in which a pilot could learn to fly and to fire at the enemy in all kinds of circumstances and configurations.

I told Grover he had convinced me of this young man's talent but what I was really interested in was what he himself was up to. He was beginning to think more about the time when he could be designing commercial and private planes again, but now, he explained, he was devoting full time to military planes, mostly bombers.

Then he suddenly asked me if I had seen Joe, meaning our common friend, Joe Kennedy, since his tragedy. I told him that I had not and that I knew it was the mention of bombers that prompted this sharp shift in our conversation. The tragedy in Joe's life was the death of his oldest and greatly cherished son, Joe Jr., in a bomber over England. Young Joe was stationed in the US Air Force in England and had volunteered for an especially hazardous mission about a year ago. He and a co-pilot were to fly a Liberator bomber, which had been reconfigured so that it could carry a thousand pounds of explosives. At a designated time Joe and the co-pilot would put the plane on automatic, which then pinpointed the plane toward German installations on the Belgian coast to deliver that thousand pounds of explosives. Joe and his co-pilot would have already parachuted out of the plane. Meanwhile, a number of Air Force pilots would be waiting below, poised to pick up them up as they landed. The timing had been checked over and over and over again and the mechanism worked perfectly.

However, something went desperately wrong. No one would ever know how it happened, but the Liberator suddenly blew up minutes before its scheduled time. It exploded in midair with both of the pilots trapped inside. No trace of them was ever found.

Grover had seen father Joe several times since then, he said, and he had not believed anyone could be as wretched as he was. It wasn't just a heartbreaking loss to Joe, Grover said. "It was as if his heart had been amputated right out of him."

I said I had called Joe the minute I heard the tragic news and had talked to him once more since, and he sounded like the mere shadow of his former self. His grief seemed to be gnawing at his very vitals.

Not directly a Kennedy, Grover said, but another example of what could be included in the "Kennedy Trail of Tears," was the death in the killing fields in Belgium of Kick Kennedy's husband, Billy Hartington. Young Billy and Kick had been married in a great splash of a wedding that united the son of the Duke of Devonshire, a Protestant family famous for its anti-Catholic history, to the well-known daughter of the former Catholic American ambassador to England. The young couple had a life together of only a few months before he, as an officer in the famous Coldstream Guards, went off to join his troop in Belgium. Billy was shot and killed by a German sniper soon after arriving there.

Kick had given up her profoundly deep Catholic faith to marry Billy (had he lived, he would have been someday the Duke of Devonshire, and Kick would have been the Duchess). Happily for Kick, Joe Jr. was already in England with the US Air Force, and he stood by her side at the wedding and her father had offered his blessings to the couple, but Rose Kennedy never forgave Kick and felt, to her dying day, that Kick had "sinned." While Grover and I talked about Rose's attitude, I pointed out that an additional problem for Rose was that if the couple had ever had children, they would have been considered illegitimate in Catholic eyes.

Grover said he thought there was "one more milestone in the Kennedy Trail of Tears," the lobotomy operation that Rosemary had undergone. Joe had been convinced that such a procedure would improve the status of what was called her mental retardation. Instead the procedure had turned out disastrously: Rosemary was now more brain-damaged then ever. Joe, who had authorized the operation with such high hopes, was shattered to realize the sad life that now lay ahead forever for Rosemary. And on top of his anguish over that, he was haunted with guilt that the idea for the operation had been his very own.

Of course, as Grover said, all this had happened since the amazing tale of the wreckage of Jack Kennedy's boat in the south Pacific, his incredible rescue of a wounded shipmate, and their eventual rescue. Jack's P.T. boat had been sliced in two by a Japanese destroyer. Jack had hauled his wounded shipmate by gripping the strap of the man's life jacket in his teeth and swimming for miles across unknown seas. Jack toted the wounded sailor until he and his burden landed on a deserted island. It was there they were later rescued. At least, Grover pointed out, this was a story about a Kennedy with a happy ending, and it had triggered a bunch of colorful newspaper and magazine articles stressing Jack's heroism.

***

After dinner I chatted briefly with Bob Fulton, who seemed pleasant. He had a nice quiet smile and amazingly sharp eyes and on closer inspection didn't look so much like a fox as I had thought. He and Frazer seemed to have already established a friendship.

On the way driving home that evening, Frazer told me that Bob Fulton had asked him to join his team, which is building an automobile-airplane. A prototype had already been built and it worked, Bob had told him. "It flies and can be converted to a car or put the other way around, it works as a car and can be converted to an airplane. Bob Fulton is calling it an Airphibian and it needs to be tweaked and perfected," Frazer said.

"He has already bought land next to the Danbury airport and hopes I will join him as soon as the war is over. I have told him that I think it sounds wonderful."

There was a long pause. "And you," he said, "what do you think?" After the idea sank in a little I told him that I, too, thought it sounded wonderful. Wonderful, I repeated. We were both silent for a while.

"Frazer," I said, sort of laughing, "I think it sounds great as long as your role wouldn't be fundraising for the project." He joined me in laughing because he knew too that his forte wasn't anything that involved money. His mother had once suggested to me that his financial appetite was larger than his financial stomach.

"No, darling, he wants me to help with the design in any way I can, and to be the test pilot." Frazer sounded delighted. "So we'll

have that fantastic project to look forward to soon's peace breaks out."
I suggested that I bet General Hunter will think that's an exciting
prospect and Frazer said he couldn't wait to tell him.

***

What Frazer and I were really thinking about then was that, although
our brave Allies were slogging along in their resolute drive toward
Berlin, the Nazis were fighting for their very skins. So Frazer made a
conscious decision not to get too excited about the Fulton project—
yet. Instead he continued to like working for General Hunter and
to welcome the added responsibilities that fell on him. I, too, managed to postpone thinking about a combination auto-airplane until
the future. I saw it as pie in the sky. When the nightmare war and the
appalling killing are finished, I'll think about it.

As Yogi Berra puts it, I thought to myself, "it ain't over 'til it's
over."

We Learn About the Holocaust

It was some time early in 1945 that a line from an old Hemingway
story sprang to mind. He had written that "all our words from loose
using have lost their edge."

The reason I had thought about that Hemingway line was
because late one January evening, Frazer and I had heard on the radio
that a unit of the Russian army had fought its way into Poland and
there had discovered a Nazi concentration camp. It consisted of over a
dozen buildings, devoted mainly to the gassing of Jews. Bones of the
dead were piled like firewood outside of the brick building which had
housed the gas chambers, the Russian troops reported.

I knew Hemingway was right. At least, there were no words left
in my vocabulary adequate to describe the horror I felt. Ones I might
have known before that night which could have applied had gotten
blunted from overuse. I couldn't find appropriate words now.

When the commandants of the killing camp heard that the
Russians were nearing they had tried to destroy some of the crematoria and had sent many of the starving inmates out of the camp before
the Russians got there. But the searing evidence could not be hidden. The gruesome stories of what the Russians had found were now
spread in newspapers and over the radio all over the non-German
world. We had learned that Jews from all over Nazi-occupied Europe,

men, women, and children, had been forced into gas chambers to their deaths, in pursuit of Hitler's avowed drive to wipe the Jews out of Europe.

As American troops made their way deeper into Germany, we learned they, too, were to find more death camps. Dozens more. Probably the worst of all the dreadful camps unearthed was one called Auschwitz, which would ever be the symbol of the barbarianism of all the Nazi concentration camps. General Hunter, who was at our house the night we heard about Auschwitz, said "that word will stink to all humans to the last syllable of recorded time."

From every newspaper and every radio broadcaster, we learned that advancing Allied troops discovered that of the scores of thousands of victims killed, not all had been Jews. The dead included political dissidents and religious adherents, such as Jehovah's Witnesses, of which Hitler disapproved, Gypsies, homosexuals, and others who just did not fit the Nazi concept of the ideal Aryan.

Some of them had been victims of disease or starvation or what was known as "individual execution," and some even of medical experiments. There were also many who had been forced to build weapons and uniforms for the Nazi army. They, too, could be sent to the crematoria if they were no longer useful.

Many of the worst camps were built in Poland, we learned, because the Germans thought that their existence could be better hidden there from the rest of the world. But the Nazis did not just favor Poland. They were found in many other occupied countries, including France, Holland, and Belgium.

If there had previously been disbelief in the rumors of the depravity of the camps, as there was on the part of many, it was because people could not conceive that civilized human beings would commit the atrocities of which the Germans were accused. As the Allied troops freed the emaciated living and discovered the evidence of the dead, anyone who had doubted now had to accept the unbelievable truth.

***

What had seemed most incomprehensible to Frazer and me in our endless nighttime discussions was that such a debasement of humanity had taken place in what many of us had considered a country at the center of the civilized world. And, we wondered if the conception of killing a whole religious group as well as thousands of others in categories which the Nazis hated, was obscene, it was its very implementation that was obscene to the nth degree. Why were there so few in Germany in the middle of the twentieth century to cry out "halt" and refuse to be functionaries in the execution of the cruelty and savagery of Hitler's nightmare?

That's what I kept asking myself when I thought of the huge organization the killing apparatus involved. It obviously took untold millions of people to run the machinery for what later came to be known as the Holocaust. First, vast numbers of people had to ferret out the large groups of people to be incarcerated. This involved thousands of trained SS agents. Most of the victims were transported by rail, therefore a huge new train system had to be built, organized, and run efficiently. Of particular importance were the large numbers of "cattle cars" we heard about, used for transportation to the killing camps. Scores of architects and workers of all kinds had to construct the camps in which the prisoners would be kept. Countless experts on the properties of asphyxiating gas were involved and numbers of people with the right credentials had to build the chambers in which the people were to be killed. And, of course, skilled Germans had to have the responsibility of controlling the gas, the quantity to be used, etc., to accomplish its purposes.

We in the outside world had learned of brave German soldiers who risked their lives trying to kill Hitler. I never heard or read of any of the hundreds of thousands it took to run the Holocaust who risked their lives by refusing to be a cog in that machinery. Were there no decent Germans left in the world, we wondered? Did no one stand up for justice? I told Frazer at length of Noel's discussions of how the famous German writer Heine had said a hundred years ago that Germans were like slaves who, without chains, without a whip, would just "accept his master's word."

The American and other Allied solders were discovering these hell camps as they got further into Germany. They reported on the savagery they found as they were fighting on what was being seen as the long, rough road to Berlin.

Part Six

The Moon, the Stars, and the Planets

"Last night the moon, the stars, and the planets fell on me."

-PRESIDENT HARRY TRUMAN

Victory in Europe Day

In the summer of 1945, our dogged troops slogged their way across the Rhine River. This very feat had huge symbolism for General Hunter, with his interest in history. He told Frazer and me that it was the first time since Napoleon's invasion of Germany that an enemy army had crossed the Rhine.

The following spring, those of us in the US could begin to believe that the Allies were actually beginning to emerge from the long dark tunnel. We knew it when our armies came close to the outskirts of Berlin.

The night before they actually crossed into Berlin, Hitler realized that his cruel dream of unlimited conquest was over and he killed his mistress, Eva Braun, and himself. Meanwhile, the "Sawdust Caesar," as we in England used to call Mussolini, and his mistress were captured and killed by a band of partisans on Lake Como as they tried to flee to Switzerland.

***

On May 7, 1945, Germany surrendered unconditionally in the Allied Headquarters in Reims. "So, at least, the war in Europe is over," I exulted, thanking whatever gods there be.

***

The rejoicing over VE (Victory in Europe) Day reverberated to the skies, but there was still a formidable Japanese enemy to defeat before the Second World War would be a part of history. Even so, I could not help casting my life into a peaceful future, with Frazer home and Fray and the baby who would be born in the fall.

***

Franklin Roosevelt, that most valiant of men who had fought so courageously for the defeat of the Nazis, did not live to see the end of the war. About a month before the unconditional surrender of the Germans, President Roosevelt died of a cerebral hemorrhage in Warm Springs, Georgia.

He had recently returned from a conference in Yalta, in Ukraine, where he and Stalin and Churchill had laid out their now famous plans for the defeat of Germany. I got dizzy thinking of how much those heads of state had traveled, and often such staggering distances.

President Roosevelt had gone to the Little White House in Warm Springs, as he had often done, seeking relief from the pain in his legs, which still bothered him although his polio attack had happened some twenty years before. Further, the polio had disabled him so completely that forever afterwards he had had to depend on heavy steel leg braces as well as a stalwart shoulder next to him on which to lean in order to walk, or even to stand. Or else he had to use a wheelchair. I had witnessed that procedure myself in that weekend at Hyde Park some nine years ago.

***

I was on a train going from Washington to New York when I learned about the President's death. I had been in Washington seeing my mother and the obstetrician who would deliver my baby that fall. I had told my sister Rosalind that now that I knew how to have a baby, I didn't have to go to Johns Hopkins. This time instead I would go to the Georgetown University Hospital in Washington, conveniently around the corner from Mother's house.

At the stop in Wilmington, Delaware, a male passenger got on the train and promptly announced in a loud voice, to everyone in our car, that President Roosevelt had died. He made his comment as if he was a town crier, and added simply that it had happened in Warm Springs. He walked briskly down the aisle of our car and went into the next one. We could hear him repeating his sad news to the people in that car.

I was surprised to find myself weeping so unabashedly that a conductor, walking past, approached me and asked if he could help me.

I mumbled my request for a glass of water, which he brought me and which I immediately spilled down the front of my dress. At least the cold water stemmed my blubbering. Then I remembered to thank him.

I started to wonder why I was so unprepared for Roosevelt's death. There had actually been many tell-tale warnings of serious health problems for the President. For a while pictures of him had shown him looking pale and tired. At his unprecedented fourth inauguration only a few months ago, the press had written about how frail he looked (although no one wrote about his disability and he was never photographed in his wheelchair), but despite those auguries of his maxed-out look, I figured this heroic man would live forever. And now, as I mourned his loss to the world, I thought back to that special weekend I had spent at Hyde Park in the summer of 1936 when he was running for his second term. I remembered, with a fresh burst of tears, the evening there when he had converted me from a conservative Republican into an impassioned liberal Democrat.

When I got to New York and thence by bus, and further by taxi, to our little house on Long Island, Frazer and I gobbled up the news on the radio and later in the newspapers of Roosevelt's last days in Warm Springs. With him at the time was an artist who was painting his portrait when he toppled from the chair in which he was posing. He died shortly thereafter. The painter finished the painting, we learned from the news, and photographs of it appeared sometime later. I felt that she had bleached out the tired lines in his face and that he came out as a handsome middle-aged man, but not surprisingly, nowhere in the portrait was there a trace of the invincible spirit, the unwavering drive, and the ebullient personality.

Also with the President at Warm Spring, we learned later, was a woman named Lucy Mercer, who many years ago had been Eleanor Roosevelt's secretary. That role had crashed to a resounding end when Mrs. Roosevelt found a bunch of love letters from her secretary to her husband in a drawer in his desk. At that time, Franklin Roosevelt was Assistant Secretary of the Navy, so the relationship had started a long time ago and had been sustained over all these years. Lucy Mercer's presence at the Little White House in Warm Springs was not officially announced at the time of the President's death, but stories of the affinity between her and the President drifted out, embellished with more details of their early romance.

There was worldwide sympathy for Eleanor Roosevelt over the death of her husband. Fortunately, as history has shown us, she was also a strong personality and she had shared with the President his commitment to lift this country up by its bootstraps to get us out of the worst depression the world had ever seen and thus also to improve the lives of the most vulnerable in this country. And, obviously of major importance, was her spirited support of all his struggles to win the war that had been thrust on his presidency. She not only worked for the issues he cared about, she added others of her own all the rest of her life. She was held in vast esteem, abroad certainly, and mostly throughout the US, too. Her extensive travels studying various working conditions in the US were sometimes treated with gentle humor. One example which I especially liked was a *New Yorker* cartoon of a group of coal miners working deep underground. Far away in the distance, one could see a vague figure approaching and in the caption, one of the miners is calling out, "My God, here comes Mrs. Roosevelt." Later I found another in the *New Yorker*. There a young officer was reviewing a small group of his troops. He told them that if they had a problem, to come to him. "Don't write to Mrs. Roosevelt," he added.

A few days after Roosevelt's death, General Hunter was at our house for supper and he commented that he hoped the President had known how closely the Allies were to victory and realized that the surrender of the Nazis was only few days away. I proposed a multiple toast to Monk Hunter, Frazer, victory, President Roosevelt, and our new President, Harry Truman.

Part Seven

The War is Over

"Thank God the war is over, but..."

-EVERYONE I KNEW

Truman's World-Shaking Decisions

Former Vice President Harry Truman, the newly sworn-in President, had spoken to the press the morning after Roosevelt's death. "Last night the moon, the stars, and all the planets fell on me," he told the reporters. Then he added, "If any of you fellows ever pray, pray for me." And well he might have pleaded for prayers because before him lay decisions so momentous that they could effect the fate and destiny of a large part of the world.

Anyway, he was off to a lucky start: he had been in the White House for a few days only when the Allies' drive was so successful that the Germans surrendered. Now, with them out of the picture, the new president and Winston Churchill could concentrate fully on the defeat of Japan. Further, shortly after the Japanese attack on Pearl Harbor, China had joined the United States in declaring war on Japan. China had suffered—and was still suffering hideously—from the Japanese invasion of that country which had started as far back as 1932.

In the spring of 1945, the Allies were chalking up great victories against Japan on land and on the sea. Frazer wished often that he was there with the Americans, especially in the Air Force, flying closer to the famous island itself, and I knew his heart was with them all the time. He followed their movements with a deep and sympathetic interest. He read about them in the papers, listened on the radio, or heard about them one way or another, occasionally from old Air Force friends he ran across. For my part, I thanked God he was here and not there.

Now huge bombers were hitting Japanese cities with deadly devastation. For instance, according to US newspapers, ninety B-29 bombers had attacked Tokyo at one point. Despite the increasing onslaughts there were no hints, according to what we read and heard, that the

259

Japanese were ready to give up the ghost. Indeed, just the opposite. No matter what the Allies threw at them, they continued to fight on.

"What would it take to force the Japanese to admit defeat?" seemed to be the question asked by the columnists, editorial writers, broadcasters, our friends, and every taxi driver I ran across on my forays into New York City. That question automatically triggered another one. "Is invasion of Japan the only answer?"

When the conversation among so many of us came to wild, uninformed guesses of how many Allied troops it would take to invade Japan, the numbers were so gigantic that they seemed ludicrous and yet I never heard anyone suggest any strategy for the defeat of Japan other than invasion. That would make the invasion of Europe look like a picnic, I once heard someone say. "The Normandy invasion in spades!" I shuddered to myself.

I know that when we discussed with General Hunter the range of numbers of troops, ships, specialty aircraft carriers, and planes it would take to invade Japan, he said he wouldn't even hazard a guess as to what it would take. Naturally, he said, he had not been in on any official consideration of this since it wasn't his bailiwick, but that it made his blood turn to ice at the thought of a land invasion. To tell you the truth, he said, he'd just fall back on humorist Will Rogers' comment, which was that all he knew was what he read in the newspapers.

***

Of course, as we learned a little later, invasion was not the only way. There was another way to compel Japan to admit defeat.

What we had not known then was that early in the war, Albert Einstein had warned President Roosevelt that the Nazis had been trying to "split the atom" and thus create what would be the ultimate energy of the universe and therefore be able to create the greatest weapon of all.

The president responded immediately: distinguished scientists— American, Canadian, and British, as well as Hungarian and German refugee scientists—were organized in a secret enterprise in New Mexico to build this weapon before the Germans were able to.

Hiroshima

On August 5, 1945, the US, Britain, and China demanded that Japan surrender unconditionally with a warning that if she did not, she would suffer dreadful devastation. The Japanese rejected the ultimatum.

The following day a US plane dropped an atomic bomb on the city of Hiroshima and its military base. Russia declared war on Japan the same day, which understandably got little attention. What the plane dropped was the equivalent of twenty kilotons of TNT. If those figures meant little to most Americans (including me, for sure) the descriptions of the dead and dying as a result of the bombing were blood-curdling and gut-wrenching enough to make us understand the full impact of an atomic bomb.

That bomb destroyed more than four square miles and killed or injured over 100,000 people in one fell swoop.

***

After the pulverization of Hiroshima, the Japanese were faced with a second ultimatum, with the same dire warning. They ignored the second ultimatum, too. On August 9, the US dropped an atomic bomb on the city of Nagasaki and its naval base.

I had been horror-struck by the first atomic bomb attack, but as soon as I heard about Nagasaki, I got a sharp pain that ran from the back of my head all the way down my spine. It was nearly gone by the next day, but ever since, just a picture of the atomic mushroom-shaped cloud triggers a pain that starts in the back of my head.

The atomic bomb on Nagasaki brought the Japanese government to its knees, and five days later the Emperor of Japan finally conceded defeat. As part of the treaty, the victors allowed him to keep his throne.

***

The unconditional surrender of Japan on August 14—VJ Day—was announced to the world by President Harry Truman and British Prime Minister Clement Attlee (Churchill was no longer PM of Great Britain). President Truman would state later that at least 200,000 American lives would have been lost in an invasion, to say nothing of the lives of the soldiers of other nations, especially the Japanese.

A few weeks after the Japanese surrender, General MacArthur set up Allied headquarters in Yokohama, thus making it clear, Monk Hunter explained to me, that Japan had suffered its first conquest by a foreigner in 2,000 years. It has always struck me as a marvel that Japan developed as a bona fide democracy under General MacArthur's hierarchy there, since I have always thought that of all our American generals, he was probably the one least addicted to my concept of democratic values.

The Forever Hiroshima Problem

Frazer and I and our families and friends, and everyone we knew, were ecstatic that at long, long last the worst war the world had ever known was over, but at the same time it seems that nearly everyone we knew spent hours trying to resolve an irresolvable problem: our attitude toward our own country for having used atomic bombs on Hiroshima and Nagasaki. We heard endless discussions of how the US had abandoned what some called an older morality, which had prohibited the deliberate destruction of non-combatants, and instead had assumed one which stressed that today's wars called for total war. The Allies had had no compunction against dropping regular bombs (what I called "old-fashioned" bombs) where we knew there were large numbers of non-combatants in our attempt to destroy civilian support for the war. The fire-bombing of Dresden over two days and two nights in February 1945 was a prime example of such total destruction that I heard that even Churchill afterwards questioned the use of such excessive bombing.

The Germans had already thrown everything they could on the citizens of countless English cities who lived nowhere near sites of military importance in a concerted effort to break British morale. Their wanton demolition of Coventry was a prime example. Granted, these attacks by the Nazis and equally ghastly ones by the Allies were picayune compared to the devastation of the atomic bomb.

***

The entire world now knew that one single word, "Hiroshima," symbolized the dawn of the nuclear age; the age in which a weapon of incalculable human suffering and of massive material destruction had not only been invented but had been used. And who had used it? The country which was always boasting about its "exceptionalism." For many of us, that was the basic problem: It was our own country that had used it. We were the citizens who touted ourselves as the ones who held the highest ethical ground.

Over the history of war, weapons had graduated, if that is the proper word, I thought, from the club wielded by one person to the atomic bomb with its apocalyptic implications.

Furthermore, how, how, how, I wondered, would we ever get that evil genie back in the bottle? What was to be the fate of humankind, now that humans had the power to destroy it?

Of course, we had no answers to the above questions, but there was a simpler one, too, which many people asked and to which I, like everyone else, had no real answer. The answer went something like this: "Obviously horrified, but what else could we do?"

General Hunter was among those whose values I admired hugely and he was one of the "obviously horrified, but" people, and I know it wasn't just because he was a soldier. Indeed, several of my friends, all strictly civilian, including my old pal, Jane Stevenson, and many of my old newspaper friends had fallen into the "obviously horrified, but" category.

A short while after the end of the war I came across a piece of paper I had completely forgotten about and was reminded that I had read it some dozens of years ago. It is typed, more neatly than I type, and I remembered vaguely that someone had given it to me, and I have completely forgotten who gave it to me and why she—or he—had done so.

At the top of the page, it reads, "Excerpts from the sixth song of the Sumerian poem, Lament, on the ruin of the city of Ur, from the second millenium B.C." I read it with horror then, and I print part of it now, again with horror.

> *Then the fair wind forsook the city, the city lies in ruins.*
> *The city has been turned to ruins: the people are lamenting.*
> *On all the places where they rejoiced in the festivals of the land,*
> *the people*
> *Lie in heaps*
> *The blood of the country has been spilled like*
> *Molten bronze or lead from the pot.*
> *Dead bodies have melted like the fat of lambs put out in the sun.*

I shook my head in a kind of disbelief at how nearly the old lament could now be applied to Hiroshima. As I looked at the piece of paper, I saw that I had scrawled in pencil at the top of the page a note which said "the dawn of history." Now I dared to say to myself, "Are we now thinking about the sunset of history?"

***

Then I realized I could no longer think cosmically. I had to turn inward, come down to earth, and concentrate on getting ready to have my wonderful new baby.

Nannie had gone to stay with Huidy in Milton and turned her house over to us for the next month or so. Frazer had long ago asked General Hunter if he could have a couple of weeks of leave to take our little family to Washington to add to it when the appropriate time came. "For God's sake, yes," General Hunter barked. "You haven't had any leave since you've been here. Take as long as you need to deliver that baby and make certain, Frazer, that this new one is as smart as the kid you already have."

***

Frazer and Fray and I had driven to Washington on October 20, about a week before my "due date." Late the night of October 27, my labor pains started and soon they were coming thick and fast. Frazer called the dear neighbor, Kerry, who was poised to come over and stay with Fray in this happy contingency. She turned up immediately, in her pajamas and curlers, and prepared to fall into the bed next to the little room where Fray was sleeping. I gave him a kiss on his cheek, which he must have thought was a fly or some such because he tried to wipe it away. I called the hospital number my doctor had given me, on his promise that he would come to the hospital as soon as I called. The voice that responded said that the doctor was at mass but was expected at the hospital shortly.

Frazer treated me as if I were made of spun sugar as he led me to our car. This was his first experience in this role and I thought he seemed apprehensive or maybe just bewildered about the whole procedure. At the hospital door we embraced warmly and I told him he would see me in a while with a howling little creature to introduce him to.

At that time the Georgetown University Hospital, or at least that part of it, was housed in an ancient, dismally-decrepit building with inadequately lit hallways and a creaky elevator. When I reached the floor I wanted, at first I saw no one except a small woman with wispy hair. Latina, I figured on getting closer to her. She was busily engaged scrubbing the floors. She looked up at me as I approached and we smiled to each other. For a couple of minutes I didn't see anyone else. I reckoned she could deliver a baby all right if she was called upon. I wished then that I spoke more Spanish than the "buenos noches" with which I had greeted her, just in case I needed Spanish a little later.

In a moment a competent-looking, very young doctor, accompanied by a nurse, materialized out of the shadows. He told me to go with the nurse, who would get me prepared, actually I think he said "prepped," that ridiculous word that has sneaked into the medical vocabulary.

After he had checked me out, I was put on a gurney. While I tried not to moan and groan too loudly, I was wheeled into the delivery room. I remember some whopping pains and then I was given an anesthetic, which alleviated the pain considerably. Professionals call it a "saddle block" because it blocks the saddle section of the body from pain. I call it a "miracle."

The next thing I was aware of was that my obstetrician, looking pious, was telling me I had an admirable little boy, and as soon as I was taken to my room the baby would be brought to me. I presumed that it was this doctor who had delivered my baby, but I will never know for sure.

In a few minutes I had Rush Huidekoper Dougherty in my arms. He was named for a beloved uncle of my father's, a distinguished doctor in Philadelphia who had decided he liked animals more than people and had become a veterinarian. If my baby had been a girl, she would have been named Pandora, after this uncle's famous little mare. Nannie had said she wouldn't mind having a granddaughter named after a horse, but Pandora was the source of so many troubles!

Anyway, there I was with my wriggly pink beautiful baby, my little Rushiepie, in my arms, when his father came in to congratulate me and to meet his child. I now remembered that it was the first time he had seen a newborn and I think he expected something a little bonnier, but anyway he was obviously thrilled to hold his second little boy. And to be there when this one was born! That was a special treat for me, too.

After three days, during which time Rush seem to have developed a nearly insatiable appetite, which fortunately I was able to satisfy, he and I went back to Nannie's house.

We rode home in style! I sat comfortably in a hospital wheelchair, nestling my baby tight to me, with Frazer pushing us.

We ran across several people on our way who seemed to think it odd to find an entourage such as ours on a sidewalk, but as they got closer they looked at my baby and cooed and clucked and laughed.

At home the baby's big brother and our dear neighbor, now dressed more formally, with curly hair, awaited our arrival. Someone had been peddling to Fray the idea that he was so lucky now to have a little brother who could be his playmate, and if he had expected a more "playmatey" package and was disappointed, he showed no evidence of it. He kept staring, wide-eyed, and smiling sweetly at the baby, and soon started offering him toys of totally inappropriate sorts. I recall that a whistle was among them.

While all this was going on, he and I had to make up for three days of hugs and kisses we had missed while I was in the hospital. When we had finished our cuddles, I asked him if he wanted to touch Rush and showed him how he could pat the baby very gently. With every little pat, his smile grew larger. I figured that he looked upon this little episode as a new adventure.

Later, his father carried Fray in the wheelchair when he returned it to the hospital. When Fray got home, beaming, he told me he had had adventures all day long.

Part Eight

Future Landscape

What new adventures will I be having, I wondered? I took a quick mental survey of the landscape of my life. The Second World War, the cruelest war the world had ever suffered, was over. Hiroshima lay behind us. There was peace on earth. Now, I thought, we'd better learn how to preserve peace.

Better yet, we must learn how to cherish it.

On a cosmic level—the end of the war—I am content. On a personal level, despite that we live in a crazy, mixed up world, with two fabulous little boys and a loving husband, I am ecstatic. Now that the war was over, Frazer will be demobilized soon and will be a civilian again.

And I am no longer going to be an innocent bystander. I am going to grab life by the throat and work forever for justice in this world.

About the Author

Page H. Wilson is a Washington writer and a social justice activist. Her writing includes articles in the *New York Times*, the *Washington Post,* and the *Baltimore Sun*. She wrote a political satire in 1963, published by Americans for Democratic Action, called *Through the Looking Glass Darkly: A Day with President Garry Boldwater*. She was co-editor of a cookbook with recipes of leading Democratic politicians called *How to Cook Reagan's Goose*, published by the Woman's National Democratic Club in 1984.

She was born in Richmond, Virginia, January 15, 1918, several days before her father, Prescott F. Huidekoper, had to leave her, her mother, and her two older sisters for France in the First World War as a captain in a machine gun company. On his return, the family lived in the countryside near Baltimore.

Page was educated at private schools until she rebelled at what she called the "narrowness of her world" and left school. Despite the raging depression in 1936, she was able to find a job. She worked for a store in Baltimore run by Samuel Tissanbaum, and took a secretarial course. She tried to take a course in international relations at Johns Hopkins University, but the professor did not allow women in his class.

From 1938 to 1940 she was in London working on the staff of Ambassador Joseph P. Kennedy as a special assistant to his press attaché. On her return to the US, she was a reporter on the *Washington Times Herald*; she also wrote a Washington column for *Town and Country*. In 1943, she married Frazer L. Dougherty, a pilot in the US Air Force. During the war, he flew bombers attacking the Japanese in the South Pacific. After some fifty missions there, he was appointed aide to and pilot for the general who was head of the First Air Force, stationed in New York. After the war, he helped to develop a combination automobile-airplane. In 1956, her marriage to Frazer Dougherty ended in divorce. In 1958, she married the brilliant author, Thomas W. Wilson, Jr., who among other things started the first environmental program for the Aspen Institute. Page says one of the exciting political events of their life was their being on President Nixon's enemies list.

She was the director of public relations for Americans for Democratic Action, especially when it was most involved in the battle for civil rights. She was among the crowd cheering for Dr. Martin Luther

King during his 1963 speech " I Have A Dream." She was also among a much smaller group that marched with Dr. King from Selma to Montgomery, Alabama in 1965 as a pressure for black voting rights.

She served on the Population Crisis Committee in 1965 and there initiated the first international meeting of third-world women to discuss population and development. She currently serves on the Advisory Board to the United Nations Association of the National Capital Area, on the Founding Board of the District of Columbia Law School (one of the best public interest law schools in the country), and on the Board of Directors for the Frameworks Institute.

She has four children: Frazer P. Dougherty of Greenport, NY; Rush H. Dougherty of Tucson, Arizona; Ariel Dougherty, of Truth or Consequences, New Mexico; and Page Delano, of Brooklyn, NY. She has six grandchildren and six great-grandchildren. She also has three step-children and their families. Tom Wilson died in November 1997. Page says she misses him "inordinately. I garden alone now, I drink my martini alone, and saddest of all, I laugh out loud alone."